Equivalences

Any expression may validly be inferred from any other that is equivalent to it, according to the following principles:

"p" and "$p \lor p$" and "$p \mathbin{\&} p$" all are equivalent.
"$p \supset q$" and "$-p \lor q$" and "$-(p \mathbin{\&} -q)$" all are equivalent.
"$p \equiv q$" and "$(q \supset p) \mathbin{\&} (p \supset q)$" are equivalent.

Double negation:	"p" and "$-(-p)$" are equivalent.
Contraposition:	"$p \supset q$" and "$-q \supset -p$" are equivalent.
Commutation:	"$p \lor q$" and "$q \lor p$" are equivalent.
	"$p \mathbin{\&} q$" and "$q \mathbin{\&} p$" are equivalent.
Association:	"$p \lor (q \lor r)$" and "$(p \lor q) \lor r$" are equivalent.
	"$p \mathbin{\&} (q \mathbin{\&} r)$" and "$(p \mathbin{\&} q) \mathbin{\&} r$" are equivalent.
Distribution:	"$p \mathbin{\&} (q \lor r)$" and "$(p \mathbin{\&} q) \lor (p \mathbin{\&} r)$" are equivalent.
	"$p \lor (q \mathbin{\&} r)$" and "$(p \lor q) \mathbin{\&} (p \lor r)$" are equivalent.
De Morgan's laws:	"$-(p \lor q)$" and "$-p \mathbin{\&} -q$" are equivalent.
	"$-(p \mathbin{\&} q)$" and "$-p \lor -q$" are equivalent.
Exportation:	"$(p \mathbin{\&} q) \supset r$" and "$p \supset (q \supset r)$" are equivalent.

ABSORPTION $p \supset q$ AND $p \supset (p \mathbin{\&} q)$ ARE EQUIVALENT

Tautologies

We may add any tautology we please as a line in a deduction, provided we are prepared to show by a truth table that it is a tautology. Some examples of tautologies are:

$p \lor -p$	$p \equiv p$	$(p \mathbin{\&} q) \supset (p \lor q)$
$-(p \mathbin{\&} -p)$	$p \supset (p \lor q)$	.
$p \supset p$	$(p \mathbin{\&} q) \supset p$	.
		.

THE ELEMENTS OF LOGIC

THE ELEMENTS
OF LOGIC

THIRD EDITION

STEPHEN F. BARKER

Department of Philosophy
Johns Hopkins University

McGRAW-HILL BOOK COMPANY

New York   St. Louis   San Francisco   Auckland   Bogotá   Hamburg
Johannesburg   London   Madrid   Mexico   Montreal   New Delhi   Panama
Paris   São Paulo   Singapore   Sydney   Tokyo   Toronto

THE ELEMENTS OF LOGIC

Copyright © 1980, 1974, 1965 by McGraw-Hill, Inc. All rights reserved.
Printed in the United States of America. No part of this publication
may be reproduced, stored in a retrieval system, or transmitted, in any
form or by any means, electronic, mechanical, photocopying, recording, or
otherwise, without the prior written permission of the publisher.

1 2 3 4 5 6 7 8 9 0 DODO 7 8 3 2 1 0 9

This book was set in Melior by Monotype Composition Company, Inc.
The editors were Richard R. Wright, Rhona Robbin, and Laura D. Warner;
the designer was Anne Canevari Green; the production supervisor
was Donna Piligra.
R. R. Donnelley & Sons Company was printer and binder.

Library of Congress Cataloging in Publication Data

Barker, Stephen Francis.
    The elements of logic.

    Includes bibliographical references and index.
    1. Logic. I. Title.
BC108.B25 1980   160   79-16871
ISBN 0-07-003720-5

CONTENTS

PREFACE

This book is intended both for the individual reader who wishes to become acquainted with logic and for use as a textbook in courses in elementary logic at the undergraduate level. It aims to combine practical ideas useful to the criticism of reasoning, technical ideas of modern symbolic logic, and philosophical ideas relevant to logic.

The book is not novel in its range of topics or radical in its approach to them. It contains no single big innovation, but there are quite a number of small ones. My hope is that this book succeeds in expressing various points of logical doctrine in clearer and slightly better ways. Among these points are, for example, the notion of distribution in traditional logic; the notion of the material conditional in the logic of truth functions; the technique of natural deduction in the logic of quantification; the classification of fallacies; and the nature of reasoning by analogy.

I hope I have been able to write concisely, and I have almost completely resisted the temptation to coin technical terminology, of which logic already has enough. I have tried to construct exercises which actually illustrate what they are supposed to illustrate, and some of which will have intrinsic interest. Also, I have given somewhat more attention than is usual to the connections between philosophy and logic, for I think that logic should to some extent be studied as a branch of philosophy.

In this third edition many small improvements and clarifications have been made in the exposition. The division into sections has been altered so that they are now more nearly uniform in length and difficulty. Exercises now accompany every section. Most of the exercises are new, and their number has been appreciably increased. Also, an indication of level is now given: groups of easier, more basic examples or questions are marked with an asterisk (*); groups of examples that are considerably more difficult or considerably less essential are marked with a dagger (†); and groups of examples intermediate in level are given neither sign.

The book contains somewhat more material than can conveniently be covered in an average one-term course. Since the chapters are largely independent of one another, however, a teacher can omit one or more of them without appreciable loss of continuity. Chapter 2 can be omitted by those who do not wish to cover the traditional logic of the syllogism in their courses; Chapter 4, which is perhaps somewhat more difficult than the other chapters, can be omitted by those who want a comparatively relaxed course; and Chapter 8 can be omitted by instructors who wish to deal differently with philosophical problems concerning logic.

Some able professors of logic feel that an elementary course attempting to include such traditional topics as the theory of the syllogism, fallacies, and induction must become a rather disreputable 'grab bag.' They prefer a more highly unified approach that omits these traditional topics in favor of an abstract exposition of deduction, mathematical in rigor and style and with up-to-date emphasis on the nature of formalized systems. By teaching undergraduate logic in this way, they have the satisfaction of being able to put directly to use the knowledge of mathematical logic which they themselves have acquired in their graduate studies. Now, I certainly recognize that a first course in logic conceived in this more abstract spirit can be a good course. However, the advocates of that approach seem to me to overlook the fact that such a course is likely to appeal to and benefit only the minority of undergraduate students who have a definitely mathematical turn of mind. Furthermore, I believe that they overlook the real intellectual benefits that the traditional 'grab bag' affords: it has a considerably greater chance of giving useful guidance to students in their actual thinking, and it has a closer connection with philosophical terminology and with traditional philosophical problems. In my view, this more traditional style of logic instruction has a greater prospect of being of intellectual benefit to most students who take a single course in logic than has a course in the more abstract style. This is a question of pedagogy about which each teacher must decide, however. I have no wish to win over to my view any reluctant converts. I feel that almost any teacher teaches best when teaching whatever he or she thinks is best.

If masculine pronouns have been used in some places in the text to refer to people in general, this is for the sake of succinctness only and no bias is intended.

For helpful and constructive suggestions about specific ways in which the book could be improved, I am indebted to many people who have communicated with me. They are too numerous to list, but I extend to all of them my warm thanks.

Stephen F. Barker

CHAPTER 1

INTRODUCTION

LOGIC AND ARGUMENTS

Most courses in the curriculum of a university today are relatively new ones, which were not taught in the universities of a few generations ago. Logic is an exception. Courses in logic have been offered to students ever since the first universities came into existence some 800 or 900 years ago. What is there about logic that for so many centuries has made people regard it as deserving to be a part of higher education? There are two kinds of reasons: logic—the critical study of reasoning—is a subject having both theoretical interest and practical value.

On the one hand, the study of logic can be intellectually rewarding as knowledge for its own sake on account of the clear and systematic character of many of its principles and its close relations with basic philosophical questions and with the foundations of mathematics.

On the other hand, the study of logic is also of practical use because a mastery of its principles can help us become more effective in recognizing and avoiding mistakes in reasoning— both in the reasoning we do ourselves and in the reasoning that others use in trying to convince us of things. A person who can recognize and avoid logical mistakes in reasoning will be able to think more clearly and correctly, more soundly and surely, whatever may be the subjects about which he is going to think. To be sure, the practical value of logic should not be overstated; the study of logic cannot by itself make people who reason poorly into good reasoners. This is because good reasoning is a very complex skill which requires sound judgment and broad knowledge concerning the subject matter about which one is going to reason; a course in logic cannot supply these. But it is reasonable to expect that people who already have some skill at reasoning can improve and refine that skill through studying logic.

This book will deal with both theoretical and practical aspects of logic because both are important and both have educational value. Although it is not always easy to relate both aspects closely to each other, ideally the theoretical principles of elementary logic should be studied in living connection with their application to actual reasoning of various types.

Logic and Philosophy

Logic is a subject with a long history. Like so much of our intellectual heritage, it goes back to the ancient Greeks, among whom the formal study of logic began with Aristotle in the fourth century B.C. Aristotle's most important contribution to logic was his theory of the syllogism. (The nature of the syllogism will be discussed in Chapter 2.) Later, Stoic philosophers worked out some of the principles of truth-functional logic. (Truth functions will be explained in Chapter 3.)

During medieval times, Aristotle's writings on logic were admired far more than anyone else's, and so thinkers in the medieval tradition came to regard the theory of the syllogism as the central and most important part of logic. This view persisted into modern times; as late as the eighteenth century, the great German philosopher Kant reflected the opinion of most thinkers of that time when he declared that logic was a completed science, a subject whose essentials were fully understood and in which no new principles remained to be discovered.

This opinion proved to be mistaken, however. In the nineteenth century the Irish logician Boole showed that the field of truth functions was far richer than had previously been realized, and he devised powerful new methods for treating problems in that branch of logic as well as for generalizing the theory of the syllogism. Also, the German mathematician Frege originated the theory of quantification. (Quantification will be discussed in Chapter 4.) The new developments in logic were systematized by Whitehead and Russell in their famous work *Principia Mathematica,* written early in the twentieth century. In that work they not only undertook to develop the new logic in a systematic manner but also tried to establish the thesis that the laws of pure mathematics can be derived from those of logic alone.

This modern logic, when properly understood, does not in any way contradict the traditional aristotelian logic, when that is properly understood. However, modern logic differs from the traditional aristotelian logic in two important ways. It is much more general, dealing with a far wider variety of forms of reasoning; and it uses more symbolism, and in its style and method is more akin to mathematics. In what follows, we shall be concerned both with the main ideas of traditional aristotelian logic and with some of the ideas of modern symbolic logic.

The more advanced logical studies nowadays have taken on a character like that of pure mathematics, while elementary parts of logic have their especial interest because of their practical value in helping to detect mistakes in reasoning. Thus it perhaps seems that logic does not have much relation to philosophy. Yet logic has always been regarded as a branch of philosophy, and there are good reasons for this. Let us briefly consider what some of the various branches of philosophy are, and what they have in common.

Moral philosophy, or *ethics,* is the branch of philosophy that investigates the notions of good and evil, right and wrong, duty and obligation, and the like. It tries to clarify the nature of these notions in order to answer general questions about their meaning; about whether there are objective standards of value and rightness; about how we determine what things are good or right; about what things are good and right; and so on. In dealing with such questions, moral philosophy seeks to analyze the critical standards used in making moral judgments.

Metaphysics is the branch of philosophy that tries to understand the nature of the real universe considered in its most general aspect. It considers questions about what kinds of things really exist (Is everything physical, or are there nonphysical realities?); about the nature of space and time; about whether everything that happens has a cause; and so on. Metaphysics seeks to analyze the standards employed in judgments about reality.

The *theory of knowledge,* or *epistemology,* is the branch of philosophy that investigates the nature and scope of knowledge. It asks what it is genuinely to know something; whether we can have knowledge of things outside our minds; whether all knowledge depends upon experience; and so on. The theory of knowledge seeks to analyze the standards employed in judging the genuineness of claims to the possession of knowledge.

Aesthetics is the branch of philosophy that deals with the notions of beauty and ugliness, and with the value of works of art. It asks what the nature of beauty is; whether there are objective standards of beauty; whether experiencing beautiful things can give us insight into the nature of reality; and so on. Aesthetics tries to deal with such questions by examining the critical standards used in making judgments about beauty and ugliness.

Four of the main branches of philosophy have been mentioned, and they are akin to one another in important ways. They deal with questions which are extremely general and which are not dealt with by the methods of the special sciences. These philosophical questions are ones with which we can make headway only through reflecting upon our own standards of various kinds (our moral standards, our standards of what counts as reality, our standards of what counts as knowledge, and so on). By obtaining a clearer view of these standards, we may be able to make progress toward unraveling philosophical questions: toward answering them in some cases, and in other cases toward clarifying the misconceptions that have given rise to the questions.

Although the study of logic differs in some ways from the pursuit of other branches of philosophy, it is no accident that in the past logic has always been classified as a branch of philosophy. Logic has a basic kinship with these other branches. Like them, it deals with some very general questions: questions about what good reasoning is and about the difference between correct and incorrect steps in thinking. Moreover, like other branches of philosophy, logic is a reflective study; experiments are not necessary, and no laboratory work is appropriate for verifying its principles. Like other branches of philosophy, logic concerns itself with the critical analysis of standards. In logic, it is standards of correctness in reasoning which are central.

Someone might object that reasoning is a phenomenon

which can be studied empirically by the science of psychology and that there is no need for a reflective, philosophical approach to it. This objection is misguided. To be sure, observations could be made and experiments conducted to find out how people reason and to find the causes that make them reason as they do. But there is a difference between studying how people reason (a matter of psychology) and studying the nature of correct reasoning (a matter of logic). Logic does not undertake to describe or explain how people think; it has the different and legitimate aim of analyzing what correct reasoning is, irrespective of whether people do, in fact, reason correctly.

Arguments

In elementary logic we shall be studying the difference between good reasoning and bad. But just what is reasoning? How is it to be identified? For the moment, let us not worry about the difference between good and bad reasoning, but simply consider what reasoning is.

To start with, we can say that reasoning is essentially a process of marshaling *reasons*, where the point is to show that some things one believes to be true are reasons for believing something else to be true. Reasoning can take place when one is thinking privately to oneself, but also, of course, it can take place when someone is trying to prove something to someone else. Let us look at an example of each kind.

Consider an example of reasoning where a person is thinking to himself. Suppose Smith expects that his income will rise by 10 percent for the coming year, and at first he is cheerful about this thought. But he also believes that the prices of the goods and services he buys are going to rise by 10 percent for the coming year, and he further realizes that if the dollar amount of his income increases, this will put him into a higher income-tax bracket so that a larger percentage of his income will go for taxes. He puts these thoughts together in his mind and becomes aware of what they imply: "Next year I'll be *less* well off financially."

Here Smith is making an *inference*. He starts from some assumptions which he accepts as true. Then he comes to accept a consequence because he regards it as something that *follows from* his assumptions, that is, something his assumptions provide *good reason* for believing. Smith makes a transition from his assumptions (or *premises,* as we shall call them) to believing the consequence (or *conclusion,* as we shall call it). He comes to believe the conclusion *because* he has come to regard it as having to be true, since the premises are.

The situation is a little different when the person who is to come to believe the conclusion is a different individual from the person who presents the reasoning. For example, suppose that Jones has always rejected astrology, while Robinson has been inclined to believe in it. Jones now tries to show Robinson that astrology is unsound. Jones argues that if a person's fate were determined by the positions of the stars and planets at the time and place of the person's birth, then any two people born at the same time and place would have the same fate. But, Jones says, twins born at the same time and place sometimes grow up to have very different destinies. And therefore, he says, it follows that astrology is unsound.

Here, Jones wants to start from premises which Robinson will accept. Then he wants to get Robinson to agree that from these premises the conclusion that astrology is unsound does follow. Jones hopes, in this way, to get Robinson to come to believe the conclusion. Jones's own belief is not going to change; he presents his reasoning merely to change Robinson's belief. If Jones is candid and sincere, he will use only premises that he himself believes; if he is not, he will use premises that he thinks will help to convince Robinson, even ones that he, Jones, does not believe.

To generalize, we may say that reasoning is a process of thinking directed toward showing that conclusions are to be accepted (either by the reasoner himself or by those whom he addresses) because there seem to be good reasons for believing them.

When the reasoning is put into words, we shall call it an *argument.* An argument may have just one premise, or there may be two or more. But we shall say that each step of an argument has just one conclusion. Where several conclusions are drawn, either there are several separate arguments or there is one longer chain of argument consisting of several distinct shorter arguments as its steps.

In the examples considered so far, the person doing the reasoning actually comes to accept the conclusion, or actually tries to get his audience to do so. He does not just suggest a possible conclusion, which someone *might* believe. When he puts his thinking into words, his words form an *actual* argument, not just a *potential* argument.

In contrast, suppose that Smith thinks to himself, "If I can get a 20 percent raise for next year, and if the consumer price index rises by no more than 10 percent, then next year I'll be better off financially." Here Smith is getting clearer in his mind about the logical connection between one possibility and another; and so, in a sense, he could be said to be doing reasoning. However, he has not actually put forward any argument, for he has not actually asserted any premise or drawn any conclusion. Such cases are significantly different from cases in which actual arguments are present.

For the purposes of logic, we shall be using the words "argument" and "inference" very differently from the ways in which they are often used in ordinary language. In ordinary talk, the word "argument" often is used to mean almost any sort of quarrel, disagreement, or debate carried on through use of language. For example, if two people are shouting insults at each other, we say they are having an argument. And in ordinary talk the word "inference" usually means reasoning whose conclusion is quite speculative or doubtful. Thus, when a detective guesses that someone is guilty of a crime, the accused person may object, "But that's mere inference; you don't have any positive evidence against me."

What we shall mean by an argument (or reasoning, or inference, or proof) involves two essential features. In the first place, the person who presents the argument must be claiming that if certain things (the premises) are true, then something else (the conclusion) should be true also. That is, he is claiming that the premises would support the conclusion, would make it reasonable to believe. In the second place, he must be claiming that the premises are indeed true.* In making both these claims together, he aims to give a reason for accepting the conclusion as true. We shall say that there is an actual argument (or reasoning, or inference, or proof) when and only when both these claims are present.

---

* Perhaps the person presenting the argument does not *explicitly* make this claim with respect to each of his premises—some of the premises may be left unstated. But at any rate he is *committed* to the claim that each premise is true.

In everyday language, arguments can be expressed in many ways. Sometimes the premises are stated first; sometimes the conclusion is stated first. For example, the following are arguments: *CONCLUSIONS UNDERLINED*

National income rose for the year, and the population did not increase. Therefore per capita income must have risen.

The barometer has been falling rapidly, so there's bound to be a change of weather.

This liquid is acid, since it turns blue litmus paper red.

Octane has a higher boiling point than butane, and butane has a higher boiling point than methane; it follows that octane has a higher boiling point than methane.

There must not be any life on Venus; the atmosphere there is unsuitable, and the temperature is too extreme.

Words like "therefore," "since," and "it follows" are often signs that an argument is being presented. "Therefore" and "it follows" are used to introduce the conclusion of an argument, while "since," "for," and "because" are used to introduce premises. Words like "must," "should," and "ought" in a sentence often serve to show that the sentence is a conclusion being derived from premises. However, none of these words is an infallible sign of an argument; in order to tell whether something that has been said embodies an argument, we need to reflect with care about its intended meaning. And remember also that, for our purposes, in classifying something as an argument we are not necessarily saying that it is a *good* argument.

To scotch one kind of misunderstanding, consider the two remarks:

NOT AN ARGUMENT → If today is Tuesday, tomorrow will be Wednesday. (1)
Since today is Tuesday, tomorrow will be Wednesday. (2)

Example (1) is not an actual argument. A speaker who says (1) is not making or asking his hearers to make any inference, for he is not claiming that today is Tuesday. No premise is asserted and no conclusion is drawn. All that is claimed in (1) is that if today were Tuesday, then tomorrow would be Wednesday. We shall classify this as just a single sentence, not as an argument. Example (2) is an argument, however. In (2) it is being claimed that today is Tuesday (the premise), and from this the speaker infers or wants us to infer that tomorrow will be Wednesday (the conclusion). Here one thing is presented as an actual, not just a hypothetical, reason for believing another.

To scotch another sort of misunderstanding, consider these examples:

> I am a Democrat, so I voted for the incumbent Democrat.   (3)
> He didn't vote in the Democratic primary, so he's a
>   Republican.   (4)

If you think about the circumstances in which these remarks are likely to be made, you can see that they are different. The person who says (3) probably is not trying to prove to himself or to others that he voted for the Democrat; that interpretation does not fit most contexts in which this remark would occur. More likely, he is not trying to prove anything (he is not giving an argument). Instead, he is explaining what motivated him to vote as he did. Example (3) is more likely to be a statement about the motive which led the speaker to act than an argument in which one thing is being presented as a reason for believing another. Example (4) is different; here the speaker probably is trying to prove that the person under discussion is a Republican, and he cites a reason for believing this. Hence, (4) is an argument.

We are dealing here with the interpretation of what people say, or write. Of course, cases can arise in which it is not obvious what the correct interpretation is. Occasionally, two or more interpretations of a remark can be equally plausible. But this certainly does not mean that any interpretation is as good as any other. We should try to be fair and accurate in interpreting examples, and usually it will be possible to determine fairly definitely what the correct interpretation is.

Unclarity in this respect can arise of course when a speaker does not indicate whether he is presenting an argument or not. Sometimes a remark can suggest or hint at an argument without explicitly stating one. For example:

> Drink Extra-Light beer! It's the beer of champions!   (5)
> The Dolores Speedster goes from 0 to 60 in eight
>   seconds. You should be in the driver's seat.   (6)
> William McKinley smoked Cigarillos. Shouldn't you?   (7)

Should we classify remarks like these as arguments? They certainly do not have the form of explicit arguments. No conclusions are explicitly stated, and the 'premises' are not identified as reasons for believing anything else. To be sure, in each case the speaker is trying to convince us of something: that we should drink Extra-Light, buy a Dolores Speedster, or smoke Cigarillos. But his way of trying to convince us is not putting forward anything that he or anyone else could seriously imagine was a good reason. So, for our purposes, we shall classify examples that are like (5), (6), and (7) as efforts at verbal persuasion that are not arguments.

So far, we have considered only very simple examples. Let us now look at one example of more intricate reasoning involving several steps, an example that has the flavor or real-life reasoning. In this piece of discourse, the French philosopher Descartes is discussing the question whether animals (brutes) can think.*

Although the brutes do nothing which can convince us that they think, nevertheless, because their bodily organs are not very different from ours, we might conjecture that there was some faculty of thought joined to these organs, as we experience in ourselves, although theirs be much less perfect, to which I have nothing to reply, except that, if they could think as we do, they would have an immortal soul as well as we, which is not likely, because there is no reason for believing it of some animals without believing it of all, and there are many of them too imperfect to make it possible to believe it of them, such as oysters, sponges, etc.

Let us consider what is being inferred from what in this example. The main thoughts are:

The bodily organs of brutes are not very different
from ours. (1)
Brutes have some faculty of thought less perfect
than ours. (2)
If brutes could think, they would have immortal souls. (3)
If some animals have immortal souls, all animals do. (4)
Many animals, such as oysters and sponges, are very
imperfect. (5)
Many animals do not have immortal souls. (6)

* Descartes, Letter to the Marquis of Newcastle.

In analyzing this passage, our problem is to tell what inferences are being made. Descartes starts by considering a possible inference, the inference of (2) from (1); he does not himself make this inference, although he seems to grant that (1) constitutes evidence tending to support (2). Descartes then goes on to argue that (2) is untrue, and he presents his argument in a backward manner that is common in informal reasoning. Statements (3), (4), and (6) constitute the premises from which Descartes infers that (2) is untrue. But (6) itself is the conclusion of another piece of reasoning, for it is inferred from (5). We can describe the whole thing as two steps of reasoning: from (5), (6) is inferred; and from (6), (4), and (3) together it is inferred that (2) is untrue. Here then is a case in which we can work out the structure of the reasoning. However, there are no hard-and-fast rules that enable us automatically to recognize arguments or to analyze their structure in cases like this; there is no substitute for a sensitive understanding of the language we speak.

Now, if we look for arguments in the books we read and in the conversations we hear, we find that most writers and speakers are seriously presenting arguments only a small fraction of the time. The larger portion of most discourse consists merely of assertions made one after another, without any of them being put forward as reasons on the basis of which others are arrived at. And this is perfectly justified where the matters discussed are not dubious or controversial. But whenever we are concerned with assertions that are doubtful or that have been challenged, there arguments are appropriate. Thoughtless people can make up their minds whether to accept doubtful beliefs without even considering arguments pro and con, but a reasonable person will demand arguments before he makes up his mind and will want to make up his mind in accordance with the best arguments.

Although they are closely related in meaning, the words "argument," "reasoning," "inference," and "proof" are not synonyms. *Inference*, in the basic sense of the word, is the mental act of reaching a conclusion from one's premises, the achievement of coming to believe the conclusion because one comes to see (or thinks one sees) that it follows from premises already accepted as true. *Reasoning* is the mental activity of marshaling one's premises, reflecting upon their weight, and making inferences. An *argument* is a formulation in words or other symbols of premises and of a conclusion that the speaker has inferred from them, or that he is urging his audience to infer. A *proof*, in the more basic sense of the term, is an argument which successfully establishes the truth of its conclusion.

However, mathematicians and logicians often use the word "proof" in a weaker sense: showing that a certain conclusion would strictly follow from certain premises they sometimes call a proof, even though the person presenting the demonstration does not accept the premises and has no reason to accept the conclusion. Even further removed from the basic sense of the term is the way of using the word "proof" that has been introduced by recent mathematical logicians who define proofs as sequences of marks that fulfill certain formalistic requirements—their use of the word "proof" is perfectly legitimate, but it has only a distant kinship with the basic, central meaning of the term.

For simplicity of presentation, we have concentrated on arguments whose conclusions are sentences of the type that are capable of being true. With this standard kind of argument that we have been discussing, a person who finds an argument convincing will believe that its conclusion is true. We should notice in passing, however, that there can also be arguments whose conclusions are not like this. Suppose someone reasons "We need a car; the Torpedo is the safest car available, and it's moderately priced. Therefore, let's buy a Torpedo." Here the conclusion "Let's buy a Torpedo" is not something which it would make sense to regard as *true*; instead, to accept it is to have decided to *do* something. If the persons to whom the argument is addressed find the argument convincing, they will decide to go out and buy this make of car. Arguments like this have been called "practical" arguments, and their distinctive trait is that the conclusion, instead of saying something that is supposedly true, says something that is to be done, or preferred, or sought after. If we were trying to give a complete account of arguments, what was said earlier in this section would have to be modified to allow for practical arguments. Such arguments are not of central importance to logic, however, and to simplify our studies we shall not devote further attention to them.

EXERCISE 1

CONCLUSIONS UNDERLINED

A *Interpreting each example in the way it is most likely to be intended, say whether it contains an actual argument. If so, what is the conclusion and what are the premises?*

1 I hate you. You're disgusting. Why, oh, why did I ever get involved with an idiot like you?

2 No man who has defrauded his own ailing mother is worthy to hold public office. Congressman Green did just that, so he's not fit to represent us.

3 She's lovely! She has a wonderful complexion! She uses Oil of Mandalay.

4 Probably few of these rose bushes will bloom here, because the soil is poor and there is little sunshine.

5 Believe me, officer, I wasn't driving 70 in a 30-mph zone, honestly. You've got to believe me, I really mean it.

NO ARGN → **6** Ever since she went away, he has been tormented by remorse.

7 Bolivia lost its struggle for access to the sea because its army was smaller and less well equipped than those of Chile and Peru.

8 Smith will win the election, I think, because the polls show her with a strong lead.

9 We all know that Smith won the last election; that was because the voters wanted a new face.

NO ARGN **10** If they build the new airplane of titanium, it should be able to withstand supersonic speeds.

11 Any integer divisible by 10 is divisible by 2. Any integer divisible by 2 is divisible by 3. Therefore, any integer divisible by 10 is divisible by 3.

NO ARGN **12** The federal government recently gave $258,000 to a psychology professor at Harding University to study why Americans have children. Asked how the nation's taxpayers will benefit from his survey, he replied, "I don't understand that question."

13 Is aluminum chemically stable? It seems to be stable, but this is only because the thin oxide coating first formed is very adherent and impervious. If the surface is wetted with mercury, the film no longer adheres and the metal oxidizes with great rapidity.

14 Although the pressure exerted by a gas depends upon the velocity of its molecules, it is not directly proportional to the speed; if the speed is doubled, not only does each molecule hit the vessel walls twice as often, but also twice as hard, for the momentum of each molecule is doubled by doubling the speed.

† **B** *Construct a clear step-by-step argument establishing what the answer is to each of the following problems.*

1 Whoever leaked the report had top-secret clearance, was in the office on Tuesday, was expert in toxicology, and had access to the telex. Only those who know chemistry are expert in toxicology. All who have access to the telex have top-secret clearance. No one but Sean, Hilary, Maria, and Germaine was in the office on Tuesday. Sean does not have access to the telex unless Maria is expert in toxicology.

Germaine lacks top-secret clearance. Maria knows no chemistry. Who leaked the report?

2 The average temperature in Bellvue on New Year's Day (expressed to the nearest degree) has been different for each of the last five years. The product of these temperatures is 12. What were the five temperatures?

3 Mrs. Jones, her brother, her son, and her daughter are all on the federal payroll. Of them, the one who draws the highest salary is of the opposite sex to the twin of the one whose salary is lowest. The one who is highest-paid and the one who is lowest-paid are the same age. Who is the highest-paid and who is the lowest-paid?

4 Ten disks, bearing the numbers 1 to 10 inclusive, were put into a bag. Alice, Bill, Carol, Don, and Eva, in that order, drew out and kept two disks each. The sum of the two numbers drawn in each case was: Alice, 16; Bill, 11; Carol, 4; Don, 17; and Eva, 7. What were the numbers on the disks actually drawn by each person?

CONCLUSIONS UNDERLINED

C *For each of the following examples, decide whether the author is advancing an argument. If he is doing so, explain what his conclusion is and what his premises are.*

1 You admit then that I believe in divinities. Now if these divinities are a species of gods, then there is my proof that . . . I do believe in gods. If, on the other hand, these divinities are sons of gods, their natural sons, as it were, by nymphs or some other mortal mothers, as rumor makes them, why, then, let me ask you, is there any one in the world who could suppose that there are sons of gods and at the same time that there are no gods?   PLATO, *Apology*

2 The sun was shining though 'twas November: he had seen the market-carts rolling into London, the guard relieved at the palace, labourers trudging to their work in the gardens between Kensington and the City—the wandering merchants and hawkers filling the air with their cries. The world was going to its business again, although dukes lay dead and ladies mourned for them; and kings, very likely, lost their chances. So night and day pass away, and to-morrow comes, and our place knows us not.

WILLIAM THACKERY, *Henry Esmond*

No argument

INDUCTIVE

3   The pure and genuine influence of Christianity may be traced
in its beneficial though imperfect effects on the barbarian
proselytes of the North.   If the decline of the Roman empire
was hastened by the conversion of Constantine, his victorious
religion broke the violence of the fall and mollified the
ferocious temper of the conquerors.

EDWARD GIBBON, *The Decline and Fall of the Roman Empire*

4   Since . . . it necessarily belongs to rulers, for the subjects'
safety to discover the enemy's counsel, to keep garrisons, and   *DEDUCTIVE*
to have money in continual readiness; and . . . princes are,
by the law of nature, bound to use their whole endeavour
in procuring the welfare of their subjects: it follows, that it is
not only lawful for them to send out spies, to maintain
soldiers, to build forts, and to require monies for these purposes; but also not to do thus is unlawful.

THOMAS HOBBES, *De Cive*

5   Upon separation of this little finger, should this consciousness go along with the little finger, and leave the rest of the   *DEDUCTIVE*
body, it is evident that the little finger would be the person,
the same person; and self then would have nothing to do with
the rest of the body. . . .   This may show us wherein personal identity consists: not in the identity of substance, but,
as I have said, in the identity of consciousness.

JOHN LOCKE, *Essay Concerning Human Understanding*

6   Every man has a right to risk his own life in order to preserve
it.   Has it ever been said that a man who throws himself   *DEDUCTIVE*
out of the window to escape from a fire is guilty of suicide?
Has such a crime ever been laid to the charge of him who
perished in a storm because, when he went on board, he
knew of the danger?

JEAN-JACQUES ROUSSEAU, *The Social Contract*

7   I do not think that one should have children.   I observe   *DEDUCTIVE*
in the acquisition of children many risks and many griefs,
whereas a harvest is rare, and even where it exists, it is thin
and poor.   DEMOCRITUS, *Fragments on Ethics*

8   [W]e have believed in Jesus Christ, that we might be justified   *ABDEDUCTIVE*
by the faith of Christ, and not by the works of the law [i.e.,
by obeying the old laws]. . . .   [But] . . . if righteousness

come by the law, then Christ is dead in vain. . . .   O foolish Galatians, . . .   This only would I learn of you, Received ye the Spirit by the works of the law, or by the hearing of faith? . . .   He therefore that ministereth to you the Spirit, and worketh miracles among you, doeth he it by the works of the law, or by the hearing of faith? . . . that no man is justified by the law in the sight of God, it is evident: for, [it is written that] The just shall live by faith.   And the law is not of faith.   ST. PAUL, *Galatians* 2, 3

DEDUCTION AND VALIDITY

"Divide and conquer" is a fine old maxim, as valuable in the intellectual sphere as in the political.   If we are to gain mastery over arguments, let us divide them into different types which can be considered separately.   We shall begin by distinguishing between what are called deductive and what are called inductive arguments.   There are good and bad arguments belonging to both types.

Deductive and Inductive Arguments

The basic distinction between deduction and induction has to do with the strength of the logical link that is supposed to hold between premises and conclusion.   In some cases when a person argues, he is claiming that the truth of his premises is strictly sufficient to establish the truth of his conclusion.   In other cases he is not claiming that the link is this strong, but is claiming that it is strong enough so that his premises do support or confirm his conclusion, making it reasonable to believe.

First let us consider arguments like these:

> Green belongs to the American Federation of Teachers.
>   All members of the AFT pay union dues.
>   Therefore, Green must pay union dues.   (1)
>   White is a bachelor.   Hence, he has no wife.   (2)

Here we have arguments that are *demonstrative.*   That is, each argument has premises whose truth would ensure that necessarily the conclusion would have to be true also; knowing that the premises are true would give us strictly sufficient reason for believing the conclusion. Thus an inconsistency would be involved in accepting the premises but denying the conclusion.

Arguments of this kind are *deductive* arguments. An argument that succeeds in being demonstrative is a good deductive argument, but we also want to allow for the possibility of bad deductive arguments. We shall therefore say that if the premises are put forward with the claim that the conclusion strictly follows from them, then the argument is deductive, even when this claim is mistaken. For example, suppose someone argues:

> Black pays union dues. All members of the AFT pay union dues. Therefore, Black must belong to the AFT. (3)

Here the wording indicates that the speaker is claiming that his premises are strictly sufficient to yield the conclusion, so we shall classify his argument as deductive, although it is a bad deductive argument (the truth of the premises would not in this case guarantee the truth of the conclusion). Thus the essential feature of a *deductive* argument is that its premises are strictly sufficient to ensure the truth of the conclusion, or at any rate that the speaker claims they are so.

Now let us look at some contrasting examples:

> Brown belongs to the National Rifle Association. Most members of the NRA are opposed to gun control. Therefore, Brown probably opposes gun control. (4)
> When I bought a pair of shoes of this brand and style once before, they lasted a long time. If I buy another pair, most likely they will last a long time too. (5)

We shall regard these arguments as having the sentences "Brown opposes gun control" and "If I buy another pair, they will last a long time" as their conclusions. We interpret the words "probably" and "most likely" not as parts of the conclusions but as indicators of the degree of connection claimed to hold between premises and conclusions.

An important feature of these two arguments is that in each

case the conclusion makes some prediction or expresses some conjecture which goes beyond what the premises say but about which we can find out by further observations. (We can wait until there is an election in which gun control is an issue and then see how Brown votes; we can test the shoes over a period of time to discover how long they wear.) Arguments that are not deductive and that possess this feature we shall call *inductive* arguments. That is, inductive arguments are nondeductive arguments whose conclusions go beyond what their premises say and yet can in principle be tested by further observations.*

To say that the conclusion of an argument 'goes beyond' what the premises say means that there would be no contradiction involved in accepting the premises but denying the conclusion. Thus, the truth of the premises cannot provide a strictly demonstrative reason for believing the conclusion. The premises of such an argument may give good reason for accepting the conclusion. They may render the conclusion highly probable. But always it remains logically possible that the premises are true and the conclusion nevertheless is false.

Deductive and inductive arguments are the only types of argument that are much studied by logicians; indeed, logicians have studied deduction much more extensively than induction because deductive reasoning can be described more readily in terms of definite general rules. Whether there is any genuine reasoning that is neither deductive nor inductive is a question to which we shall briefly return later (in Chapter 7).

In practice, when we encounter arguments it is not always possible to classify them definitely as deductive or inductive, for the speaker may not have made clear how tight a link he is claiming that there is between premises and conclusion (he may even be unclear in his own mind about this question). In such cases we can at least consider which way of classifying the argument would be more sympathetic to the speaker's concerns.

---

* There is no unanimity among logicians about the definition of induction; the definition adopted here is not the simplest in current use, but it is perhaps the least likely to be misleading in the long run. An old-fashioned idea was that deductive arguments always move from the general to the less general and that inductive arguments always move from the less general to the more general; however, this idea is too inaccurate to be helpful.

Truth and Validity

Next we shall consider the notion of truth, which relates to the premises and conclusions of arguments, and the notion of validity, which relates to arguments themselves. While these two notions should be distinguished, they are connected in an important way.

What sort of items are the premises and conclusions of arguments? We shall speak of them as being sentences. A *sentence* may be defined roughly as a series of words that form a complete utterance in accordance with the conventions of language. The sentences that serve as premises and conclusions of arguments ordinarily are what grammarians call declarative sentences, and they differ from other kinds of sentences in that they have the distinctive feature of being used to say what is *true* or *false*. Other kinds of sentences, such as questions and exclamations, ordinarily would not be appropriate as parts of an argument, for they are not ordinarily used to say anything true or false. (In the first example of Exercise 1, part C, above, a question does serve as a premise, but it is a rhetorical question—one that does not call for an answer and is being used instead to state that something is so.)

Naturally, a sentence that is a premise in one argument may be a conclusion in some other argument. Suppose I am trying to prove a conclusion, and in doing so I advance an argument that uses another sentence as its premise. My opponent, even if he grants that my conclusion follows from my premise, may question whether my premise is true; he may say that he will not accept my conclusion until I prove my premise. If he challenges my premise in this way, it may become my duty to try to construct a new argument to establish that premise, that is, a new argument that will have as its conclusion the premise of the first argument. I would hope to be able to choose as the premise of my new argument something my opponent will not challenge; if he challenges this new premise also, then perhaps I can prove it too.

We noted earlier that an argument has two essential features: The speaker who presents the argument is claiming that his premises are true, and he is also claiming that if these premises are true, the conclusion should be true also (the strength that the logical link is claimed to have can vary, as we noticed). Every argument, whether good or bad, must have these two features if it is to be an actual argument in our sense of the term. Now we can see from this that there are two chief ways in which a person can err when he advances an unsatisfactory argument. On the one hand, the person presenting the argument may make a mistake in claiming that his premises are true. In this case he is making a *factual* error. (Here we suppose that his premises are false but not logically inconsistent.) His mistake is that his facts are wrong, and he has reasoned from assumptions that are untrue.

On the other hand, a second kind of mistake would be the mistake of claiming that if the premises are true, the conclusion should be true too, when this is not so (and a milder form of this mistake would be the error of claiming this more strongly than is justified). This would be a *logical* error, resulting from misunderstanding the logical relation between premises and conclusion. Logic, insofar as it is concerned with errors, is primarily concerned with errors of this second sort. It is not the business of logic to tell us what premises to start with in our thinking (except that we should start with premises that are logically consistent), but it is the business of logic to help us see how conclusions ought to be related to their premises.

The first kind of mistake is the mistake of using false sentences as premises. Sentences can be said to be true or false, but whole arguments should not be spoken of as being true or false. When the premises of an argument are linked to the conclusion in the right sort of logical way, the argument is called *valid*.* That is, in a valid argument the premises really do support the conclusion; if the premises are true, then the conclusion should be true too. And in a valid argument the claim that is being made as to the strength with which the premises support the conclusion corresponds to the strength of the link that does hold between premises and conclusion. An argument is *invalid* if its premises are not related to its conclusion in this way. Thus

---

* Some writers on logic restrict the term "valid" to good deductive arguments. They do not choose to call an inductive argument valid, no matter how good it is. We shall not follow that usage, however. Note that we are using the word "valid" in a somewhat special sense, and are applying it only to arguments; in ordinary language the word is used more broadly and vaguely as a synonym for "true," as when people speak of valid opinions, viewpoints, beliefs, etc.

---

the second kind of mistake is the mistake of employing an invalid type of argument.

To see clearly that there is a difference between truth and validity, let us think about deductive arguments. (For inductive arguments, truth and validity are related in a somewhat more complicated way, which will be discussed in Chapter 6.) A deductive argument is valid provided that if its premises are true, its conclusion must necessarily be true also. Notice, however, that even when a deductive argument is valid its conclusion may not be true. For example, the argument "All creatures that fly have wings; all pigs fly; therefore all pigs have wings" is an argument that is deductively valid; that is, if the premises are all true, the conclusion necessarily must be true also. But the conclusion is false, and that is possible because the premises are not all true.

We should note also that a conclusion invalidly reached may happen to be true. For example, the argument "All birds have wings and all chickens have wings; therefore all chickens are birds" is an argument whose conclusion happens to be true even though the argument is invalid.* The one thing that cannot happen is for a false conclusion to be validly deduced from premises all of which are true; this cannot happen, in virtue of what we mean when we call a deductive argument valid.

One further bit of terminology: In ordinary language the word "imply" means "hint" or "suggest," but in logic this word is used in a different and stronger sense. When we say that the premises of an argument *imply* the conclusion, we mean that the argument is a valid deductive argument. More generally, to say that one sentence or group of sentences implies another sentence means that if the former are true, the latter must necessarily be true also.† We do not say that the premises infer the conclusion

---

* If someone does not see that this example is invalid, a good way to show him is to make use of an *analogy*. We say to him, "If you say that this is valid, then you might as well say that 'All birds have legs and all pigs have legs, and so all pigs are birds' is a valid argument." Thus we show him that in this style of reasoning the premises do not support the conclusion with the strictness that valid deduction requires.

† This is the only notion of implication that we shall employ. However, many modern logic writers follow the somewhat confusing precedent set by Russell, who used the word "implication" as a name for the truth-functional conditional (which we shall discuss in Chapter 3).

---

in a valid deductive argument, as that is not good English. Implication is a logical relation that can hold between sentences; inference is an act that people perform when they derive one sentence from another.

° To say say that the premises and conclusions of arguments are sentences (as was said earlier in this section) is a serviceable but crude way of speaking. It is serviceable in enabling us to talk about parts of arguments without our having to speak in tedious circumlocutions. It is crude, however, because it glosses over the distinction between a declarative sentence and the statement, or assertion, that a speaker makes by uttering the sentence on a particular occasion. Saying that the premises and conclusion of an argument are sentences suggests that sentences as such are true or false and that we can analyze the logic of an argument merely by studying the sentences (the series of words) that occur in it. But we cannot do that. Suppose a speaker argued:

If Jones is mad, he needs psychiatric treatment. Jones is mad. Therefore, Jones needs psychiatric treatment.

Whether this argument is logical depends, for one thing, upon whether the word "mad" is used in the same sense in both premises. If in uttering the first sentence the speaker was asserting that if Jones is insane then he needs treatment, while in uttering the second the speaker was asserting that Jones is angry, then the argument is not good logic. Merely by inspecting the words themselves one cannot determine how the speaker is using them, and one cannot determine whether the argument is good or bad logic. To determine those things one must consider the *context* in which these sentences are uttered. Perhaps one must take account of what the speaker said before or afterward, what he saw and knew, perhaps his gestures and tone of voice.

A less crude way of stating this would be to say that the premises and conclusions of arguments are not the sentences that speakers utter but rather are the things they are saying by uttering these sentences. The difficulty is that this way of speaking would be very cumbersome later on, when we come to discuss the logical forms of arguments. In the rest of this book, whenever a remark is made about some logical aspect of a sentence, the meticulous reader should understand this as short for a more cumbrous remark about some aspect of what it is that a speaker would normally be saying by uttering that sentence.

Writers on logic have used various terms for referring to the premises and conclusions of arguments. Some have spoken of *propositions*, some of *judgments*, some of *statements*.

EXERCISE 2

* **A** *Examine each example and decide whether it contains an argument. If it does, decide whether it makes better sense to in-*

*terpret the argument as deductive or inductive; also, identify the
conclusion and the main premises.*

1 This pasture can support three sheep per acre, and we have
500 acres. So there's room enough for our 800 sheep.

2 Jim's been hiking in the woods all day, so he'll be tired and
hungry when he gets home.

3 It isn't prudent to keep vipers or piranhas as pets. They are
dangerous. It's never prudent to keep any dangerous creatures as pets.

4 Since neither of the parents-to-be has blue eyes, their baby
probably won't have blue eyes either.

5 Our neighbor's lights are on, so he must be at home.

6 The statue, made of Greek marble, represents a draped female
figure. The pose, the way the garments are draped, and their
transparency are the clues that lead to the identification of
the figure as a Muse, for the type is similar to a figure on
a relief now in the British Museum which is signed by
Archelaus of Priene and shows all nine Muses.

7 There are already fifty drilling rigs probing deep beneath the
surface at West Pembina. Given the cost of drilling down to
the 9000-foot level, where new oil strikes have been taking
place, it seems obvious that oil companies would not be
spending millions of dollars on oil leases and additional
millions on drilling wells unless they were satisfied that the
potential payoff could be very big indeed.

B *For each example, discuss whether it makes better sense to
interpret it as deductive or as inductive.*

1 "How, in the name of good fortune, did you know all that, Mr.
Holmes?" he asked. "How did you know, for example, that I
did manual labor? It's true as gospel, for I began as a ship's
carpenter."

   "Your hands, my dear sir. Your right hand is quite a size
larger than your left. You have worked with it and the
muscles are more developed."

   A. CONAN DOYLE, *The Red-Headed League*

2 A struggle for existence inevitably follows from the high rate
at which all organic beings tend to increase. Every being,
which during its natural lifetime produces several eggs or

seeds, must suffer destruction during some period of its life, and during some season or occasional year, otherwise, on the principle of geometrical increase, its numbers would quickly become so inordinately great that no country could support the product. Hence, as more individuals are produced than can possibly survive, there must in every case be a struggle for existence, either one individual with another of the same species, or with the individuals of distinct species, or with the physical conditions of life.

CHARLES DARWIN, *The Origin of Species*

3 "Sperrit? Well, maybe," he said. "But there's one thing not clear to me. There was an echo. Now, no man ever seen a sperrit with a shadow; well, then, what's he doing with an echo to him, I should like to know? That ain't in natur', surely?" R. L. STEVENSON, *Treasure Island*

IMPLIED THERE IS NO SPERRIT

4 [Flaubert in his] letters to Louise Colet . . . boasts of amorous exploits, which must be true, since he is addressing the only person who can be both witness and judge of them.

JEAN-PAUL SARTRE, *Search for a Method*

5   . . . You are wise;
Or else you love not; for to be wise and love
Exceeds man's might; that dwells with gods above.

WILLIAM SHAKESPEARE, *Troilus and Cressida*

6 It is necessary that the land and the surrounding waters have the figure which the shadow of the earth casts, for at the time of an eclipse it projects on the moon the circumference of a perfect circle. Therefore the earth is not a plane, as Empedocles and Anaximenes opined . . . or again a cylinder, as Anaximander . . . but it is perfectly round. . . .

COPERNICUS, *On the Revolutions of the Celestial Spheres*

7 The nature of the mind and soul is bodily; for when it is seen to push the limbs, rouse the body from sleep, and alter the countenance and guide and turn about the whole man, and when we see that none of these effects can take place without touch nor touch without body, must we not admit that the mind and the soul are of a bodily nature?

LUCRETIUS, *On the Nature of Things*

* **C** *Each of the following is a deductive argument. In each case, is the argument valid? Are its premises all true? Is its conclusion true? Notice how each example differs from every other.*

1 All Germans are Europeans, and all Berliners are Germans. Therefore, all Berliners are Europeans. *VALID*

2 All Germans are Europeans, and all Berliners are Europeans. Therefore, all Berliners are Germans. *N.V.*

3 All Germans are Africans, and all Berliners are Germans. Therefore, all Berliners are Africans. *V*

4 All Germans are Africans, and all Berliners are Africans. Therefore, all Germans are Berliners. *N.V.*

5 All Germans are Africans, and all Berliners are Africans. Therefore, all Berliners are Germans. *N.V.*

6 All Germans are Africans, and all Nigerians are Germans. Therefore, all Nigerians are Africans. *V*

7 All Germans are Europeans, and all Berliners are Europeans. Therefore, all Germans are Berliners. *N.V.*

EMPIRICAL AND
NECESSARY SENTENCES

The sentences that serve as premises of an argument are supposed to be true, and their being true is supposed to provide a reason for accepting as true the sentence which serves as the conclusion. However, true sentences (and false ones also, for that matter) can be divided into rather different kinds, depending on how we can come to know whether they are true.

Most of the sentences encountered in ordinary discourse are empirical ('based on experience'). Consider a few examples:

Lead is cheaper than copper.
Some pigs can fly.
Caesar conquered Gaul.
Ted's age plus Jim's age equals thirty-two.

Each of these sample sentences is 'based on experience'; but in what sense? Not merely in the comparatively trivial sense that to know whether the sentence is true one must have had the experience involved in learning the meanings of its words—for us, all sentences are 'based on experience' to this extent. No, these sentences are connected with experience in a stronger sense: to know whether one of these sentences is true or false, an ordinary person must possess *evidence* of its truth (or falsity) *drawn from experience*—sensory evidence regarding what has been seen or heard or felt or smelled or tasted. This evidence might consist of comparatively direct observations made by oneself, or it might be more indirect, consisting, say, of what one had heard concerning observations made by others. Now, to be sure, a person lacking such evidence drawn from experience could still *believe* it to be true that lead is cheaper than copper, or *believe* it to be false that some pigs can fly; but then he would not *know* these things, for it would be merely accidental that his beliefs were correct. For ordinary people like ourselves (who lack extraordinary faculties such as extrasensory perception), beliefs about such matters are not knowledge unless they are properly based on direct or indirect evidence obtained by use of our senses.

Thus an empirical sentence is a sentence such that merely understanding its meaning is not sufficient to enable us to know whether it is true; in addition to understanding the sentence, we must have sensory experience on which to base our knowledge of that. Empirical sentences are said to be known *a posteriori*, because whether they are true is known only after appropriate experience has been had. Also, empirical sentences are said to be *contingent*, in that their truth or falsity depends on more than merely their meaning: an empirical sentence is a sentence which, if true, might conceivably have been false, or which if false, might conceivably have been true.

However, there are other sentences whose truth or falsity is knowable without reliance upon sensory evidence. Such sentences are said to be knowable *a priori* (because we can know whether they are true before we observe the phenomena of which they speak). And among sentences whose truth is knowable a priori we shall concentrate on *necessary* sentences: sentences that, if true, are necessarily true because to deny them would involve an inconsistency; or that, if false, are necessarily false because to affirm them would involve an inconsistency.* Some examples:

---

* Let us leave it an open question whether there are other sentences knowable a priori which are not necessary in this sense. If there are any contingent but

Snow is white or it is not.
All dogs are animals.
Caesar conquered Gaul, but it is not the case that he did.
Fifteen plus seventeen equals thirty-two.

When these sentences are understood straightforwardly in their likeliest senses, the first, second, and fourth are necessarily true, for to deny them would involve inconsistency—something illogical or inconceivable, e.g., snow that is both white and not white, dogs that are not animals. The third is necessarily false, for to affirm it would involve inconsistency. And all are a priori, in that there is no need to have evidence from sense experience in order to know whether they are true. One can come to know whether they are true just by understanding the meanings of the words employed and reflecting upon what has to be involved, granted that the words mean what they do. For instance, the realization that it would not be literally correct to *call* anything a dog unless it was an animal enables us to know a priori that all dogs are necessarily animals. But no sense experience, beyond what was involved in learning the meanings of the words, is required in order to enable one to know this.

In logic we are interested in learning to tell the difference between arguments that are valid and arguments that are invalid. But to understand that the argument "No gentlemen are tactless; all baboons are tactless; therefore no baboons are gentlemen" is a valid deductive argument amounts to the same thing as to understand that the sentence "If no gentlemen are tactless and if all baboons are tactless, then no baboons are gentlemen" is a necessarily true sentence. The argument differs from the sentence in that it is an argument rather than a single sentence. (It consists of a series of sentences: premises that are asserted and a conclusion derived from them.) But to recognize the deductive validity of the argument is to recognize that the premises imply the conclusion. To say that the premises imply the conclusion amounts to saying that this "if-then" sentence is necessarily true.

---

a priori sentences (such as Descartes's "I am thinking" and "I exist"), they are rather rare and special cases, with which we shall not be concerned. Also we shall not be concerned with weaker senses of necessity—e.g., the 'physical necessity' supposedly expressed by sentences like "Taking arsenic must be fatal."

Thus logic is very much concerned with necessary sentences. It is especially concerned with sentences that are necessarily true in virtue of their *logical form*. The logical form "If no # # # are *** and if all /// are ***, then no /// are ###" is such that, with whatever three words or phrases we consistently fill the gaps, provided we make sense, we always get an overall "if-then" sentence that is true. Regardless of its subject matter, any sentence of this form is bound to be true. Thus we say that this particular sentence about gentlemen and baboons is true in virtue of its logical form, and the corresponding argument is valid in virtue of its logical form. We shall learn more about logical form in later chapters.

We should notice in passing, however, that not all valid arguments are valid in virtue of their logical forms. For instance, the argument "This glass is red; therefore this glass is colored" is a valid piece of deductive reasoning. (The truth of the premise would be absolutely sufficient to guarantee the truth of the conclusion.) But we cannot usefully analyze the logical form of the argument except as " . . . is ***, therefore . . . is ///." Since many arguments having this form are invalid, we cannot say that this argument is valid because of its logical form. Instead, its validity results from the special connection in meaning between the words "red" and "colored." However, in logic, and especially in deductive logic, we are mainly interested in considering arguments whose validity depends upon their logical forms, that is, on the ways in which certain logical words such as "all," "some," "not," and "or" are arranged in them.

Returning to our distinction between empirical and necessary sentences, we must recognize that this is not an absolutely precise distinction; there are plenty of borderline cases of sentences that do not clearly belong in one category rather than the other. For example, consider the sentence "All spiders have eight legs." When straightforwardly understood, is this a necessary a priori truth or is it an empirical truth? Is there or is there not an inconsistency involved in supposing that there might be a species of spiders that did not have eight legs? (Suppose explorers found a species of creatures that looked like spiders, behaved like spiders, and were directly descended from spiders—but which had evolved ten legs instead of eight. Would it be incorrect to call such creatures spiders?) There are no definite answers to these questions because the word "spider" is somewhat indefinite in its meaning. Because of this indefiniteness, there is no answer to the question whether the sentence as ordinarily understood is necessary or empirical. We could decide to change or sharpen the meaning we attach to the word "spider"; then the sentence could become either definitely empirical or definitely necessary—but that does not alter what has just been said.

Thus some sentences cannot be definitely classified as necessary or empirical. However, the distinction between necessary and empirical sentences still has value, in spite of such borderline cases, for many sentences with which we ordinarily are concerned do fit fairly definitely into these categories. And even with sentences that do not fit definitely into either category, it can often be helpful to ask: *To what extent* are they necessary, to what extent are they empirical? How could they be understood so as to be necessary, how could they be understood so as to be empirical? By thinking about sentences in this way we can often come to understand them better.

Moreover, the distinction between necessary and empirical sentences is of interest in two further ways, one theoretical and the other practical.

First, the distinction helps us to understand a philosophical difference between two types of knowledge: the a priori knowledge involved in logic and mathematics, on the one hand, and the empirical knowledge involved in the experimental sciences, on the other hand. The sentences in which are expressed the laws of physics, chemistry, and other experimental sciences typically are empirical sentences. They tell us about what actually is so, although it might have been otherwise. Scientists must make observations and conduct experiments in order to know whether the sentences in which they are interested are true.

In pure mathematics, however, and in logic, we do not have to employ observations or experiments; the sentences in which laws of mathematics and logic are expressed are a priori necessary sentences. The principles of mathematics and logic give us no specific information about this particular world that happens to exist but apply equally to all conceivable worlds. Such of these principles as we attain knowledge of, we can know by means of reflection without appeal to sense experience.

Second, a practical reason why the distinction between

necessary and empirical sentences is worth noticing is that it can help us to evaluate sentences met in ordinary discourse. Sometimes a person wishes to assert an informative, empirical thought, but without realizing the difference, he asserts something necessarily true but trivial instead. His hearers give the wrong weight to what he said and may ask for the wrong kinds of reasons in its support if they are not aware of this distinction. Also, speakers sometimes utter necessarily false sentences without realizing that they are doing so; here too their hearers will give the wrong weight to what is said and may try in the wrong way to refute it if they are not aware of the distinction.

Obviously, trying to distinguish between empirical and necessary sentences brings us face to face with problems about language. One problem is that many words in our language are *vague:* it is unsettled just where correct use of a word begins and where it leaves off, as things vary in degree. For instance, the word "bald" is vague, for baldness is a matter of degree, and we cannot say just how many hairs must be missing before it is correct to describe a man as bald; there is a 'gray area' between being bald and not being bald. Vagueness on the part of the words a sentence contains can sometimes make for vagueness about whether that sentence is empirical or necessary. For example, the sentence "Bald men have little hair on their heads" is impossible to classify definitely as empirical or as necessary because it contains two quite vague words, "bald" and "little." If by "bald men" were meant "very bald men," then the sentence would be necessarily true; but if by "bald men" were ment "men at least slightly bald," then the sentence would be empirical and false. So vagueness can cause trouble here.

Another problem is that many words in our language are *ambiguous;* they have two or more different meanings. For instance, the word "heavy" in the sentence "This is a heavy book" is ambiguous, for it may have either of two quite different meanings: "hard to read" or "hard to lift." Ambiguity on the part of the words a sentence contains can make for difficulty about telling whether that sentence is empirical or necessary. Thus, "Heavy books are massive" would be a necessary truth if "heavy" means "hard to lift," but would be empirical if "heavy" meant "hard to read." In cases like this it is necessary to determine what meaning is intended for the ambiguous word before the sentence can be classified.

Some people who study logic get the impression that vagueness and ambiguity are always bad features for language to have, and they imagine that ideally we ought to use words that have no vagueness or ambiguity. This is a misunderstanding. It would be impossible to eliminate all vagueness and ambiguity from our language. And, in any case, it would be undesirable to do so; often we want to speak vaguely or ambiguously, and we need language that permits this. What we should do is become aware of the vagueness and ambiguity in our language so that in particular cases where these features might cause trouble we can be armed against it. (There will be further discussion of ambiguity in Chapter 5.)

EXERCISE 3

* **A** *When each sentence is straightforwardly understood, does it say something necessarily true, necessarily false, or empirical? Try to give the most reasonable answer in each case. If there seems to be no one best answer, discuss and explain the best alternative interpretations.*

1 All flying machines are aircraft.

2 Only a few kinds of dinosaurs lived in the Triassic period.

3 Any building constructed of granite is built of stone.

4 No neutrons are electrically charged particles.

5 There are no elephants in Patagonia.

6 If you are a Capricorn, dating an Aries will lead to trouble.

7 Some rodents can survive without ever drinking liquids.

8 Under purely competitive conditions, marginal unit revenue and average revenue will be equal for a firm.

9 Crocker Corporation increased its earnings during each quarter of the year just ended. However, the gains were not sufficient to bring the corporation's earnings for the full year up to the level of the preceding year.

10 The Mbongo are a fascinating tribe found on Ndugu, an uninhabited island off the coast of Africa.

11 If you eat an adequate, well-balanced diet, you will get all the vitamins your body normally needs.

12 The centerfielder leaped in vain for McGurk's towering drive; luckily it was foul by inches.

13 Turn on the pressure and the good ones always come through.

ϝ 14 The tiny island nations of Liechtenburg and Luxenstein have a long history of border skirmishes.

Ɛ 15 All known matter in the solar system is made up of chemical elements.

ϝ 16 No statement is wholly true.

B *In each case, if your answer is "yes," give an example to establish your answer. If your answer is "no," explain why there can be no example.*

1 Can there be a valid deductive argument consisting entirely of empirical sentences?

2 Can there be a valid deductive argument consisting entirely of necessary sentences?

3 Consider a valid deductive argument all of whose premises are necessarily true. Can its conclusion be an empirical sentence?

4 Consider a valid deductive argument all of whose premises are true empirical sentences. Can its conclusion be a necessary sentence?

5 Consider a valid deductive argument all of whose premises are false empirical sentences. Can its conclusion be a necessary sentence?

† C *In logic it is important to distinguish between what necessarily follows from a remark and what is merely suggested by it. In each of the following cases, suppose that someone says (a). Then is (b) something that follows as a valid deductive conclusion? If you find an example to be ambiguous, discuss alternative interpretations.*

1 (a) Only residents of the city are allowed to run for mayor.
  ~~NOT VALID~~ **(b)** Any resident of the city is allowed to run for mayor.

2 (a) All who love virtue love angling.
  VALID **(b)** All who don't love angling don't love virtue.

3 (a) Havre de Grace is east of Port Deposit.
  VALID **(b)** Port Deposit is west of Havre de Grace.

4 (a) Boy Scouts are as clean as they are reverent.
  NOT VALID **(b)** Boy Scouts are clean and reverent.

5 (a) Taxes won't have to be raised, if expenditures are cut.
  NOT VALID **(b)** Taxes will have to be raised, if expenditures aren't cut.

a) IF E THEN ~T   NOT VALID
b) IF ~E THEN T

SOME MEANS AT LEAST ONE, POSSIBLY ALL.

6 **(a)** Some of my neighbors are honest. — *NOT VALID*

(b) Some of my neighbors are not honest.

7 **(a)** The pool is open to anyone who is a club member or a guest of a member. — *NOT VALID*

(b) The pool is open to anyone who is both a club member and a guest of a member.

8 **(a)** Not all cases of rabies are fatal. — *VALID*

(b) Some cases of rabies are not fatal.

9 **(a)** Only buses are permitted in the right lane. — *NOT VALID*

(b) Buses are permitted only in the right lane.

10 **(a)** If this substance dissolves in sulfuric acid, then it isn't gold. *IF P THEN -Q* — *VALID*

(b) If this substance is gold, then it doesn't dissolve in sulfuric acid. *IF Q THEN -P*

11 **(a)** Carelessly he anchored in the target area. — *NOT VALID*

(b) He anchored carelessly in the target area.

12 **(a)** Each thing that happens has a purpose.

(b) There is a purpose behind all things that happen.

ALL DOGS ARE ANIMALS.   VALID

ALL NON-ANIMALS ARE NON-DOGS.

IF P THEN Q.   VALID

IF NOT-Q THEN NOT-P.

CHAPTER 2

THE LOGIC OF
CATEGORICAL SENTENCES

In this chapter we shall consider the traditional logic of categorical sentences, a part of logic first worked out by Aristotle. This part of logic deals with arguments whose premises and conclusions all can be expressed as sentences of the kind called categorical. This was the kind of logic mainly studied by logicians of medieval and early modern times, and they came to regard it as the principal part, perhaps even the whole, of logic. Nowadays it can be seen that such a view is far too narrow; there are many valuable forms of argument not comprehended within this traditional part of logic, and the limited range of arguments that it treats is not of great theoretical importance. Nevertheless, this traditional part of logic still deserves attention, for arguments that can be analyzed in this traditional style occur very frequently in ordinary thinking.

CATEGORICAL SENTENCES

We find it useful in logic to study the logical properties of certain basic standard forms of sentence. Then later we shall see how a wider range of arguments are capable of being translated into these basic forms so that their validity can be determined from our knowledge of the logical properties of the basic forms.

The Four Categorical Forms

Let us focus our attention upon four specific forms of sentence, forms important enough so that they were long ago given the special names "**A**," "**E**," "**I**," and "**O**." These four forms of sentence are:

A: All so-and-so's are such-and-such's.
E: No so-and-so's are such-and-such's.
I: Some so-and-so's are such-and-such's.
O: Some so-and-so's are not such-and-such's.

Sentences of these four forms, and only these, we shall call *categorical* sentences.* Thus, for example, the sentence "All unicorns are animals" is a categorical sentence of **A** form; the sentence "No natural satellites of the earth are self-luminous bodies" is a categorical sentence of **E** form; and the sentence "Some birds are not dodoes" is a categorical sentence of **O** form.

To be in categorical form, a sentence must start with a *quantifier* (the word "all," "no," or "some"), followed by the word or phrase called the *subject* of the sentence, then the *copula* ("are" or "are not"), and finally the word or phrase called the *predicate*. The words or phrases that serve as subjects and predicates in categorical sentences are called *terms*.

The **A** and **E** sentences are said to be *universal* because sentences of these forms sweepingly speak of the whole of the class of things to which the subject term applies. The **I** and **O** forms are said to be *particular* because sentences of these forms give definite information only about part of the class of things to which the subject term applies. This is called *quantity*. **A** and **E** are said to be universal in quantity, and **I** and **O** are said to be particular in quantity.

---

* The term "categorical" traditionally has been used because of its connection with the term "category," which comes from the Greek word for predicate. Thus, categorical sentences are sentences in which a predicate is connected with a subject. In Aristotle's philosophy, predicates were classified into some ten basic types, such as substance (e.g., "man"), quantity (e.g., 2 feet long"), quality (e.g., "white"), and others. These types of predicates, also regarded as corresponding to types of real entity in the universe, came to be called the categories. It was thought that in every categorical sentence the predicate had to belong to one of these categories.

The **A** and **I** forms say something *affirmative*, while **E** and **O** say something *negative*. This is called *quality*. **A** and **I** are said to be affirmative in quality, while **E** and **O** are said to be negative in quality. [The four letters used as names of these forms come from the vowels in the Latin words "*affirmo*" ("I affirm") and "*nego*" (I deny"); in medieval and early modern times, logic, like all university subjects, was studied only in Latin.] We can use a little diagram to sum up these facts about quantity and quality (Figure 1).

Before we can discuss the logical relationships among the four forms of categorical sentences, we must get clearly in mind what each form is to mean. With regard to the meaning of "some," two difficulties may cause misunderstanding. First, the word "some" is vague as it is used in ordinary conversation. By "some" we mean "a few"; but how many are a few? If a person says that some chairs are in the next room, is he claiming that there is at least one chair in the next room, that there are at least two, or perhaps that there are at least three? Such questions have no answer, for the word "some" is vague as it is ordinarily used. Vagueness of this kind is inconvenient for our present purposes. It will be best for us to decide more definitely what meaning we shall assign to the word "some." The most convenient way to do this is to assign it the minimum meaning: We shall stipulate that "Some so-and-so's are such-and such's" is to mean that there is *at least one* so-and-so that is a such-and-such.

A second difficulty is that the word "some" can give rise to ambiguity as it is ordinarily used. The ambiguity involved with

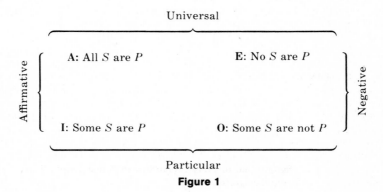

Figure 1

"some" comes to light if we consider a man who says that some people are boring. Is he thereby claiming that some people are *not* boring? In ordinary discourse this occasionally may be part of what his remark means, although more often it is not. For example, a student who says in an acid tone, "*Some* members of the faculty are worth listening to" is strongly suggesting that some are not, and perhaps we should regard his remark as asserting that some are and some are not worth listening to. But usually to say that some so-and-so's are such-and-such's is not to say that some are not.

For the purposes of logic, it is best to choose the minimum meaning of "some." We shall interpret sentences of the form "Some so-and-so's are such-and-such's" as meaning merely that there is at least one so-and-so that is a such-and-such. (This leaves it an open question whether there is any so-and-so that is not a such-and-such.) Similarly, we shall interpret the **O** sentence as meaning merely that at least one so-and-so is not a such-and-such, leaving it an open question whether any is.

Our consideration of categorical sentences will be smoother and clearer if we adhere to this comparatively strict and narrow point of view concerning the form of categorical sentences. (This will facilitate our discussion of immediate inference, later on, when we shall want to talk about letting the subject and predicate terms trade places.) Accordingly, let us insist that in a sentence in strictly categorical form the copula must be plural, and consequently the terms must be plural substantive general terms. Thus, the sentence "All gold is valuable" will not be regarded as strictly in categorical form because its copula is "is" rather than "are" and because its predicate is an adjective rather than a substantive (that is, nounlike) expression. However, if we reword it as "All pieces of gold are valuable things," then we have a sentence that is strictly categorical.

The distinction between general terms and singular terms is of some importance for logic. A *general term* is a word or phrase whose grammar allows it to apply to many individual things, to just one, or to none. Thus, the general term "dog" happens to apply to millions of individual dogs, the general term "natural satellite of the earth" happens to apply just to the moon, and the general term "unicorn" happens to apply to nothing. (Of course, merely from knowledge of its grammar you usually cannot tell how many things a general term applies to; observations will often be required to find that out.) A speaker can use a general term (e.g., "dodoes") in saying many things that he knows to be true (e.g., in saying "No dogs are dodoes," "Some birds are not dodoes," etc.), irrespective of whether there is anything to which the term applies. Some general terms require plural verbs (e.g., "dodoes"), while others take singular verbs (e.g., "gold"). In contrast, a *singular term* is a word or phrase whose grammar makes it purport to refer to one thing on any particular occasion. When the subject or predicate of a sentence is a singular term, the verb must be singular, not plural. A speaker can use a singular term (e.g., the proper name "Bruno") in saying a variety of things that he knows to be true (e.g., in saying "Bruno is an intelligent dog," "Bruno is not a cat," etc.) only if the term as he is using it does refer to just one individual thing. If he had made a mistake and there were no one such dog as the dog he thought he was referring to, then he would not have said anything either true or false by uttering those sentences.

One further distinction which it is useful to notice here is the distinction between compound sentences and atomic sentences. Sentences are said to be *compound* if they contain other simpler sentences as logical components within themselves; sentences are said to be *atomic* if they do not contain other simpler sentences as logical components of themselves. Thus the sentences "Birds have wings and birds can fly," "If birds have wings, then birds can fly," and "Birds can fly because birds have wings" are examples of compound sentences, for each contains as logical components the shorter sentences "Birds can fly" and "Birds have wings." Such sentences as "It is not the case that fish can fly," "Smith believes that fish can fly," and "It is impossible that fish can fly" also may conveniently be classified as compound sentences, for each contains as a component the shorter sentence "Fish can fly." This shorter sentence, however, would be classified as atomic insofar as it does not have any other still simpler sentence as a component of itself.

Categorical sentences are not compound, as such. That is, a categorical sentence does not need to contain other simpler sentences as logical components of itself, and most ordinary examples of categorical sentences do not. However, it would be incorrect to say that all categorical sentences are atomic, for some categorical sentences do contain other simpler sentences. For example, the sentence "All persons who believe that birds can fly are persons who believe that birds have wings" is a compound sentence containing the simpler sentences "Birds can fly" and "Birds have wings." The best way to describe the situation is to say that a categorical sentence need not be compound, although it need not be atomic either.

Venn Diagrams

The meanings of the four forms of categorical sentence can be brought out especially clearly if we illustrate them by means of Venn diagrams. These diagrams were devised by the nineteenth-century English logician John Venn.*

---

* Another type of diagram, invented by the eighteenth-century mathematician Euler, can also be used to represent categorical sentences. Venn diagrams are preferable, however, as with them it is always possible to illustrate exactly what the categorical sentence says, no less and no more, whereas Euler diagrams must sometimes appear to express more information than is contained in the sentences being diagrammed.

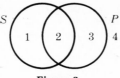

Figure 2

Let us draw two overlapping circles (Figure 2) and consider two classes of individuals, Swedes and Protestants. We shall now imagine that all the Swedes in existence are herded inside the left-hand circle; no one else and nothing else is allowed within that circle. Into the right-hand circle all Protestants are herded; no one else and nothing else may enter. In region 1 of this diagram we now shall find Swedes who are not Protestants, if there are any. In region 2 we would find Swedes who are Protestants. In region 3 of the diagram we would find Protestants who are not Swedes. And in region 4 will be all persons and things that are neither Swedes nor Protestants.

We now consider the **I** sentence "Some Swedes are Protestants." To illustrate what it says, we put an asterisk in region 2 to indicate that this region is not empty (Figure 3). This picture indicates that region 2 is occupied by at least one thing, and so it exhibits exactly the information conveyed by the **I** sentence, no less and no more. All other regions are blank in the diagram, indicating that the **I** sentence tells us nothing about whether they are vacant or occupied.

Using the same method, we can illustrate what the **O** sentence says (Figure 4). Here the asterisk in region 1 means that there is at least one thing that is an S but not a P.

Diagrams also can be drawn for the universal sentences. Here we shade a region to indicate that it is empty. The **A** sentence says that there are no S's that fail to be P's (Figure 5). The

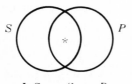

I: Some S are P

Figure 3

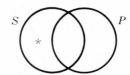

O: Some S are not P

Figure 4

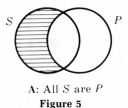

A: All *S* are *P*

Figure 5

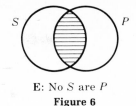

E: No *S* are *P*

Figure 6

E sentence says that there does not exist any S that is a P (Figure 6). Notice that neither of the universal sentences asserts the existence of anything.

Distribution of Terms

The notion of distribution of terms in categorical sentences is a bit of medieval logical lore which will be useful to us later on. Traditional definitions of this notion were rather unsatisfactory, but we may redefine it as follows: A term S occurring as the subject of a categorical sentence is said to be distributed in that sentence if and only if the sentence, in virtue of its form, says something about *every kind of S*. Similarly, a term P occurring as the predicate of a categorical sentence is said to be distributed in that sentence if and only if the sentence, in virtue of its form, says something about *every kind of P*.

Consider the sentence "All Slavs are promiscuous persons." This sentence says something about every kind of Slav: young Slavs, old Slavs, male Slavs, female Slavs, blond Slavs, dark Slavs, and so on. Thus the subject term "Slavs" is said to be distributed in it. However, the sentence does not say anything about every kind of promiscuous person; it speaks only of Slavic ones and tells us nothing about non-Slavic kinds of promiscuous persons. Thus the predicate term is undistributed. In this **A** sentence the subject is distributed and the predicate is undistributed.

Consider next the sentence "No Slavs are promiscuous persons." Here again our sentence says something about every kind of Slav; it says that large ones, small ones, fat ones, slim ones are none of them promiscuous. And this sentence, though more indirectly, says something about all kinds of promiscuous persons; concerning promiscuous persons, whether happy or sad, wise or foolish, it says that none of them are Slavs. Thus both the subject and the predicate of this **E** sentence are distributed.

Now consider the sentence "Some Slavs are promiscuous persons." This sentence does not say anything about every kind of Slav; it speaks only about such of them as are promiscuous. Neither does it say anything about every kind of promiscuous person; it speaks only about such of them as are Slavs. Thus in this **I** sentence neither the subject nor the predicate is distributed.

Finally, consider the sentence "Some Slavs are not promiscuous persons." Here again nothing is said about every kind of Slav. However, in a roundabout way, a claim is made about every kind of promiscuous person. For this **O** sentence says that whatever kind of promiscuous persons we consider, sane ones, mad ones, tall ones, short ones, each of these kinds of promiscuous individuals is such as not to include all Slavs. This is, our sentence implies that some Slavs are not sane promiscuous persons, that some Slavs are not mad promiscuous persons, and so on. Thus in this **O** sentence the subject is undistributed but the predicate is distributed.

What has been said about these sample sentences clearly holds true in general. In any **A** sentence the subject is distributed and the predicate is undistributed; in any **E** sentence both subject and predicate are distributed; in any **I** sentence neither subject nor predicate is distributed; and in any **O** sentence the subject is not distributed but the predicate is.

One way of remembering these facts is to remember that in any universal sentence the subject is distributed, while in any negative sentence the predicate is distributed. Another way of remembering them is to remember the mnemonic word "As Eb In Op," which means that in **A** the subject is distributed, in **E** both subject and predicate, in **I** neither, and in **O** the predicate.

A more rigorous formulation of the definition of distribution is as follows: Suppose that T is a term which occurs as subject or predicate in a categorical sentence s. Where T' is any other term, let s' be the sentence that is exactly like s except for containing the compound term T' & T, where s contains T. Now, T is said to be distributed in s if and only if, for every term T', s logically implies s'.

To see the meaning of this definition, consider an example. Suppose that T were the term "prohibitionists" and s were the sentence "Some seamen are not prohibitionists." Then if T' were the term "rich," s' would be the sentence "Some seamen are not rich prohibitionists." To say that T is distributed in s is to say that every sentence of the form "Some seamen are not . . . prohibitionists" is logically implied by s.

Old-fashioned logic books do not explain the notion of distribution in this way. They usually say that a term in a categorical sentence is distributed if and only if the sentence 'refers to' all members of the class of things to which the term applies. But this explanation is obscure and misleading. The sentence "All equilateral triangles are equiangular triangles" 'refers to' all equilateral triangles, and since necessarily these and only these are equiangular triangles, the sentence would appear to 'refer to' all equiangular triangles also. Thus, according to the old-fashioned account, it would seem that the predicate ought to count as distributed in this A sentence. The predicate is not considered to be distributed, however, and this illustrates one unsatisfactory aspect of the old-fashioned explanation of distribution.

Another unsatisfactory aspect of the old-fashioned account is that it is unclear in its treatment of the predicate of the O form. To claim that the sentence "Some seamen are not prohibitionists" 'refers to' all prohibitionists is to make an obscure and unsatisfactory claim. The notion of 'reference' employed in this old-fashioned account is too hazy.

EXERCISE 4

* **A** *Which of the following sentences are in categorical form just as they stand? For those which are in categorical form, name their form, say what their quantity and quality are, draw their Venn diagrams, and say which of their terms are distributed. For those which are not in categorical form, explain why they fall short of being categorical.*

1 All emeralds are gems. *A*
2 Some Lebanese are Moslems. *I*
3 Some iguanas are aquatic. *I* SOME IGUANAS ARE SWIMMERS.
4 No leukocytes are phagocytes. *E*
5 All Britain is an island. *A*
6 Some rock gardens require no care. *O*
7 No chemical additive is a proven way of prolonging battery life. *E*
8 Some real numbers are not rational numbers. *O*
9 Most plant viruses are elongated in shape. *I*
10 Some well-known Roman emperors are not historical figures whom we can admire. *O*
11 A mature beech tree has as many as 200,000 leaves. *A*
12 No alleged cases of precognition are phenomena that have actually occurred. *E*

B *Criticize, explain, or discuss the following.*

1 **White:** There are some cars in the parking lot.
Black: There is only one. What you said is false!

2 **White:** Some members of your family are honest.
Black: What a shocking thing to say! You're accusing some members of my family of not being honest.

3 Draw Venn diagrams for the following sentences. First do it using circles labeled "nonmosques" and "nontemples," then do it using circles labeled "mosques" and "temples."
(a) All nontemples are nonmosques.
(b) No nonmosques are nontemples.
(c) Some nonmosques are nontemples.
(d) Some nontemples are not nonmosques.

4 In the following sentences, is the term "engines" distributed, or does this question lack an answer? Explain.
(a) All motorcars are vehicles with engines.
(b) If all engines are devices needing servicing, then some mechanics are people who will be in demand.
(c) All diesel engines are efficient power plants.

5 **Student:** I'll have to be excused from my examinations tomorrow. My sister Jane is critically ill.
Vice-dean: There's no such person as Jane, and you've never had any sister. So the phrase "My sister Jane" as you are using it doesn't refer to anyone. Your second sentence is false.
Dean: There's no such person as Jane, and you've never had a sister. So that second sentence is neither true nor false.

6 **Black:** No animals on Maryland farms are unicorns.
White: There aren't any unicorns at all, so the word "unicorn" doesn't apply to anything. Hence your sentence is neither true nor false.

THE SQUARE OF OPPOSITION

Suppose that we have categorical sentences of different forms but with the same subject and the same predicate: "All S are P," "No S are P," "Some S are P," and "Some S are not P." What logical relations will hold among them? Before we can answer this question in any particular case, we first have to make a decision concerning the viewpoint from which the relations among these **A**, **E**, **I**, and **O** sentences are to be discussed. As we discuss these relations, are we allowing for the possibility that *S*'s do not exist, or are we excluding that possibility by presupposing that at least one *S* exists? It makes a difference.

If we consider the logical relations among these categorical sentences from a viewpoint which presupposes that there exist things of some specified kind, then we shall be adopting what we shall call an *existential viewpoint*. The existential viewpoint we shall discuss now presupposes that there exist things to which the subject term, *S*, applies. If we consider the relation among these categorical sentences without taking for granted that any things exist, then we are adopting what we shall call the *hypothetical viewpoint*. Each of these viewpoints is worthy of consideration.

First, let us consider how the four categorical forms are related to one another if we do not presuppose the existence of anything. Let us consider the logical relations among the sentences "All succubi are poltergeists," "No succubi are poltergeists," "Some succubi are poltergeists," and "Some succubi are not poltergeists." Here we shall not exclude the possibility that succubi may not exist. The relationships can be exhibited in a diagram that is called the square of opposition (Figure 7).

As the Venn diagrams show, **A** and **O** are opposite as regards their truth and falsity. **A** says exactly what **O** denies, no less and no more. **A** and **O** are said to be *contradictories* of each other. **E** and **I** are also contradictories, for what **E** says is exactly what **I** denies, no less and no more.

Is **A** related to **I**? You might have thought that **A** would imply **I**, but this is not so. The truth of **A** would not guarantee the truth of **I**, for it is possible that **A** might be true and **I** false—that is to say, **A** does not imply **I**. There is no logical connection between **A** and **I**; knowledge of the truth or falsity of one of these sentences does not by itself enable us to tell whether the other is true or false. Similarly, **E** does not imply **O**, for **E** could be true but **O** false; this would happen if *S*'s do not exist, for in that case it would be true that no *S* are *P* but false that some *S* are not *P*. There is no logical connection between **E** and **O**.

Is **A** related to **E**? You might have thought that it would be impossible for them both to be true, but this is not so. These sentences will both be true if there are no *S*'s at all. When

Square of Opposition

Hypothetical viewpoint: We do
not presuppose that any S exists.

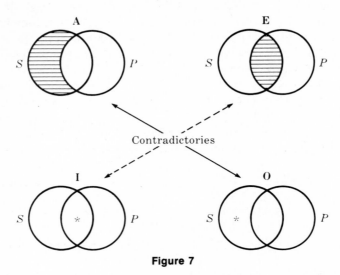

Figure 7

nothing is an S, there certainly are no S that fail to be P, and
there are no S that are P, so both the **A** and the **E** sentences would
be true.   Thus there is no logical connection between **A** and **E**;
knowing the truth or falsity of one of them does not enable us to
tell the truth or falsity of the other.   How about **I** and **O**?   You
might have thought that they cannot both be false, but this is not
so either.   **I** says that there is at least one S that is P, while **O** says
that there is at least one S that is not P; both these sentences
will be false if there are no S's at all.   Thus there is no logical
connection between **I** and **O** either.

Now let us go over the matter again, but this time from an
existential rather than the hypothetical viewpoint.   Let us consider the four sentences "All Samoans are pantheists," "No
Samoans are pantheists," "Some Samoans are pantheists," and
"Some Samoans are not pantheists."   We want to know how
these sentences are related, under the presupposition that there
are Samoans.   Our results will be brought together in Figure 8.

If it is true that all Samoans are pantheists, then (since we
take for granted that at least one Samoan exists) it must be true

that some Samoans are pantheists. Thus the truth of the **A** sentence will guarantee the truth of the **I**, and in this sense **A** implies **I**. On the other hand, that some Samoans are pantheists does not guarantee that all of them are (since some might be and some not). Thus we can fully describe the relation between **A** and **I** by saying that **A** implies **I** but **I** does not imply **A**.

Similarly, if it is true that no Samoans are pantheists, then (since we take for granted that there are Samoans) it must follow that some Samoans are not pantheists. Thus the **E** sentence implies the **O**. However, that some Samoans are not pantheists does not guarantee that no Samoans are (for perhaps some of them are and some are not). Thus we can describe the relation between **E** and **O** by saying that **E** implies **O** but **O** does not imply **E**.

As for **A** and **E**, neither implies the other. But if we take for

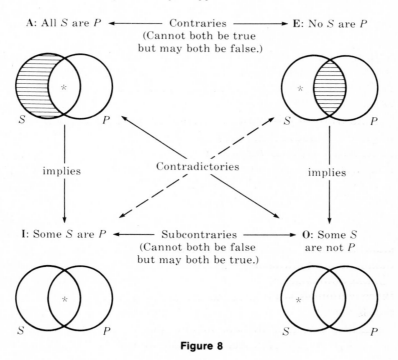

Square of Opposition

Existential viewpoint: We presuppose that at least one S exists.

A: All S are P ⟵——— Contraries ———⟶ E: No S are P
(Cannot both be true
but may both be false.)

implies   Contradictories   implies

I: Some S are P ⟵——— Subcontraries ———⟶ O: Some S
(Cannot both be false   are not P
but may both be true.)

Figure 8

granted that there are Samoans, it cannot be true both that all Samoans are pantheists and that no Samoans are pantheists; that is, **A** and **E** cannot both be true. Might **A** and **E** both be false? Surely, for if some Samoans are pantheists and some are not, then neither **A** nor **E** is true. Thus the relation between **A** and **E** may be described by saying that they cannot both be true but they may both be false. The traditional way of referring to this relationship was to call **A** and **E** *contrary* sentences.

The relationship between **I** and **O** is different but analogous. Neither implies the other. Both may be true. But if we take for granted that Samoans exist, then **I** and **O** cannot both be false; if there are Samoans, then either some of them are pantheists or some of them are not pantheists (or perhaps both). Thus **I** and **O** are related in such a way that they cannot both be false, although they may both be true. The traditional way of referring to this relationship was to call **I** and **O** *subcontraries*.

Now consider the relationship between **A** and **O**. If it is true that all Samoans are pantheists, it must be false that some of them are not pantheists. And if it is false that all Samoans are pantheists, then it must be true that some of them are not. Conversely, if it is true that some Samoans are not pantheists, it must be false that all Samoans are; and if it is false that some Samoans are not pantheists, then it must be true that all of them are. Thus **A** and **O** cannot both be true and they cannot both be false; they are opposite as regards truth and falsity. They are called *contradictories* of each other.

Similarly, **E** and **I** are related in such a way that if **E** is true, **I** must be false, and if **E** is false, then **I** must be true. **E** and **I** are always opposite as regards their truth and falsity, and so they too are contradictories of each other.

These relationships can be displayed in a diagram for the square of opposition under an existential interpretation (Figure 8). Here each of the four component Venn diagrams contains an asterisk because we are presupposing throughout that at least one S exists.

> Some of the words used to describe the relationships of this traditional square of opposition for the existential viewpoint are used *loosely*; this is a point that old-fashioned logic books often do not make clear.
>
> In the strict sense, to say that one sentence *implies* another is to say that if the first is true, that alone is sufficient to guarantee that the second must necessarily be true also. **A** does not imply **I**, nor does **E** imply **O** in

this strict sense. These pairs of sentences involve implication only in the looser sense that if the existential presupposition is true, then if **A** is true **I** must be true; and if the existential presupposition is true, then if **E** is true **O** must be true.

Similarly, to say that two sentences are *contraries* in the strict sense is to say that it is logically impossible for them both to be true. **A** and **E** are not contraries in this strict sense. They are contraries only in the looser sense that if the existential presupposition is true, then **A** and **E** cannot both be true. Also, **I** and **O** are subcontraries only in a corresponding loose sense. Furthermore, it is only for nonnecessary sentences that we can count on **A** and **E** to be contraries and **I** and **O** to be subcontraries; for some necessary sentences these relationships fail to hold: e.g., "All men are humans" and "No men are humans" fail to be contraries, as they cannot both be false.

To say that two sentences are contradictories in the strict sense is to say that one asserts just what the other denies, no more and no less. As we have been understanding them, **A** and **O** are contradictories in this strict sense, as are **E** and **I**.

If we had regarded the existential assumption that at least one S exists, not as a presupposition but as part of the meaning of each universal categorical sentence, the situation would have been different. Then **A** would have been understood as meaning "If anything is an S, it is a P, and there is at least one S," and **E** would have been understood as meaning "Nothing is both an S and a P, and there is at least one S"; **I** and **O**, which already affirm that at least one S exists, would have remained unchanged in meaning. Under these circumstances, **A** would not have been the contradictory of **O**. **A** would have asserted more than what **O** denies, since **A** would contain the assertion that there exists an S, an assertion not denied by **O**, which merely says that there exists an S that is not a P. Also, **I** and **O** would not have been subcontraries, for it would have been possible for them both to be false, as would happen if nothing is an S. Because these consequences are inconvenient, we shall regard the existential claim not as part of the meaning of universal categorical sentences but rather as a presupposition that underlies our discussion of the interrelations among categorical sentences.

We have discussed the square of opposition both from the hypothetical viewpoint and from an existential viewpoint; in handling actual examples sometimes the former viewpoint is definitely called for, but often the latter viewpoint is more appropriate. Let us consider an example of each situation.

Suppose that a landowner has said "All trespassers are people who will be prosecuted"; and then we wonder about the logical relation of his remark to the sentence "Some trespassers are people who will be prosecuted." Does believing the former commit him to believing the latter too? Here our answer must depend on whether the possibility is left open that perhaps no one trespasses. In this example it is better to regard that possibility as indeed left open, and therefore our answer should be that it does not follow. There are two reasons for keeping open the possibility that trespassers may not exist: first, that the landowner, in speaking as he did, probably did not specifically intend to exclude this possibility—he may even have hoped that his remark would serve as an effective warning, preventing all trespassing; and, second, that the possibility that there may be no trespassers is a reasonable sort of possibility, so far as we know. Thus, the hypothetical viewpoint is appropriate in this case.

On the other hand, suppose an honest, sincere woman says "All my jewels are diamonds." Does "Some of my jewels are diamonds" follow from this? Here it would be inappropriate to say that it doesn't follow because perhaps she has no jewels. Such a comment would be reprehensible logic-chopping. By speaking as she did, the woman quite clearly indicated that she believes she owns jewels, and normally it is reasonable to take for granted that a woman knows what she owns. The sensible thing for us to do is to carry on our discussion presupposing that she does have jewels. Hence, the best answer would be that the **I** sentence does follow from the **A** in this case.

Traditional aristotelian logic considered categorical sentences only from an existential viewpoint. Modern symbolic logic almost always treats them from the hypothetical viewpoint. But the best approach is to understand both viewpoints and to be able to use whichever one is more appropriate in a particular case. Of course, it can sometimes happen that one encounters a case where the two viewpoints give different answers, yet neither viewpoint is clearly preferable to the other. Then there is no definitely right answer, and the best we can do is to recognize what the situation is and why it is ambiguous.

EXERCISE 5

* **A** *In each case, (a) suppose you know that the first sentence is true. Can you then infer that the second is true or that the second is false, or can you infer nothing about the second? (b) Suppose you know that the first sentence is false. What can*

you infer regarding the second? (c) Suppose you know that the second sentence is false. What can you infer regarding the first? In this exercise, where does it make a difference if you adopt an existential rather than the hypothetical viewpoint?

1 Some theologians are theists.   All theologians are theists.
2 No utilitarians are ethical relativists.   Some utilitarians are ethical relativists.
3 No cuts in taxes are causes of inflation.   Some cuts in taxes are causes of inflation.
4 Some monists are not materialists.   Some monists are materialists.
5 Some unsolved problems are not solvable problems.   All unsolved problems are solvable problems.
6 All mathematical logicians are lovers of classical music.   No mathematical logicians are lovers of classical music.

B *Should an existential presupposition be made in the following cases?*

1 In his sermon the priest declares that no true Christian envies others.   Should this be understood as logically implying that some true Christians do not envy others?
2 A student complains that all the courses he is taking are boring.   Should this be understood as logically implying that some courses are being taken by him?
3 The physics book states that for any ideal gas, PV always equals RT.   Should this be understood as logically implying that there is at least one ideal gas, for which PV equals RT?
4 The Watusi chieftain boasts that none of his sons is less than 7 feet tall.   Does this logically imply that some of his sons are not less than 7 feet tall?
5 The economist says that under conditions of free competition, firms will adjust their levels of output so that, at equilibrium, marginal costs exactly equal marginal revenues.   Does this logically imply that there are firms whose marginal costs sometimes exactly equal their marginal revenues?
6 In a discussion among Bible scholars, one asserts that none of the Old Testament prophets were women.   Should this be understood as logically implying that some Old Testament prophets were not women?

IMMEDIATE INFERENCE

Next we shall consider some important relationships between pairs of categorical sentences that do not have exactly the same subjects and predicates. The operations involved here have traditionally been called immediate inferences, because they correspond to simple, immediate types of argument in which only one premise yields the conclusion. In discussing these relationships we do not need to worry about any contrast between hypothetical and existential viewpoints, except when we come to conversion by limitation; only there will it make any difference among the relationships we shall consider.

Conversion

A simple way to alter a categorical sentence is to make the subject and predicate trade places. This is *conversion*, and the new sentence obtained by this operation is called the *converse* of the original sentence. (It is sometimes called the *simple converse*, to contrast it with the converse by limitation, which will be discussed presently.) Let us consider how the meanings of the various forms of categorical sentence are affected by conversion.

Suppose we start with the **E** sentence "No syllogisms are perplexing things." When subject and predicate trade places, we get the converse "No perplexing things are syllogisms." A pair of Venn diagrams drawn from the hypothetical viewpoint (Figure 9) can help us to see how the original and its converse are related. Two sentences are said to be *equivalent* if they are necessarily alike as regards truth and falsity. Here the diagrams are just the same, showing that the **E** sentence and its converse

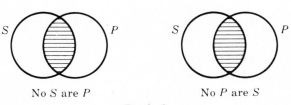

No S are P No P are S

Figure 9

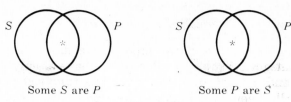

Figure 10

are equivalent. Notice that a pair of Venn diagrams for these sentences drawn from an existential viewpoint (putting in an asterisk in the S region of each diagram) would give us the same result: both sentences are alike in their diagrams, from either viewpoint.

The **I** sentence "Some syllogisms are perplexing things" has as its converse the sentence "Some perplexing things are syllogisms." Here again it is clear that conversion has left the meaning of the sentence basically unchanged; the **I** and its converse are equivalent, as the diagrams (Figure 10) show.

Next let us consider the **A** sentence "All syllogisms are perplexing things." When subject and predicate trade places, we obtain the converse "All perplexing things are syllogisms." Has conversion altered the meaning of the sentence? From the diagram (Figure 11) it is clear that conversion has completely changed the meaning of the **A** sentence; the converse is an independent sentence that says something entirely different from what the original sentence said.

Finally, if we convert the **O** sentence "Some syllogisms are not perplexing things," we obtain "Some perplexing things are not syllogisms." Here too it is clear from the diagram (Figure 12) that the original sentence and its converse are not equivalent.

What holds good in this example holds good in general. We can sum up by saying that any **E** or **I** sentence is equivalent

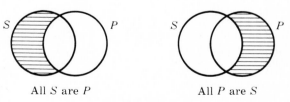

All S are P All P are S

Figure 11

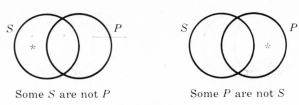

Some S are not P Some P are not S

Figure 12

to its converse, whereas no **A** or **O** sentence is equivalent to its converse. Another way of describing the matter is to say that when subject and predicate in the original sentence are alike as regards distribution (either both distributed or both undistributed) then the converse will be equivalent to the original sentence, but when the subject and predicate in the original sentence differ as regards distribution then the converse will not be equivalent to the original sentence.

Conversion by Limitation

Although an **A** sentence is not equivalent to its simple converse, we can validly derive from the **A** sentence another sentence in which subject and predicate have changed places. This is a feeble substitute for a simple converse, and it is called the *converse by limitation* (or the *converse per accidens*). This new sentence will be an **I**. From "All syllogisms are perplexing things" we may validly derive "Some perplexing things are syllogisms" (Figure 13). This process is legitimate only from an existential viewpoint; it is the existence of syllogisms that must be presupposed here. Moreover, the converse by limitation is not equivalent to the original sentence but is merely implied by it.

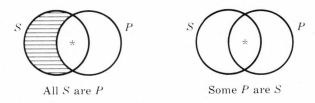

All S are P Some P are S

Figure 13

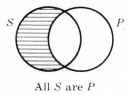 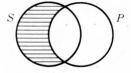

| All S are P | No S are non$P$ |
| | (There are no S outside P circle.) |

Figure 14

Obversion

The operation of conversion has the disadvantage that we cannot always convert a categorical sentence without changing its meaning. Obversion is an operation free from this disadvantage. However, it involves a slightly more complicated alteration. To form the *obverse* of a categorical sentence we do two things: We change the quality of the sentence, and we negate the predicate term as a whole.

Suppose we start with the **A** sentence "All saints are puritans." This is a universal affirmative sentence, and so to change its quality we must make it into a negative sentence. We leave the quantity unaltered, thus obtaining a universal negative sentence, that is, a sentence of the **E** form. Also we negate the predicate, replacing it by its contradictory "nonpuritans." The subject we leave unaltered. Thus we obtain the new sentence "No saints are nonpuritans," which is the obverse of our original sentence. Here we can see (Figure 14) that the **A** sentence and its obverse are equivalent.

If we start with the **E** sentence "No saints are puritans," we form its obverse by changing the quality from negative to affirmative and by negating the predicate. Thus we obtain the obverse "All saints are nonpuritans." Here again we can see from the diagram (Figure 15) how the original sentence and its obverse are equivalent.

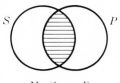 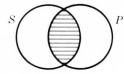

| No S are P | All S are non$P$ |
| | (All S are outside P circle.) |

Figure 15

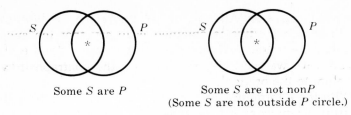

Some *S* are *P*   Some *S* are not non*P*
(Some *S* are not outside *P* circle.)

Figure 16

If we start with the **I** sentence "Some saints are puritans," we form its obverse by changing it from particular affirmative to particular negative and negating the predicate. We obtain "Some saints are not nonpuritans." It is clear (Figure 16) that this is equivalent to our original sentence.

Finally, if we begin with the **O** sentence "Some saints are not puritans," we change from particular negative to particular affirmative and negate the predicate, thus obtaining the obverse "Some saints are nonpuritans." In this case the obverse is so very similar to the original sentence that it almost looks as though no change had taken place. But a change has taken place, for we consider the obverse to be in **I** form and to have the negation as part of its predicate, while the original sentence is in **O** form and has the negation as part of its copula. When we write such sentences, it will help to avoid confusion if "non" is used by us to express negation that belongs to the predicate or subject and "not" is reserved to express negation that is part of the copula. (However, we may have to fall back on "not" for negating subjects or predicates which are longer phrases instead of single words.)

Contraposition

Suppose we start with an **A** sentence "All S are P" and obvert it into "No S are nonP," then convert that into "No nonP are S," and finally obvert that into "All nonP are nonS." These steps are performed in such a way that each new sentence is equivalent to the previous one. The final result is equivalent to the original, and it is related to the original in a way interesting enough to have a special name. "All nonP are nonS" is called the *contrapositive* of "All S are P." A briefer way of describing how the contrapositive is obtained is to say that the subject and predicate of the original sentence trade places and each is negated. As we see, with the **A** form, the contrapositive is equivalent to the original.

With the **E** form, this process of obverting, converting, then obverting again cannot be carried out without changing the meaning; the second step would involve converting an **A** sentence, and an **A** is not equivalent to its converse. If the original **E** sentence were "No S are P," its contrapositive would be "No nonP are nonS"; this is not equivalent to the original.

If we start with an **I** sentence, obvert it, then convert it, and obvert it again, we would likewise find that the meaning is changed. In this case the second step would involve converting an **O** sentence, and the **O** is not equivalent to its converse. Thus the **I** sentence "Some S are P" is not equivalent to its contrapositive "Some nonP are nonS." However, if we start with an **O** sentence, we can obvert, convert, and obvert again without basically altering the meaning. The **O** sentence "Some S are not P" is equivalent to its contrapositive "Some nonP are not nonS."

Thus we see that while conversion preserves the meanings of **E** and **I** but not of **A** and **O**, contraposition preserves the meanings of **A** and **O** but not of **E** and **I**.

If we list only the cases where the original sentence is equivalent to the one obtained from it, we may sum up as follows all the relationships that have just been discussed. The original sentence is listed on the left, and its converse, obverse, or contrapositive is listed on the right.

Conversion (No existential presupposition needed.)

E	No S are P	No P are S	*E*
I	Some S are P	Some P are S	*I*

Conversion by limitation (Must presuppose there are S's.)

A	All S are P	Some P are ~~not~~ S	*I*

Obversion (No existential presupposition needed.)

A	All S are P	No S are nonP	*E*
E	No S are P	All S are nonP	*A*
I	Some S are P	Some S are ~~not~~ nonP	*I*
O	SOME S ARE NOT P	SOMES ARE NON-P	*I*

O ⊃ (⊋ ∪ (handwritten top-left)

Contraposition   (No existential presupposition needed.)

~~Some S are not P~~   ~~Some S are nonP~~

A All S are P   All nonP are nonS *A*

O Some S are not P   Some nonP are not nonS *O*

E NON S ARE P (handwritten)   SOME NONP ARE NOT NONS O (handwritten)

Symmetry of These Relations

It is worth noticing that the relation between any categorical sentence and its converse is a symmetrical relation: If sentence r is the converse of sentence q, then sentence q is the converse of sentence r.   That is to say, if we obtain r by transposing the subject and predicate of q, then were we to start with r and transpose its subject and predicate the result would be q.

Similarly, the relation between any categorical sentence and its obverse is a symmetrical relation.   If r is the obverse of q, then q must be the obverse of r.   For example, if q is "All S are P," its obverse r is "No S are nonP."   What is the obverse of r?   If we change the quality and negate the predicate of r, we get "All S are non-nonP," and, letting the double negation in the predicate cancel out, we have "All S are P," which is q. (This sort of double negation cancels out, but we must beware of supposing that two negatives of different types always cancel each other.   For example, "No nonS are P" is not equivalent to "All S are P.")

Also, the relation between a sentence and its contrapositive is symmetrical.   If r is the contrapositive of q, then q is the contrapositive of r.   For instance, if q is "All S are P," then r, its contrapositive, is "All nonP are nonS."   But what is the contrapositive of r?   If we transpose the subject and predicate of r and negate each of them, we obtain "All non-nonS are non-nonP"; letting the double negations within the terms cancel out, we have "All S are P," which is exactly q.

The relation between an **A** sentence and its converse by limitation is not a symmetrical relation, however.   Instead it is asymmetrical.   If r is the converse by limitation of q, then q never is the converse by limitation of r.

EXERCISE 6

A *State in each case how the conclusion is related to the premise (converse, obverse, etc.), and indicate whether the argu-*

ment is valid, making clear any existential presuppositions that may be required.

1 No rationalists are mystics. Therefore, all rationalists are nonmystics.

2 All bacteria are organisms. Therefore, all organisms are bacteria.

3 No pagans are heretics. Therefore, no heretics are pagans.

4 Some miracles are not natural phenomena. Therefore, some natural phenomena are not miracles.

5 Some positivists are not theists. Therefore, some positivists are not nontheists.

6 All revolutionaries are radicals. Therefore, no revolutionaries are nonradicals.

7 All acids are corrosives. Therefore, some corrosives are acids.

8 Some noncombatants are not neutrals. Therefore, some nonneutrals are not combatants.

B *By means of what sequence of operations can (b) be validly inferred from (a)? Operations of immediate inference and implications from the square of opposition may be used. Make clear any existential presuppositions.*

1 (a) Some metals are liquids.
   (b) Some liquids are not nonmetals.

2 (a) No Africans are Buddhists.
   (b) Some Africans are non-Buddhists.

3 (a) No Greek epics are poems about courtly love.
   (b) Some poems about courtly love are not Greek epics.

4 (a) No senators are infants.
   (b) All infants are nonsenators.

5 (a) All insects are nonquadrupeds.
   (b) All quadrupeds are noninsects.

6 (a) All antiques are things over 100 years old.
   (b) Some things that are not antiques are things that are not over 100 years old.

C *Explain why each of the following arguments is not valid.*

1 No nonresidents are members of the city council. Therefore, all residents are members of the city council.

2 Some numbers are not rational. Therefore, some numbers are not irrational.

3 Some sons of his are not fat giants. Therefore, some sons of his are nonfat giants.

4 No non-Americans are nonforeigners. Therefore, all Americans are foreigners.

5 All French generals are dignified patriots. Therefore, all undignified patriots are non-French generals.

6 No members of this faculty are unrecognized geniuses. Therefore, all members of this faculty are recognized geniuses.

THE SYLLOGISM

The categorical syllogism is a particularly familiar form of reasoning, valuable because arguments encountered in ordinary discourse can very frequently be analyzed in terms of it. An argument is a *categorical syllogism* (or *syllogism,* for short) if and only if it consists of three categorical sentences containing three terms in all, each term appearing in two different sentences. The argument "All Pakistanis are Mohammedans; no Sinhalese are Mohammedans; therefore no Sinhalese are Pakistanis" is an example of a syllogism. It consists of three categorical sentences that contain three different terms, each term appearing in two different sentences.

The term appearing as the predicate of the conclusion (in this case "Pakistanis") is called the *major term* of the syllogism; the term appearing as subject of the conclusion (in this case "Sinhalese") is called the *minor term* of the syllogism; and the term appearing in the premises but not in the conclusion (in this case "Mohammedans") is called the *middle term.* The premise containing the major term is called the *major premise,* and the premise containing the minor term is called the *minor premise.* For the sake of having a standard procedure, let us always put the major premise first, then the minor premise, and last the conclusion.

In order to describe fully the logical form of a syllogism, we need to specify the forms of the categorical sentences in it, and we need to specify how the terms are arranged in these sentences. The example just given is a syllogism whose logical form may be exhibited as follows:

All *P* are *M*
No *S* are *M*
∴ no *S* are *P*

To give the *mood* of a syllogism is to state the categorical forms of its sentences. We mention these in the standard order: major premise, minor premise, conclusion. In our example of a syllogism, its major premise is an **A** sentence, its minor premise is an **E**, and its conclusion is an **E**; therefore this particular syllogism is in the mood **AEE**.

But there is more to say about its form, for other different syllogisms can share with it this mood **AEE**. For instance, a syllogism also is in the mood **AEE** if it has the structure:

All *M* are *P*
No *S* are *M*
∴ no *S* are *P*

But this sort of syllogism differs from the previous example in an important way because of the different arrangement of its terms; one syllogism is valid, the other invalid. To specify fully the structure of a syllogism, we must say how its terms are arranged within the sentences in which they occur. This is called giving the *figure* of the syllogism.

There are four possible arrangements, four different figures, of syllogisms. We can represent these four figures as follows:

	1			**2**			**3**			**4**	
M	*P*		*P*	*M*		*M*	*P*		*P*	*M*	
S	*M*		*S*	*M*		*M*	*S*		*M*	*S*	
S	*P*		*S*	*P*		*S*	*P*		*S*	*P*	

It is easy to remember which figure is which if we think of the positions of the middle term as outlining the front of a shirt collar (Figure 17). The first form of syllogism we considered was **AEE** in the second figure; the second form was **AEE** in the first figure.

How many different kinds of syllogisms are possible? There

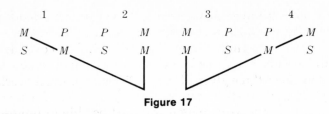

Figure 17

are four possibilities as regards the form of the major premise (**A, E, I, O**), four possibilities as regards the form of the minor premise, four possibilities as regards the form of the conclusion, and four possibilities as regards the figure of the syllogism. This means that there are $4 \times 4 \times 4 \times 4$, or 256, possible forms in all. Any two syllogisms having the same form, that is, the same mood and figure, are bound to be alike as regards formal validity.

How can we tell whether a given form of syllogism is valid? Venn diagrams provide the most straightforward method. The method is this: We draw a diagram showing exactly what the two premises of the syllogism say; then, by looking at it, we can see whether or not the conclusion necessarily follows from those premises.

The syllogism "All Pakistanis are Mohammedans; no Sinhalese are Mohammedans; therefore no Sinhalese are Pakistanis" is in the mood **AEE** and in the second figure, as we saw. To test its validity, we form a diagram showing exactly what the premises say. Since the premises contain three terms, the diagram must show relations among three classes of beings: Pakistanis, Sinhalese, and Mohammedans (Figure 18).

We now imagine that all Mohammedans are herded inside the M circle, no one else and nothing else being allowed inside it; all Pakistanis are placed inside the P circle, no one and noth-

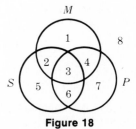

Figure 18

ing else being allowed there; and all Sinhalese are herded inside the S circle, no one and nothing else being allowed there. We must be sure to begin the diagram by drawing three circles that overlap in such a way as to allow for all possible subclasses formed by these three given classes. The circles must overlap so as to yield eight distinct regions on the diagram, for there are eight distinct subclasses which we must be able to represent.

Region 1 of the diagram is the location of Mohammedans who are not Sinhalese and not Pakistanis. Region 2 would contain Mohammedans who are Sinhalese but who are not Pakistanis. In region 3 Mohammedans who are Sinhalese and also Pakistanis would be found. Region 4 would contain Mohammedans who are Pakistanis but not Sinhalese. Region 5 is the location of Sinhalese who are neither Mohammedans nor Pakistanis. Region 6 is for Sinhalese who are Pakistanis but not Mohammedans. Region 7 is the place for Pakistanis who are neither Sinhalese nor Mohammedans. And region 8 is occupied by those who are neither Mohammedans nor Sinhalese nor Pakistanis.

The major premise of our syllogism declares that all Pakistanis are Mohammedans. This means that all who are inside the P circle are inside the M circle, that is, that the part of the P circle outside the M circle is unoccupied. We indicate this on the drawing by crossing out regions 6 and 7 (Figure 19). The minor premise of the syllogism declares that no Sinhalese are Mohammedans. This means that all who are inside the S circle are outside the M circle; that is, that part of the S circle that is inside the M circle is unoccupied. We indicate this by crossing out regions 2 and 3 (Figure 20). We now have a diagram that shows exactly what the premises say, no more and no less.*

We now inspect the diagram to see whether or not the conclusion validly follows from the premises. According to the diagram, all that part of the S circle which overlaps the P circle is unoccupied; that is, there are no Sinhalese who are Pakistanis. This means that the conclusion validly follows from the prem-

---

* The relation between the premises and the conclusion here has been considered from the hypothetical viewpoint rather than from an existential viewpoint. That is, no presupposition has been made concerning the existence of anything. More will be said soon concerning syllogisms considered from an existential viewpoint.

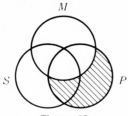

Figure 19

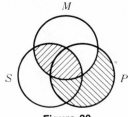

Figure 20

ises; if the premises are true, the conclusion must necessarily be true also.

If you have difficulty telling whether the diagram shows the argument to be valid, try this: See whether it is logically possible to add the *contradictory* of the conclusion to the diagram for the premises. If this is possible, the argument is invalid; if it is not possible, the argument is valid. For the syllogism we have just been considering, the contradictory of the conclusion would be "Some Sinhalese are Pakistanis"; to add this to the diagram of Figure 20 would be impossible, for it would mean putting an asterisk into an area that is entirely crossed out. This helps us to see how the diagram shows the argument to be valid.

Next let us consider the syllogism "All Mormons are polygamous persons; no Samoans are Mormons; therefore no Samoans are polygamous persons." This syllogism is in the mood **AEE** and in the first figure. To test its validity, we again draw a diagram that will show exactly what the premises say. The major premise tells us that whatever is inside the *M* circle is inside the *P* circle, that is, that the part of the *M* circle outside the *P* circle is unoccupied. Accordingly we cross out regions 1 and 2 (Figure 21). The minor premise tells us that nothing inside the *S* circle is inside the *M* circle, that is, that the part of the *S* circle overlapping the *M* circle is unoccupied, and so we add to our diagram by crossing out regions 2 and 3 (Figure 22). Here the completed diagram shows that the syllogism is invalid, for according to the diagram there may or may not be no Samoans who are polygamous persons.

Using the same method, we can deal with the syllogism "No primates are marsupials; some salamanders are marsupials; therefore some salamanders are not primates." This syllogism is in the mood **EIO** and in the second figure. When we draw its

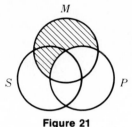

Figure 21

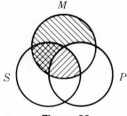

Figure 22

diagram (Figure 23) we find that the diagram shows the syllogism to be valid.

In dealing with the syllogism "All martinets are pusillanimous individuals; some sergeants are not martinets; therefore some sergeants are not pusillanimous individuals," special care must be taken in drawing the diagram. To indicate the major premise is easy (Figure 24). But the minor premise gives trouble, for we wish to indicate on the diagram exactly the information expressed, no less and no more. The minor premise is a particular sentence, and it declares that a certain space on the diagram is occupied. But what space? To put an asterisk in region 5 would be to claim that the premise tells us there are sergeants who are neither pusillanimous nor martinets; this is more than the premise says. To put an asterisk in region 6 would be to claim that the premise tells us there are pusillanimous sergeants who are not martinets; this too is more than the premise says. All the premise says is that there is at least one individual either in region 5 or in region 6 (although there may be individuals in both places).

The best way to draw the diagram is to use a bar instead of an asterisk. We draw a bar touching region 5 and region 6 but

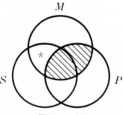

Figure 23

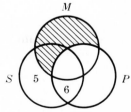

Figure 24

no other regions (Figure 25); this we interpret to mean that there is something somewhere in that space touched by the bar. Thus, according to the diagram, there may or may not be sergeants who are pusillanimous; when the premises are true, the conclusion of the syllogism may or may not be true. We see by the diagram that this **AOO** first-figure syllogism is invalid.

Various generalizations can be made concerning how the diagrams for valid syllogisms must look. For instance, any syllogism whose Venn diagram contains exactly three shaded regions is invalid. And any syllogism is invalid whose Venn diagram contains a bar that touches more than one region (that is, if the syllogism is to be valid, all but one segment of the bar must have been shaded out). However, it is better to understand how to use Venn diagrams than to memorize mechanical rules like these.

Now we must consider briefly how the difference between hypothetical and existential viewpoints relates to the validity of syllogisms. With many syllogisms, such as those we have just been considering, it makes no difference whether presuppositions about existence are made or not; such presuppositions have no effect on the validity or invalidity of these syllogisms. However, there are a few cases where it does make a difference; all of these are syllogisms having two universal premises and a particular conclusion. For instance, consider the syllogism "No persons medically fit for military service are paraplegics; all students who can run a mile in four minutes are persons medically fit for military service; therefore some students who can run a mile in four minutes are not paraplegics."

Figure 26 shows how we can diagram what the premises say. In drawing the left-hand diagram, we leave it entirely an open question whether individuals of any of these types exist; this makes the syllogism invalid. However if we may assume the

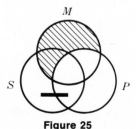

Figure 25

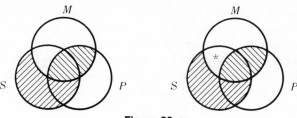

Figure 26

existence of students who can run a mile in four minutes, then we can add an asterisk to the diagram, and now the conclusion will follow. Thus this form of syllogism is invalid from the hypothetical viewpoint, but is valid from a certain existential viewpoint (notice that for this syllogism it happens to be an assumption about S's, not about M's or P's, that is required).

In this case there does not seem to be any obvious reason for regarding one viewpoint as more appropriate than the other. Perhaps in the context of an actual discussion it would be clear which viewpoint should be adopted, but when we are discussing the syllogism abstractly, the best we can do is explain the situation, pointing out the ambiguity, and leave matters at that.

EXERCISE 7

* **A** *Determine the mood and figure of each of the following syllogisms, and test the validity of each by means of a Venn diagram.*

1 No ruminant animals are predacious. All lions are predacious. Therefore, no lions are ruminant animals.
2 All proteins are organic compounds. No proteins are aluminosilicates. Therefore, no aluminosilicates are organic compounds.
3 No humanists are nihilists. Some nihilists are anarchists. Therefore, some anarchists are not humanists.
4 All even numbers are numbers divisible by 2. Some prime numbers are not even numbers. Therefore, some prime numbers are not numbers divisible by 2.
5 All existentialists are metaphysicians. Some existentialists are phenomenologists. Therefore, some phenomenologists are metaphysicians.
6 All Christian Scientists are believers in the power of prayer. Some social scientists are not believers in the

power of prayer.   Therefore, some social scientists are not Christian Scientists.

7   Some alcohols are hydroxides of paraffin radicals.   Some methanols are alcohols.   Therefore, some methanols are hydroxides of paraffin radicals.

8   No successful ballet dancers are wooden-legged men. Some Russian emigrés are successful ballet dancers.   Therefore, some Russian emigrés are not wooden-legged men.

9   No realtors are angels.   No lawyers are angels.   Therefore, no lawyers are realtors.

10   No Venetian galleys are ships that were square-rigged. Some caravels are not ships that were square-rigged.   Therefore, some caravels are not Venetian galleys.

B   *Determine the mood and figure of each of the following syllogisms, test it by a Venn diagram, and discuss whether it should be classified as valid.*

1   All compounds containing arsenic are substances dangerous to humans.   No substances dangerous to humans are good ingredients of food.   So some compounds containing arsenic are not good ingredients of food.

2   All eligible voters are residents of the precinct.   No three-legged men are residents of the precinct.   So some three-legged men are not eligible voters.

3   No mink-lined sneakers are good buys.   Some inexpensive articles are not good buys.   Therefore, some mink-lined sneakers are not inexpensive articles.

4   No Abominable Snowmen are creatures classified by biology. Some Tibetan bipeds are creatures classified by biology.   So some Abominable Snowmen are not Tibetan bipeds.

5   No persons who can run a mile in 3½ minutes are Ohioans. All persons who can run a mile in 3½ minutes are fine athletes.   So some fine athletes are not Ohioans.

RULES OF THE SYLLOGISM

Venn diagrams provide an efficient and general method for determining the validity of any syllogism.   If we were to construct a Venn diagram for each of the sixty-four possible sets of prem-mises that the 256 possible types of syllogism can have (32 diagrams would do; a tedious but instructive exercise), we would find that the following fifteen forms are valid from the hypothetical viewpoint.

Figure 1	Figure 2	Figure 3	Figure 4
AAA	EAE	IAI	AEE
EAE	AEE	AII	IAI
AII	EIO	OAO	EIO
EIO	AOO	EIO	

Nine additional forms are valid, provided appropriate existential presuppositions are made.

Figure 1	Figure 2	Figure 3	Figure 4	Presupposition required
AAI	AEO		AEO	S exist
EAO	EAO			
		AAI	EAO	M exist
		EAO		
			AAI	P exist

In medieval times each valid form of syllogism was given a name, the vowels in the name indicating its mood. Thus **AAA** in the first figure was called "*Barbara*," and **EAE** in the first figure was called "*Celarent*." In traditional discussion of the syllogism, an existential viewpoint always was adopted. Some lines of Latin verse were used to help students remember the names of the valid forms:

Barbara, Celarent, Darii, Ferioque prioris;
Cesare, Camestres, Festino, Baroco secundae;
Tertia Darapti, Disamis, Datisi, Felapton,
Bocardo, Ferison habet; quarta insuper addit
Bramantip, Camenes, Dimaris, Fesapo, Fresison.

These lines omit **AAI** and **EAO** in the first figure, **AEO** and **EAO** in the second, and **AEO** in the fourth. These five forms, though recognized as valid, were looked down upon by medieval logicians. They called these 'weakened' forms, because in each of these five cases a particular conclusion is drawn from premises from which a universal conclusion can validly be derived. Medieval logicians thought it pointless to get a particular conclusion when one could get the universal conclusion instead.

It is not necessary to memorize this list of valid forms; it is far better to remember how to test syllogisms for validity. The Venn diagrams provide one method for testing them. But, on the basis of this list, we can develop another method which does

not require pencil and paper.   If we study this list of valid forms
of syllogism, we can verify certain rules that valid syllogisms
obey.   One set of rules is the following:

1   In any valid syllogism the middle term is distributed at least
    once.
2   In any valid syllogism no term is distributed in the conclu-
    sion unless it is distributed in a premise (although we are not
    saying that a term could not be distributed in a premise with-
    out being distributed in the conclusion).
3   No valid syllogism has two negative premises.
4   Any valid syllogism has at least one negative premise if and
    only if it has a negative conclusion.
5   No syllogism valid from the hypothetical viewpoint has two
    universal premises and a particular conclusion.

If we studied the list of valid forms (which we can justify by appeal to Venn diagrams), we could prove that each of these rules
is correct.   Old-fashioned books on logic used to state such rules
without saying anything about how proof of them could be
given.   But these rules are not self-evident and call for proof;
using Venn diagrams would be a straightforward way of proving
them.

By studying the list of valid forms, we also could prove some
noteworthy facts about this specific set of rules.   Each of the
first four rules states a *necessary* condition for the validity of a
syllogism regarded from an existential viewpoint; taken together, the conditions stated in these first four rules constitute a
sufficient condition* for the validity of a syllogism regarded
from an existential viewpoint.   Moreover, each of the five rules
states a necessary condition for the validity of a syllogism regarded from the hypothetical viewpoint; taken together, these
five rules constitute a sufficient condition for the validity of such
a syllogism.

Once we have convinced ourselves of these rules, we may

---

* By saying that *B* is a *necessary* condition for *C*, we mean that nothing is a case of
C without being a case of *B*.   By saying that *B* is a *sufficient* condition for *C*, we
mean that anything that is a case of *B* is a case of *C*.   For example, being at
least thirty years old is a necessary but not a sufficient condition for being a
United States senator.   And eating a pint of arsenic is a sufficient but not
necessary condition for promptly dying.

use them instead of Venn diagrams for checking the validity of specific syllogisms. To use the rules in testing the validity of a syllogism, we simply observe whether the syllogism breaks any one of the rules; if it breaks a rule, it is invalid. A syllogism that violates the first rule is said to commit the fallacy of *undistributed middle*. A syllogism that breaks the second rule is said to commit a fallacy of *illicit process*; it is *illicit process of the major* if the major term is distributed in the conclusion but not in the major premise, and it is *illicit process of the minor* if the minor term is distributed in conclusion but not in the minor premise. No special names need be given to violations of the other rules. A syllogism that violates no rule is valid, of course.

Old-fashioned books usually also give the rule "A syllogism must have only three terms." Violation of this rule was called the fallacy of four terms. It is not necessary to include this rule, since it is part of the definition of a syllogism that it must have just three terms. The fallacy of four terms is a special kind of equivocation (which will be discussed in Chapter 5).

The set of rules stated above has been chosen so as to constitute a brief and easily remembered criterion for the validity of a syllogism. It is instructive to see how further rules can be deduced from the initial set of rules. For example, if we wish to prove that no valid syllogism has two particular premises (i.e., that every valid syllogism has at least one universal premise), we can reason as follows:

Suppose that there was a valid syllogism having two particular premises; its premises would be either (1) two **I** sentences, or (2) two **O** sentences, or (3) an **I** and an **O**. Case 1 is excluded by rule 1, since in two **I** premises the middle term would nowhere be distributed. Case 2 is excluded by rule 3. Case 3 would require the conclusion to be negative, according to rule 4; and in a negative sentence the predicate is distributed, so that by rule 2 the major term would have to be distributed in the major premise. But by rule 1 the middle term also would have to be distributed somewhere in a premise. Yet it is impossible for both the major and the middle term to be distributed, since an **I** and an **O** premise contain only one distributed term altogether. Therefore case 3 is excluded, for it would commit either the fallacy of undistributed middle or the fallacy of illicit process of the major. Hence, the rules imply that there can be no valid syllogism having two particular premises.

EXERCISE 8

A *Identify the mood and figure of each syllogism. Test its validity by the rules of the syllogism. Then check your answer with a Venn diagram, and name any fallacy committed that has a name.*

1 All less-developed countries are countries with balance-of-payments deficits. Hence, some Latin American countries are not less-developed countries, since some Latin American countries are not countries with balance-of-payments deficits.

2 All Eurocommunists are Marxists. Some members of the Chamber of Deputies are Marxists. So some members of the Chamber of Deputies are Eurocommunists.

3 All Presbyterians are predestinarians, because all Presbyterians are Calvinists, and all Calvinists are predestinarians.

4 No cars made in the United States are cars with inboard disk brakes. Some cars widely sold in the United States are not cars made in the United States. Therefore, some cars with inboard disk brakes are widely sold in the United States.

5 Some plays of Shakespeare are histories. No plays commonly read in English classes are histories. Therefore, some plays of Shakespeare are not commonly read in English classes.

6 No Malays are Buddhists, since no Moslems are Buddhists, and all Malays are Moslems.

7 No symbolist poets are romantic poets. No epic poets are romantic poets. Hence, no epic poets are symbolist poets.

8 All spherical pyramids are cubical pyramids, and all cubical pyramids are prisms. Therefore, all prisms are spherical pyramids.

9 No digital computers are analog computers. Some computers used in accounting are digital computers. So some computers used in accounting are analog computers.

10 Some variable stars are not double stars. Some double stars are not red stars. So some red stars are not variable stars.

B *Appealing only to the first four rules of the syllogism, prove that the following generalizations hold true of all syllogisms that are valid from an existential viewpoint.*

1 If one premise is particular, the conclusion is particular.
2 In the first figure the minor premise is affirmative.
3 In the first figure the major premise is universal.
4 In the second figure the conclusion is negative.
5 In the second figure the major premise is universal.
6 In the third figure the conclusion is particular.
7 In the third figure the minor premise is affirmative.
8 If the major term is the predicate of the major premise, then the minor premise must be affirmative.
9 In the fourth figure, if the conclusion is negative, the major premise must be universal.
10 In the fourth figure, if the minor premise is affirmative, the conclusion must be particular.

C *Appeal only to the first four syllogistic rules to answer the following questions. Give a proof in each case.*

1 In what syllogisms, if any, is the middle term distributed in both premises?
2 Can an invalid syllogism violate all four rules at once?
3 What is the maximum number of rules that an invalid syllogism can violate at once?
4 How many more occurrences of distributed terms can there be in the premises of a valid syllogism than there are in its conclusion?
5 In what valid syllogism is the major term distributed in the major premise but not in the conclusion? Prove that there is just one such syllogism.
6 Can a syllogism be valid from the hypothetical viewpoint but not from the existential viewpoint? Explain.

TRANSLATING INTO
STANDARD FORM

So far, we have considered ways of dealing with immediate inferences and syllogisms that are stated in standard form. Our logical techniques and rules do not apply to arguments that are not in standard form. But of course very often the arguments we meet in ordinary language are not expressed in standard form.

Putting Sentences into Categorical Form

For one thing, ordinary arguments usually contain sentences that are not categorical sentences. We cannot begin to apply what we know about the syllogism to such arguments until we have first translated the sentences into equivalent categorical sentences. Any sentence can be translated into categorical form if we exercise ingenuity, and there is always more than one correct way of doing this.* Skill at making these translations is useful, for logical relationships between sentences generally are easier to see after the sentences have been expressed in standard categorical form.

First let us examine some of the simpler kinds of cases. "Jaguars are all fast cars" becomes "All Jaguar cars are fast cars." (Note that it would be misleading to use the translation "All Jaguar cars are fast things." Here the word "fast" has a meaning that is comparative; Jaguars are fast for cars, although they are not fast compared with things like jet planes, rockets, or rays of light.) "Baboons never are courteous" becomes "No baboons are courteous creatures." "There are abstemious Virginians" becomes "Some Virginians are abstemious persons." In each case we try to construct in categorical form a new sentence that is strictly equivalent to the original one.

Sentences containing the verb "to be" in the past tense or future tense can be put into categorical form by moving the tensed verb into the predicate. Thus "Some Elizabethans were great lovers of bear baiting" can become "Some Elizabethans are people who were great lovers of bear baiting"; "No cocker spaniels will be elected to Congress" can become "No cocker spaniels are creatures that will be elected to Congress." These

---

* Some philosophers, such as Bertrand Russell, have believed that every assertion has just one essential logical form. They have held, for instance, that a sentence such as "Brutus betrayed Caesar" cannot legitimately be regarded as having the logical form of an **A** sentence; they maintain that this kind of example is essentially relational in form and that the only legitimate way of analyzing it is according to the relational style, which we shall discuss in Chapter 4. But this attitude is misguided. It is only in the context of a specific argument that we can say that a sentence ought to be analyzed as, say, relational rather then categorical. In some other argument the same sentence might properly be analyzed in the opposite fashion.

examples illustrate how, in a categorical sentence, the copula is to be understood in a tenseless sense. Also, sentences whose main verbs are verbs other than "to be" can be put into categorical form by transforming the verb into a noun. Thus "No pigs fly" becomes "No pigs are flyers," and "Some men enjoy croquet" can become "Some men are enjoyers of croquet."

Sentences like "Ohio is a state" and "Caesar conquered Gaul" are called *singular* sentences because each speaks about some single individual thing. We cannot translate "Ohio is a state" into "All Ohio is a state," because this has the wrong kind of copula (the copula should be "are") and because its subject is not a general term. To translate it into "All parts of Ohio are states" would be to alter the meaning. The best way to translate it is this: "Ohio is a state" can become "All things identical to Ohio are states." Thus we get a sentence in proper categorical form that necessarily agrees with the original sentence as regards truth or falsity, since one and only one thing is identical to Ohio (that is, Ohio itself). Similarly, "Caesar conquered Gaul" can become "All persons identical to Caesar are conquerers of Gaul." This somewhat cumbersome style of translation is required only for singular sentences, however; it would be pointless to translate "All Jaguars are fast cars" into "All things identical with Jaguars are fast cars."

Sometimes we meet sentences that contain no specific indication as to quantity. Occasionally such sentences are really ambiguous, but more often if we think about them we have no trouble seeing that they mean one thing rather than the other. Thus, someone who says "Bachelors are unmarried" surely means "*All* bachelors are unmarried persons," but someone who says "Visitors are coming" surely means "*Some* visitors are people coming." Similarly, "An elephant is a pachyderm" surely means "All elephants are pachyderms," but "A policeman is at the door" means "Some policemen are persons at the door."

Another sort of ambiguity can occur when the word "not" is inserted in the middle of a universal sentence. "All my students are not lazy" might mean "All students of mine are people who are not lazy," or it might mean "It is not the case that all my students are lazy," that is, "Some students of mine are not lazy persons." These two meanings are very different, and so we must distinguish between them; when we meet a sentence constructed in this ambiguous way we simply have to guess what is in the speaker's mind.

Sentences containing the words "only" and "none but" must be handled carefully. Thus, "Only the wealthy attend Calvin Coolidge College" does not mean that all wealthy persons are attenders of Calvin Coolidge College; what it means is "All persons who attend C.C.C. are wealthy persons." Similarly, "None but the brave deserve the fair" does not mean that all brave persons are deservers of the fair; it means "All persons who deserve the fair are brave persons." In general, "Only S are P" means "All P are S," and "None but S are P" also means "All P are S."

But "only some" has a meaning different from "only" by itself; thus "Only some students at the university attend the college" means "Some university students are attenders of the college and some university students are not attenders of the college." In the same vein, "All except employees are eligible" means "All nonemployees are eligible," and it suggests, although it does not necessarily say, that no employees are eligible. Similarly, "Anyone is eligible unless he is an employee" means "All nonemployees are eligible"; it too suggests, although it does not necessarily say, that no employees are eligible. In general, both "All except S are P" and "Anything is P unless it is S" mean "All nonS are P."

For some sentences that look quite unlike categorical sentences we may have to devise entirely new terms before we can put them into categorical form. The sentence "Whenever it rains it pours" does not appear to be categorical, but if we think of it as a sentence about times, it can become "All times when it rains are times when it pours." Analogously, the sentence "Whither thou goest I will go" can be understood as referring to places, and it can become "All places where thou goest are places where I will go." However, we have to be alert to the intended meanings of sentences like these, for "Wilbur always sleeps in class" does not mean "All times are times when Wilbur is sleeping in class"; what it surely means is "All times when Wilbur is in class are times when he sleeps." Similarly, "She goes everywhere with him" probably does not mean "All places are places to which she goes with him"; much more likely it means "All places he goes are places she goes with him."

Working out translations such as these is necessary as a preliminary to the syllogistic analysis of ordinary reasoning. But it also has an additional intellectual value in that it encourages us to learn to understand more accurately what ordinary sentences are saying.

Translating into Syllogistic Form

Not all arguments can properly be interpreted as syllogisms. However, many arguments not in syllogistic form can be analyzed for validity by being translated into syllogisms. That is, their premises and conclusions admit of being translated into equivalent sentences that constitute syllogisms, and the validity of these arguments stands or falls with that of the syllogisms into which they are translated. By translating such arguments into standard syllogistic form, we make it easier to test their validity by means of Venn diagrams, and we make it possible to test their validity by means of the rules of the syllogism.

There are two different respects in which an argument that can be translated into a syllogism may at first fall short of being in explicit syllogistic form. The argument may at first contain sentences that are not categorical sentences, or it may at first contain more than three terms. We have already discussed translating sentences into categorical form. Now we must consider how to deal with syllogistic arguments that contain too many terms.

Suppose we have an argument that is like a syllogism (that is, it contains three sentences and talks about just three classes of things) but contains too many terms, some of these terms, however, being negations of others. Whenever this happens, we can use immediate inference to eliminate some of the terms, replacing the original sentences by equivalent new ones. For instance, the argument "No millionaires are paupers; no stars of television are nonmillionaires; therefore no stars of television are paupers" as it stands is not in syllogistic form. But we can put it into syllogistic form without difficulty once we notice that two of its terms are negations of each other. The easiest thing to do is to obvert the second premise. We then obtain "No M are P; all S are M; therefore no S are P." This syllogism is **EAE** in the first figure, and since it fulfills all the rules, it is a valid syllogism.

Notice that it would have been an error to have called the original argument invalid because it contains two negative

premises. The rule that an argument with two negative premises is invalid applies only to syllogisms in standard form (and
the same is true for all our five syllogistic rules). We must translate this argument into syllogistic form before we attempt to
judge it by means of the rules; when we put it into syllogistic
form, we find that it is valid.

Immediate inference allows us to reword an argument so as
to reduce the number of terms when some terms are negations of
each other. But sometimes a deeper rewording of the argument
is required if we are to put it into syllogistic form. Where this
is so, we must be judicious about selecting our terms, trying
to word it so that we have just three terms in all, each of which
appears in two different sentences of the argument. For instance, the argument "The car doesn't start easily when the
temperature is below zero; it will be below zero tomorrow; and
so tomorrow I'll have trouble starting" does not look much like
a syllogism. Yet we can put it into syllogistic form if we select
our terms judiciously. One way of doing it is this: "All days
when the temperature falls below zero are days when the car
does not start easily; all days identical to tomorrow are days
when the temperature falls below zero; therefore, all days
identical to tomorrow are days when the car does not start
easily." Here we have **AAA** in the first figure.

EXERCISE 9

* **A** *Interpreting each of the following sentences in the way most
likely to be intended, find at least one way of translating it into
categorical form. The translation must be equivalent to the
original sentence (that is, they must necessarily agree as regards
truth or falsity).*

1 Eskimos never are vegetarians.
2 A kilogram is 2.2 pounds.
3 All politicians are not dishonest.
4 There are women judges.
5 A positive real number always has two square roots.
6 Only a millionaire can afford to own a personal jet plane.
7 There aren't any parts of physics that don't involve mathematics.
8 Socrates was the teacher of Plato.
9 The moon is the earth's only natural satellite.
10 There are no birds without feathers.

† B *Translate each sentence into categorical form.*

1 Blessed are the pure in heart.
2 Tardiness is reprehensible.
3 None but the lonely heart can know my sadness.
4 Whenever interest rates rise, bond prices fall.
5 Who lives without folly is not so wise as he thinks.
6 He jests at scars who never felt a wound.
7 No friend is better than a fair-weather friend.
8 There never was philosopher that could endure the tooth-ache patiently.
9 He cannot become rich who will not labor.
10 The unexamined life is not worthy to be lived by man.

SOCRATES

11 Whosoever loveth me loveth my hound.

SIR THOMAS MORE

12 All noble things are as difficult as they are rare.

BARUCH SPINOZA

13 He's a fool that makes his doctor his heir.

BENJAMIN FRANKLIN

14 He who knows only his own side of the case, knows little of that. JOHN STUART MILL

15 Under a government which imprisons any unjustly, the true place for a just man is also a prison.

HENRY DAVID THOREAU

C *In each case decide whether (b) is a correct translation of (a). If any translation is incorrect, explain why and correct it.*

1 **(a)** American warships are in the Mediterranean.
   (b) All American warships are vessels in the Mediterranean.
2 **(a)** Only the brave deserve the fair.
   (b) All brave persons are deservers of the fair.
3 **(a)** Wherever trade goes, the flag will follow.
   (b) All places are places to which trade goes and the flag follows.
4 **(a)** Every marriage does not end in divorce.
   (b) All marriages are relationships that do not end in divorce.
5 **(a)** None but those who love virtue love angling.
   (b) All lovers of virtue are lovers of angling.
6 **(a)** He and she do everything together.
   (b) All things are things he and she do together.

7 **(a)** It is a wise father who knows his own child.

    (b) All wise fathers are knowers of their own children.

8 **(a)** It is sharper than a serpent's tooth to have an ungrateful child.

    (b) All persons having ungrateful children are persons who suffer more sharply than do those bitten by serpents' teeth.

* **D** *Put each of the following arguments into syllogistic form, state its mood and figure, and then test its validity by means of a Venn diagram and by the rules of the syllogism.*

1 Some biologists are government employees. All who are not biologists are botanists. Therefore, some botanists are government employees.

2 All industrial workers are covered by social security. It is not the case that no industrial workers need more adequate retirement pensions. Therefore, there are some who need more adequate retirement pensions even though they are covered by social security.

3 No deficit in the federal budget is not an inflationary influence. No inflationary influences are helpful to the balance of payments. Thus some factors not helpful to the balance of payments are deficits in the federal budget.

4 No biophysicists are untrained in chemistry. Some geneticists are untrained in chemistry. Therefore, some persons who are not biophysicists are geneticists.

5 All companies that are conglomerates are speculative to invest in. Only companies that are not blue chips are conglomerates. Therefore, no blue chips are speculative to invest in.

6 No republics are dictatorships. Not all republics are democratic. Therefore, some nondemocracies are not dictatorships.

7 Only a pantheist would believe that God is physical. But Spinoza was a pantheist, so he must have believed that.

8 Whenever the soil is very acid, flowers will not grow. But flowers grow in your garden, so the soil cannot be very acid there.

9 You cannot convict someone of murder just on circumstantial evidence. There is nothing but circumstantial evidence

against the butler.   Thus the butler cannot be convicted of murder.

10 Any time the press is free, there will be active criticism of the government.   You never get active criticism of the government without some of it being unfair and harmful. So you can't have a free press without some unfair and harmful criticism of the government.

RELATED TYPES OF ARGUMENT

We can make use of what we now know about syllogisms and about Venn diagrams in order to analyze further arguments that are not quite of the types we have studied so far but are akin to them.

The Sorites

Sometimes we encounter an argument that consists of a chain of syllogisms.   When an argument has more than two premises, sometimes two of the premises can be combined to yield a syllogistic conclusion that, when combined with another premise, yields a syllogistic conclusion that, when combined with another premise, . . . yields the final conclusion.   An argument of this type is called a *sorites* (from the Greek word for a pile).   In order to show that a sorites is valid, we must show how it is possible to pass, by means of a series of valid syllogistic steps, from the premises to the conclusion.   We use our ingenuity in order to fit together the links of the chain, testing each link by means of a Venn diagram or by the rules of the syllogism. For example, consider the argument:

> Some of my uncles are really worth listening to on military subjects.
> No one can remember the Battle of San Juan Hill unless he is very old.
> No one is really worth listening to on military subjects unless he can remember the Battle of San Juan Hill.
> Therefore, some of my uncles are very old.

This can be symbolized:

Some U are W	(1)
All R are O	(2)
All W are R	(3)
Therefore some U are O	(4)

Here (1) and (3) can be combined to make a syllogism of the form **AII** in the first figure whose conclusion, "Some U are R," can then be combined with (2) to make a syllogism again of the form **AII** in the first figure whose conclusion is (4). Thus we show that the original premises validly yield the desired result.

The method just employed is a method for establishing the validity of a valid sorites. Suppose, however, that in a given case we try to pass, by means of syllogistic steps, from the premises to the conclusion but do not succeed in doing so. This may lead us to *suspect* that the sorites is invalid, but just by itself our failure does not definitely *prove* that the sorites is invalid; perhaps we simply have not been ingenious enough. To prove that the sorites is invalid by using our present method, we would have to investigate *every* possible sequence in which the premises might be combined, and we would have to show that *none* of these sequences validly yields the conclusion.

A different method for dealing with this particular example would be to use a single Venn-like diagram which can depict the interrelations among four terms. We cannot make such a diagram using overlapping circles, but we can do it with over-lapping ellipses (Figure 27). The diagram is difficult to draw, as it must contain sixteen different distinct regions. But if we draw it and enter the information contained in the premises

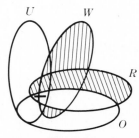

Figure 27

of the above argument, we can then see from the diagram that the conclusion has to be true if the premises are.

Further Uses of Venn Diagrams

Some arguments that cannot be translated into syllogisms or into chains of syllogisms can nevertheless be tested by means of Venn diagrams. Consider the argument "All who detest Tchaikovsky admire either Bach or Mozart (or both); some who detest Tchaikovsky do not admire Mozart; therefore, not all who admire Bach admire Mozart." Here we have an argument which is not valid as a syllogism, for if we think of the argument as containing just three terms, its premises are not all in categorical form, while if we think of its premises in categorical form, there are too many terms. But we would be too hasty if we assumed this argument to be invalid just because it is not a valid syllogism; this argument is not supposed to be a syllogism. It is the kind of argument, however, whose validity can be tested by means of a Venn diagram, since it deals with just three classes of individuals and makes appropriately simple assertions about them. We shall indicate on the diagram exactly what the premises say; then by inspecting the diagram we shall be able to tell whether the conclusion follows.

Here we need three circles representing, respectively, those who detest Tchaikovsky, those who admire Bach, and those who admire Mozart. The first premise declares that all individuals inside the *DT* circle are either inside the *AB* circle or inside the *AM* circle; that is, there are none inside the *DT* circle but outside both the *AB* and *AM* circles (Figure 28). The second premise makes the added claim that some individuals inside the *DT* circle are outside the *AM* circle (Figure 29). Inspecting the

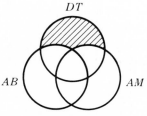

Figure 28

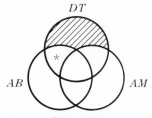

Figure 29

diagram, we see that the conclusion that not all inside the *AB* circle are inside the *AM* circle validly follows from these two premises.

* **A** *Use appropriate methods to establish the validity of the argument or to answer the question in each case.*

1 Some people are tolerated in polite society even though their manners are not beyond reproach. No one is tolerated in polite society who insists upon drinking the blood of infants. All werewolves insist upon doing just that. Therefore, some people whose manners are not beyond reproach are not werewolves.

2 All the bright students who get high grades are hard-working. Some students who get high grades are either bright or hard-working. Therefore, some students who get high grades are hard-working.

3 No one plays the harpsichord unless he is an intellectual. All dolphins are intellectuals, but they cannot read music. Only those who can read music play the harpsichord. Therefore, dolphins do not play the harpsichord.

4 Every Cypriot is either Turkish or Greek. There are non-Turkish Cypriots. Therefore, some non-Turkish Cypriots are Greek.

5 The regulations of Calvin Coolidge College contain these requirements:
All students must take logic.
All premedical students must take physics.
No one may take physics without taking the calculus.
Only those who do not take the calculus may take logic.
Would you advise a young man who wants to be a doctor to enroll at Calvin Coolidge College?

6 Derive from these three sentences a valid conclusion that follows only from all three sentences together:
Feathers of the moa bird cannot be bought for money.
Nothing is sold by barrow boys but what can be had for a song.
Anything can be bought for money that can be had for a song.

7 Derive a valid conclusion using all these premises:

Any person likely to cause trouble in cramped quarters is dangerous aboard a space capsule.

Infants are always noisy.

All distracting companions are likely to cause trouble in cramped quarters.

No one who would be dangerous aboard a space capsule is suitable as an astronaut for the trip to Mars.

Any noisy person is a distracting companion.

† **B** *Translate each argument into the form of a syllogism or a sorites, and test its validity.*

1 Some . . . have . . . expressed themselves in a manner . . . of imagining the whole of virtue to consist in singly aiming, according to the best of their judgment, at promoting the happiness of mankind in the present state; and the whole of vice in doing what they foresee, or might foresee, is likely to produce an overbalance of unhappiness in it: than which mistakes, none can be conceived more terrible. For it is certain, that some of the most shocking instances of injustice, adultery, murder, perjury, and even of persecution, may, in many supposable cases, not have the appearance of being likely to produce an overbalance of misery in the present state; perhaps sometimes may have the contrary appearance.

BISHOP BUTLER, *Analogy of Religion*

2 How can anyone maintain that pain is always evil, if he admits that remorse is painful yet is sometimes a real good?

3 Speculative opinions . . . and articles of faith . . . which are required only to be believed, cannot be imposed on any church by the law of the land. For it is absurd that things should be enjoined by laws which are not in men's power to perform. And to believe this or that to be true does not depend upon our will.

JOHN LOCKE, *A Letter Concerning Toleration*

4 Philosophy must possess complete certitude. For since philosophy is a science, its content must be demonstrated by inferring conclusions with legitimate sequence from certain and immutable principles. Now, that which is inferred by legitimate sequence from certain and immutable

principles is thereby certain and cannot be doubted. . . .
Hence, since there is no room for doubt in philosophy,
which is a science, it must possess complete certitude.

CHRISTIAN WOLFF,
Preliminary Discourse on Philosophy in General

5 The governments, not only the military ones, but the governments in general, could be, I do not say useful, but harmless,
only in case they consisted of infallible, holy people. . . .
But the governments, by dint of their very activity, which
consists in the practice of violence, are always composed of
elements which are the very opposite of holy,—of the most
impudent, coarse, and corrupted men. For this reason every
government . . . is a most dangerous institution in the world.

LEO TOLSTOI, "Patriotism and Government"

CHAPTER 3

THE LOGIC OF
TRUTH FUNCTIONS

In this chapter we shall study a type of deductive argument basically different from those dealt with in the previous chapter. Arguments of this new type essentially involve compound sentences of certain logically elementary kinds.

ARGUMENTS CONTAINING
COMPOUND SENTENCES

We may think of an argument as having two parts. One part consists of those words which make up its logical skeleton, that is, its logical form or structure; the other part consists of those words which are the flesh with which the skeleton is filled out. For instance, (1) is an argument, and (2) is its logical skeleton:

All spiders are eight-legged. (1)   All . . . are # # #   (2)
No wasps are eight-legged.   No * * * are # # #

Therefore no wasps are spiders.   ∴ no * * * are . . .

In argument (1) the words "all," "no," and "are" make up the logical skeleton, while the words "spiders," "wasps," and "eight-legged" are the flesh with which the skeleton happens to be filled out. Notice that (1) is a valid argument; it is valid *because* (2) is a valid kind of skeleton. To say that (2) is a valid kind of skeleton or logical form is to say that *any* argument having this same form will have a true conclusion if its premises are true. That is, whatever word or phrase we insert for "...," whatever word or phrase we insert for "# # #," and whatever word or phrase we insert for "* * *," we never can turn (2) into an argument having true premises but a false conclusion.

All the arguments dealt with in Chapter 2 had one important feature in common. They all were like (1) in that their logical skeletons had gaps that were to be filled by single words or phrases which we called general terms and symbolized by means of capital letters. However, not all arguments are like this. Consider argument (3) and its skeleton (4):

This is a wasp or this is a spider.	(3)	# # # or . . . (4)
This is not a wasp.		Not # # #
Therefore this is a spider.		∴ . . . .

Argument (3) is valid too, but notice the difference between (4) and (2). The gaps in skeleton (4) must be filled not by single words or phrases but by whole sentences. In argument (3) the sentences which happen to fill these gaps are the sentences "This is a wasp" and "This is a spider." Notice also that in analyzing this argument we must think of the first premise not as a categorical sentence but rather as a compound sentence; only by thinking of it in this way can we see what makes the argument valid. We shall now become acquainted with some of the main kinds of arguments that contain compound sentences like this, arguments whose fleshly parts are whole sentences.

Some of them are very simple, trivial forms of argument. You may think that they are pointless and silly. But remember that simple arguments can be combined to form chains of reasoning, and a chain of reasoning may succeed in reaching an interesting conclusion that was not obvious, even if each step in it is trivial and obvious.

Negation

The simplest way of forming a compound sentence is by prefixing the words "It is not the case that." The sentence "It is not the case that wasps are spiders" is a compound sentence, for it contains within itself the simpler sentence "Wasps are spiders."

We say that the former sentence is the *negation* of the latter sentence. The single word "not" can be used instead: "Wasps are not spiders" is another way of expressing the negation of "Wasps are spiders." But notice that the word "not" is not as reliable in forming negations as is the phrase "It is not the case that." "Some wasps are not spiders" is *not* the negation of "Some wasps are spiders"; the negation of the latter sentence should be expressed "It is not the case that some wasps are spiders," and that is equivalent to "No wasps are spiders."

The negation of a given sentence should be its *contradictory*; that is, it should deny just what the sentence says, no less and no more. Therefore, the negation of the negation of a sentence will be equivalent to the original sentence itself. This provides us with one extremely simple form of argument that involves negation only.

Double negation

Not (not p)	e.g., It is not the case that wasps aren't insects.
∴ p	Therefore wasps are insects.
p	e.g., Wasps are insects.
∴ not (not p)	Therefore it's not the case that wasps aren't insects.

Here, in representing the forms of compound sentences, we have stopped using cumbersome dots, dashes, and asterisks; instead, we use the letters "p," "q," and "r," which are to be thought of as doing just the same job, that is, marking places where sentences may be filled in.

Notice, however, that we cannot use the principle of double negation indiscriminately to cancel out negations. From "It is not the case both that there will not be rain and that there will not be snow" we are not entitled to infer "There will be rain and there will be snow." This is an example of a misuse of the principle of double negation. Here the mistake is that our premise is the negation of an "and" sentence rather than the negation of a negation. To avoid mistakes like this, we need to pay close attention to the logical forms of the expressions with which we deal. The position of a negation can make a great difference to the meaning. As another example, we have to distinguish among:

Not (p or q)	e.g., It is not the case that it will either rain or snow.
Not p or q	e.g., It will not rain or it will snow.
Not p or not q	e.g., It will not rain or it will not snow.

Here are three different forms of sentences which say three different things. They are not equivalent; that is, they do not necessarily need to be alike as regards truth or falsity.

Disjunction

A compound sentence consisting of two simpler sentences linked together by "or" (or by "either . . . or . . . ," which means just the same) is called a *disjunction* (or an *alternation*). A disjunction is symmetrical, in the sense that "p or q" always is equivalent to "q or p." We can rewrite our earlier skeleton (4) using letters:

Disjunctive argument

p or q	also: p or q	e.g., It will rain or it will snow.
Not p	not q	It will not rain.
$\therefore q$	$\therefore p$	Therefore it will snow.

These forms of disjunctive argument are valid because the first premise tells us that at least one component is true, while the second premise tells us that a certain component is not true; it follows that the other component must be true.

Sometimes there is an ambiguity about the word "or." When we say "p or q," sometimes we mean "p or q but not both." This is called the *exclusive* sense of "or." More often when we say "p or q," we mean "p or q or perhaps both." This is the *nonexclusive* sense of "or." In ordinary conversation, if a gentleman says to a lady in a tone of acquiescence "I'll buy you a Cadillac or a mink coat," he is surely using "or" in the nonexclusive sense, since she cannot accuse him of having spoken untruthfully if he then gives her both. Cases of the exclusive sense of "or" occur, though more rarely. If a father says to his child in a tone of refusal "I'll take you to the zoo or to the beach," then the mother can accuse him of having spoken falsely if he takes the child both places.

Ordinarily, unless we have some reason to the contrary, we shall interpret the word "or" in the nonexclusive sense so that we can be sure of not taking too much for granted. Therefore, we regard the following two forms of argument as invalid:

Invalid disjunctive arguments

p or q	p or q	e.g., He's guilty or she's guilty.
p	q	He's guilty.
∴ not q	∴ not p	Therefore she's not guilty.

These forms would be valid if "or" were understood in the exclusive sense, but they are invalid when "or" is understood in the commoner nonexclusive sense.

Conjunction

A compound sentence consisting of two simpler sentences linked by the word "and" is called a *conjunction*. Sometimes, as in the sentence "They got married and had a baby," the word "and" is used to mean "and then," indicating that one event occurred first and the other event occurred later. But other times, as in the sentence "I like cake and I like candy," the word "and" is simply used to join together two assertions, without indicating any temporal relationship. This latter sense of "and" is the more important one for logic. When "and" is used in this sense, conjunctions are symmetrical; that is, "p and q" is then equivalent to "q and p." In English, various other words, such as "but" and "although," often do essentially the same logical job as "and." One absurdly simple but perfectly valid form of conjunctive argument is this:

Valid conjunctive argument (simplification)

| p and q | e.g., It will rain and snow. |
| ∴ p | Therefore it will rain. |

If we combine negation with conjunction, we can obtain a slightly less trivial kind of valid conjunctive argument:

Valid conjunctive arguments

Not (p and q)	e.g., He will not give her both gems and a car.
p	He is giving her gems.
∴ not q	Therefore he will not give her a car.

Not (p and q)	e.g., It will not both rain and snow.
q	It will snow.
∴ not p	Therefore it will not rain.

The following forms, however, are invalid:

Invalid conjunctive arguments

Not (p and q)	e.g., Joe and Ted won't both come.
Not p	Joe won't come.
∴ q	Therefore Ted will come.

Not (p and q)	e.g., He won't both buy and sell today.
Not q	He won't sell today.
∴ p	Therefore he'll buy today.

Conditionals

Another important kind of compound sentence involves the word "if." A sentence consisting of two simpler sentences linked by the word "if," or by the words "if . . . then # # #," is called a *conditional*, or *hypothetical*, sentence. The part to which the word "if" is directly attached is called the *antecedent* of the conditional sentence, and the other part is called the *consequent*. To assert the conditional sentence is to say that the truth of the antecedent will ensure the truth of the consequent. For instance, someone who asserts "If tufa floats, then some rocks float" is saying that the truth of "Tufa floats" would be sufficient to ensure the truth of "Some rocks float."

Let us consider some forms of argument containing conditional sentences.

Modus ponens

If p then q	e.g., If tufa floats, some rocks float.
p	Tufa does float.
∴ q	Therefore some rocks float.

Modus tollens

If p then q	e.g., If pigs can fly, then dogs can fly.
Not q	Dogs cannot fly.
∴ not p	Therefore pigs can't fly.

Somewhat similar, but invalid,* are the following:

Fallacy of affirming the consequent

If p then q	e.g., If he wants to marry me, he'll give me mink.
q	He is giving me mink.
∴ p	Therefore he wants to marry me.

Fallacy of denying the antecedent

If p then q	e.g., If the car runs, it has gas.
Not p	The car does not run.
∴ not q	Therefore the car does not have gas.

Another valid form has three conditional sentences, the consequent of the first being the same as the antecedent of the second:

Chain argument (or hypothetical syllogism)

If p then q	e.g., If the moon can be settled, then Mars can be settled.
If q then r	If Mars can be settled, then Jupiter can be settled.
∴ if p then r	Therefore if the moon can be settled, Jupiter can be settled.

We can also construct even longer chain arguments with any number of premises. The one requirement for a valid chain argument is that the consequent of the first premise must serve as the antecedent of the next, the consequent of that premise as

---

* We say that these arguments are invalid because, for the present, we are considering only *deductive* reasoning. However, such arguments are not always fallacious when they are intended as *inductive* arguments. In inductive reasoning the speaker claims only that his premises help to make his conclusion reasonable to believe; it *sometimes* is legitimate to make this weaker claim in connection with some arguments like these and others that are classified as deductively fallacious.

the antecedent of the next, and so on, while the conclusion must have the first antecedent as its antecedent and the last consequent as its consequent.

Another style of argument involving a conditional premise goes by the name of *reductio ad absurdum* (Latin: "reduction to the absurd"). Suppose, for example, that we want to prove that there is no largest integer (a positive whole number). We may reason as follows: If there is an integer larger than every other integer, then (because adding 1 to it will yield a still larger integer) it is not an integer larger than every other integer. From this it follows that there is not a largest integer.

Reductio ad absurdum

If p then not p	e.g., If there is a largest integer, then there is not a largest integer.
∴ not p	Therefore it is not the case that there is a largest integer.

This style of reasoning may seem puzzling because one is inclined to think that a sentence of the form "if p then not p" says something impossible, something necessarily false. However, that is a mistake. A sentence of the form "if p then not p" can very well be true, but only if its antecedent is false. This is why the reasoning is valid: The premise tells us that the truth of the antecedent would carry with it a consequent inconsistent with the truth of the antecedent. Thus the antecedent is 'reduced to absurdity,' and this entitles us to conclude that the antecedent is false.

Very similar is a kindred form of *reductio ad absurdum* argument where the premise is a conditional whose consequent is a contradiction:

Reductio ad absurdum (another form)

	e.g., If I get home before dark, then I'll both have traveled at 90 mph (for it is 90 miles, and one hour till dark) and not traveled at 90 mph (for at that speed I'd crash before arriving).
If p then both q and not q	
∴ not p	Therefore I won't get home before dark.

Here the premise is a conditional whose consequent is necessarily false, but that does not prevent the premise as a whole from being a true sentence. The antecedent is 'reduced to absurdity'; this allows us to infer that it is false.

EXERCISE 11

A *Abbreviate each argument, using the suggested letters. Identify the form of each argument, and say whether it is deductively valid.*

1 The patient should take two tablets before dinner and one after breakfast. So the patient should take one tablet after breakfast. (*T, O*)

2 Jackson was either a Whig or a Democrat. He was not a Whig, so he must have been a Democrat. (*W, D*)

3 If the insurance is in force, then the premium was paid. But the premium was not paid. So the insurance is not in force. (*F, P*)

4 His car doesn't have both front-wheel drive and a rear engine. It does have a rear engine. So it doesn't have front-wheel drive. (*F, R*)

5 It's not true that you can't be both president of the company and on its board of directors. So you can be both president of the company and on its board of directors. (*P, B*)

6 If Messina is in Italy, Palermo is in Italy. If Palermo is in Italy, all Sicily is in Italy. So if Messina is in Italy, all Sicily is. (*M, P, S*)

7 Selling machine guns is permitted or selling hand grenades is. So it's not the case that either selling machine guns isn't permitted or that selling hand grenades isn't permitted. (*M, H*)

8 This field needs rain or it needs fertilizer. It doesn't need rain. So it needs fertilizer. (*R, F*)

9 Madagascar is either Malawi or Malagasy. Madagascar isn't Malawi. So it must be Malagasy. (*W, S*)

10 Rousseau didn't write both *Candide* and *The Monadology*. Now, he didn't write *The Monadology*. So he must be the author of *Candide*. (*C, M*)

11 If the testimony of the witness was correct, the defendant was guilty. The defendant was indeed guilty. So the testimony of the witness must have been correct. (*T, G*)

12 If Madeira is in the Pacific, then Pitcairn is in the Atlantic. If Captain Bligh sailed the Atlantic, then Pitcairn is in the Atlantic. So, if Captain Bligh sailed the Atlantic, then Madeira is in the Pacific. *(M, P, B)*

13 If there is no largest whole number, then the whole numbers are infinite. There is no largest whole number. So the whole numbers are infinite. *(L, I)*

14 If no acid can dissolve gold, then gold is the most noble metal. There is an acid which can dissolve gold. So gold isn't the most noble metal. *(A, N)*

15 If there are two different circles each going through three of the same points, these circles are not different. Therefore, there cannot be two different circles each going through three of the same points. *(C)*

B *Madame Fortuna tells Joan: She'll travel if she doesn't slim down; but, if she slims down, she'll either marry a rich stranger or travel and marry someone she knows. Which of the following outcomes accord with the prediction?*

1 Joan slims, doesn't travel, marries a poor stranger.
2 Joan slims, travels, marries a rich stranger.
3 Joan doesn't slim, travels, marries her cousin.
4 Joan doesn't slim, travels, marries a rich stranger.
5 Joan slims, travels, becomes a nun.
6 Joan doesn't slim, stays home, marries no one.
7 Joan slims, travels, marries her cousin.
8 Joan doesn't slim, doesn't travel, marries a rich stranger.
9 Joan slims, stays home, marries a rich stranger.
10 Joan slims, doesn't travel, marries no one.

TRANSLATING INTO
STANDARD FORM: DILEMMAS

In English, our ways of expressing negation, disjunction, and conjunction are comparatively straightforward and do not give rise to much difficulty. With the conditional, however, the situation is more complicated. In English, we have many different but equivalent ways in which conditionals can be expressed, and these are easy to misunderstand.

Consider the following formulations, all of which are equivalent:

If Jones is a senator, then he is over thirty.	If p then q
If Jones is a senator, he is over thirty.	If p, q
Jones is over thirty if he is a senator.	q if p
Jones is over thirty provided he is a senator.	q provided p
Jones is a senator only if he is over thirty.	p only if q
Jones is not a senator unless he is over thirty.	Not p unless q
Unless he is over thirty Jones is not a senator.	Unless q, not p

Here, in each sentence, "Jones is a senator" may be regarded as the antecedent and "Jones is over thirty" as the consequent. Each of these equivalent sentences claims that the antecedent expresses a *sufficient* condition for the consequent (being a senator is sufficient to guarantee being over thirty) and claims that the consequent expresses a *necessary* condition for the antecedent (being over thirty is necessary to being a senator).

An important point to notice about conditionals is that "if p then q" is not in general equivalent to "if q then p." Thus, "If he's a senator, then he's over thirty" is not equivalent to "If he's over thirty, then he's a senator." These two sentences express independent thoughts, and the truth of one does not guarantee the truth of the other.

Because of this, we have to be on our guard against mistranslating a sentence which really means "if p then q" into a sentence which means "if q then p." For example, we have to be on our guard against supposing that "if p then q" is equivalent to "q only if p." We might be misled into thinking that "if" means the same as "only if," but they are not the same at all. "If Jones is a senator, then he's over thirty" is quite different in what it says from "Jones is over thirty only if he's a senator." The general rule is that "if p then q" is equivalent to "p only if q," but not to "q only if p."

Similarly, when we translate an "unless" sentence into an "if-then" sentence, we must be careful to distinguish correctly between antecedent and consequent. A general rule for doing this is: Negate either part of the "unless" sentence and make it the antecedent of your "if-then" sentence. Thus, "p unless q" becomes either "if not p then q" or "if not q then p." For example, "He's an admiral unless he's a general" is equivalent to "If he isn't an admiral, then he's a general" and to "If he isn't a general, then he's an admiral"; but it is not equivalent to "If he's an admiral, then he isn't a general" or to "If he's a general, then he isn't an admiral."

When the antecedent and consequent trade places in a conditional sentence, we obtain what is called the *converse* of the original sentence. Thus, "If Jones is over thirty, then he is a senator" is the converse of "If Jones is a senator, then he is over thirty"; in general, "if q then p" is the converse of "if p then q." As we have already noticed, the converse is a new and different sentence which need not agree with the original as regards truth and falsity.

If, in a conditional sentence, antecedent and consequent trade places and also each of them is negated, we obtain what is called the *contrapositive* of the original sentence. Thus, "If Jones is not over thirty, then he is not a senator" is the contrapositive of "If Jones is a senator, then he is over thirty." And, in general, "if not q then not p" is the contrapositive of "if p then q." The contrapositive always is equivalent to the original sentence. This is because the original sentence says in effect that the truth of p ensures the truth of q, while its contrapositive says that the falsehood of q ensures the falsehood of p—which amounts to the same thing.

Understanding these relationships can help us deal with arguments which are not stated in standard form. If we meet an argument whose premises and conclusion can be translated into equivalent sentences that do form an argument of a standard type, then we can use what we know about the validity of the standard type to evaluate the validity of that argument. Our method here allows two sorts of moves: We may replace any premise or conclusion by a new sentence equivalent to it, and we may rearrange premises. Such moves will have no effect on the validity or invalidity of an argument. Our aim in dealing with a nonstandard argument will be to get it into some familiar standard form so that we can determine better whether or not it is valid.

For instance, we may handle an example as follows:

Mica sinks only if tufa doesn't sink. ⟶	If M then (not T)
Mica does sink. ⟶	M
Hence tufa doesn't sink. ⟶	Therefore (not T)

Here the arrows merely connect each original sentence with its translation, to indicate our moves. We use capital letters to abbreviate the sentences, and it is important always to keep clearly in mind what sentence a given capital letter is being used as the abbreviation for. (We shall not use the small letters "p," "q," and "r" to abbreviate particular sentences; they will be reserved for use when we are representing general logical forms.) The above argument is translated into a case of modus ponens, because the premise becomes a conditional whose antecedent is the same as the second premise and whose consequent is the same as the conclusion. Since the original argument can be translated into modus ponens, we know that the original argument is valid.

Here is another example:

If argon burns, neon burns.	If X then A
If argon does not burn, xenon does not burn.	If A then N
Hence xenon does not burn unless neon does. →	If X then N

Here we have replaced the second premise by its contrapositive, letting the double negations cancel out; this is permissible because our new sentence is strictly equivalent to the original one. Also, we have changed the order of the premises, as we are permitted to do. Since this new translation is an argument in the form of a valid chain argument, we know that our original argument is a valid one.

We shall conclude this section by considering one other type of standard form for arguments containing compound sentences. This type of argument is somewhat more complex than those considered in the preceding section. It combines conditional and disjunctive sentences in a special way, and sometimes includes negation also. Arguments of this type are called *dilemmas*.

Simple constructive dilemma

If p then q	e.g., If he gives her mink, he loves her.
If r then q	If he gives her a Cadillac, he loves her.
p or r	He will give her either mink or a Cadillac.
∴ q	Therefore he loves her.

Simple destructive dilemma

If p then q	e.g., If he graduates, he'll have passed physics.
If p then r	If he graduates, he'll have passed biology.
Not q or not r	Either he won't pass physics or he won't pass biology.
∴ not p	Therefore he will not graduate.

Complex constructive dilemma

If p then q	e.g., If she shot unintentionally, she's guilty of manslaughter.
If r then s	If she shot intentionally, she's guilty of murder.
p or r	She shot unintentionally or intentionally.
∴ q or s	Therefore she's guilty of manslaughter or murder.

Complex destructive dilemma

If p then q	e.g., If money gets tight, interest rates will rise.
If r then s	If prosperity increases, loan volume will stay high.
Not q or not s	Either interest rates won't rise, or loan volume won't stay high.
∴ not p or not r	Therefore either money won't get tight or prosperity won't increase.

Dilemmas have often been used by debaters, and they were a formidable weapon in the rhetoric of the ancients. Often dilemmas whose overall logical form is valid nevertheless contain logical flaws that prevent them from being good arguments. (We shall return to this point in Chapter 5.) A valid construc-

UNLESS = IF NOT

tive dilemma is like double use of modus ponens, while a valid destructive dilemma is like a double use of modus tollens. A dilemma is invalid if it resembles the fallacy of affirming the consequent or of denying the antecedent.

Invalid dilemma

If p then q	e.g., If Hugo gets all the answers right, he'll pass the test.
If r then not q	If he gets them all wrong, he'll fail the test.
q or not q	He will either pass or fail.
∴ p or r	Therefore he'll either get all the answers right or all the answers wrong.

If your opponent in a debate presents a dilemma whose conclusion you do not want to accept but which you cannot refute, you are said to be 'caught on the horns of a dilemma.' If you succeed in refuting his argument by showing that the disjunctive premise is not true, then you 'escape between the horns of the dilemma.'

EXERCISE 12

A Which of the following sentences are equivalent to "If this is a platypus, then it lays eggs"? $P \supset E$

NE 1 If this isn't a platypus, then it doesn't lay eggs. $-P \supset -E$
NE 2 This doesn't lay eggs if it isn't a platypus. $-P \supset -E$
E 3 This lays eggs provided it's a platypus. $P \supset E$
NE 4 If this lays eggs, it's a platypus. $E \supset P$
E 5 This is a platypus only if it lays eggs. $P \supset E$ ← BECAUSE OF ONLY IF,
NE 6 This lays eggs only if it's a platypus. $E \supset P$ ONLY IF SLIDES TO LEFT
E 7 This lays eggs only if it isn't a platypus. $E \supset -P$
→ E 8 This isn't a platypus unless it lays eggs. $-E \supset -P$
E 9 This lays eggs unless it isn't a platypus. $--P \supset E$
NE 10 This is a platypus unless it doesn't lay eggs. $-E \supset P$
→ E 11 This doesn't lay eggs only if it isn't a platypus. $-E \supset -P$
12 This is a platypus, but it doesn't lay eggs. $P \cdot -E$
                              AND
* **B** Abbreviate each argument, using the suggested letters; translate it into some standard form (there may be more than one correct way to do this); and say whether it is valid.

---

1 If prices do not rise, costs do not rise. But costs do rise, if wages rise. Thus, if wages rise, prices rise. (*P, C, W*)

2 If it rains, the driving will be bad; and if it snows, the driving will be bad. It will either rain or snow, and so the driving will be bad. (*R, S, D*)

3 Bolyai was not the first to conceive of non-Euclidean geometry, unless Lobachevsky came later. But Lobachevsky didn't come later. So Bolyai wasn't the first. (*B, L*)

4 Double-indemnity insurance will be paid only if the person insured has died in an accident. But he has died in an accident. Hence, double-indemnity insurance will be paid. (*D, A,*)

5 The landlord may evict the tenant only if the tenant has not fulfilled the terms of the lease. If the rent is overdue, the tenant has not fulfilled the terms of the lease. Thus, if the rent is overdue, the landlord may evict the tenant. (*E, L, R*)

6 The estate cannot be settled this year unless the house is sold by September. The estate cannot be settled this year. So the house will not be sold by September. (*E, H*)

7 If the budget is reduced, employees will have to be dismissed; and if the budget is not increased, employees will have to be dismissed. But the budget will be reduced, or not increased. So employees will have to be dismissed. (*R, E, I*)

8 If the cylinder is empty, the pump will operate. If the vapor pressure is excessive, the pump will not operate. So if the vapor pressure is excessive, the cylinder is empty. (*C, P, V*)

9 Vermin will multiply, unless strong poisons are spread. The residents will be unsafe, if strong poisons are spread. So if the residents are to stay safe, the vermin will have to multiply. (*V, P, R*)

10 If she goes into law, she'll be successful; and if she goes into banking, she'll be successful. It's not the case that she'll neither go into banking nor go into law. So she'll be successful. (*L, S, B*)

† **C** *A regulation of the U.S. Internal Revenue Service concerning domestic services performed by relatives says: "Social Security taxes now apply if you pay cash wages for domestic services to your mother or father, or your spouse's mother or father, if you meet the following conditions for at least 4 continuous weeks in*

a quarter: (1) *You have a son or daughter (including an adopted child or stepchild) in your home who is under age 18, or who has a physical or mental condition that requires the personal care of an adult; and (2) you are either a widow (widower) or a divorced person who has not remarried; or you have a spouse in your home who, because of a physical or mental condition, is not capable of caring for the son or daughter."* Try your best to interpret logically how this regulation would apply to the following cases. In each case explain whether social security tax must be paid on the wages mentioned. Be prepared to distinguish between the literal meaning of the regulation and its probable intent.

1 Mr. Robinson is divorced and has not remarried. His healthy seventeen-year-old daughter lives with him. For the month of April, Robinson was away on a business trip. He paid his mother cash wages to stay in his house for that month to keep an eye on his daughter.

2 Ms. Brown is unmarried and has no children. Her mother keeps house for her. Ms. Brown pays her mother cash wages throughout the year for these services.

3 Mrs. Green, a widow who has not remarried, has a son and a daughter, both infants. She pays cash wages all year to her mentally retarded father-in-law, who cares for the children in her home.

4 Mr. Smith's wife is crippled. He paid his mother-in-law cash wages from March 15 to May 15 for caring for his ten-year-old son in her home.

5 Mr. Jones is a widower who has remarried; his present wife is now confined to a mental hospital, and he pays cash wages throughout the year to the mother of his late first wife, hiring her to care for his paralyzed eighteen-year-old stepson in his (Mr. Jones's) home.

6 Mrs. Black's household consists of her invalid husband, her healthy eighteen-year-old son, and her mother. She pays her mother cash wages all year to keep house and care for Mr. Black.

7 Mr. Gray pays cash wages all year to his mother-in-law to nurse his invalid father and mother in his home, as his wife is mentally too unstable to care for anyone. His seventeen-year-old daughter also lives at home.

8 Mary Silver legally adopted Ann White. Later she married the latter's son, John White, Jr. After his death she went on vacation for the period September 15 to November 5, during which time she hired her father-in-law, John White, Sr., to care for her lawns and gardens, paying him cash wages. Ann White, by now divorced and elderly, continued to live in Mary's house but had become ill and needed constant nursing, although she did not receive it.

TRUTH FUNCTIONS AND THEIR GROUPING

Many compound sentences are what we call *truth-functional* sentences; this means that they are compounds whose truth or falsity is strictly determined by (is a function of) the truth or falsity of the component sentences. In other words, to say that a compound sentence is truth-functional is to say that settling the truth or falsity of each of its components is sufficient to settle necessarily whether the compound sentence as a whole is true or false. Most sentences of the kinds considered in the preceding section are truth-functional, and understanding this can help us with the logical analysis of arguments. Let us consider the ways in which various types of truth-functional sentences are related to their components. In describing this we shall also encounter some examples of *non*-truth-functional sentences.

Negation

The relation between a negation and the sentence negated is simple: They must be opposite as regards truth and falsity. Using the dash as our symbol for negation, we shall write "−p" for "not p." We can use the following little table to express the effect of negating a sentence:

p	−p
True	False
False	True

This "truth table" has two lines, covering the two cases that arise here; if p is true, its negation is false (first line); and if p is false, its negation is true (second line). We may replace "p" by whatever sentence we please, and the table will show how our chosen sentence is truth-functionally related to its negation. In using the symbol for negation, we shall always interpret the negation sign as governing as little of what follows as would make sense. For instance, in "$-p$ and q" the negation sign will be regarded as governing only "p," not "p and q"; that is, "$-p$ and q" means "$(-p)$ and q" rather than "$-(p$ and $q)$."

Conjunction

The way in which an ordinary conjunctive sentence is related to its components is also straightforward. The conjunction is true when both its parts are true; otherwise it is false. Using the ampersand as our symbol for truth-functional conjunction, we can abbreviate "p and q" as "p & q." Our truth table for conjunction will need four lines to cover the possible situations.

p	q	p & q
True	True	True
False	True	False
True	False	False
False	False	False

Thus, for instance, the sentence "It will rain and it will get colder" is true if it rains and also gets colder, but it is false if either one or both of these things fail to happen.

As was mentioned earlier, "and" is sometimes used in English to mean "and then," as in "They got married and had a baby." Such a sentence is not truth-functional, since merely knowing whether they got married and whether they had a baby does not enable you to tell for certain whether "They got married and had a baby" is true; you also need to know which happened first. Since we are using the ampersand to mean just "and," not "and then," it would be incorrect to symbolize "They got married and had a baby" as "M & B." However, when we are analyzing an argument, often it is permissible to replace a premise that is a non-truth-functional "and" sentence by a truth-functional conjunction, since ordinarily the truth-functional conjunction, though weaker, expresses that part of the meaning which is relevant to the validity of the argument.

Disjunction

The relation between a disjunctive sentence and its components is also straightforward. The disjunction is true whenever at least one of its components is true, and it is false otherwise. Here our table must contain four lines, as there are four possible situations to be considered. Using the wedge as our symbol for (nonexclusive) disjunction, we can abbreviate "p or q" as "p ∨ q."

p	q	p ∨ q
True	True	True
False	True	True
True	False	True
False	False	False

Here we may replace "p" and "q" by any sentences we please, and the table will show how they are truth-functionally related to their disjunction.

Conditionals

To say that a compound sentence is truth-functional is to say that its truth or falsity is strictly determined by the truth or falsity of its component sentences. We have seen that often conjunctive sentences are truth-functional. In order to determine whether the sentence "Ted comes and Jim goes" is true or false, all we need to know is whether "Ted comes" is true or false and whether "Jim goes" is true or false. However, not all compound sentences are truth-functional; for instance, in order to discover whether "Ted comes because Jim goes" is true or false, we need to know more than just whether "Ted comes" is true and whether "Jim goes" is true. The difficulty about conditional sentences is that although the words "if-then" are sometimes used in a truth-functional way, they are often used in ways that are not truth-functional.

Let us consider cases where "if . . . then # # #" is truth-functional. Suppose a petulant mother exclaims, "If I've told you once, then I've told you a thousand times." She means this in a sense in which it is equivalent to denying that she has told you once without telling you a thousand times. If we write "O" for "I have told you once" and write "T" for "I have told you a thousand times," then the mother's original remark may be expressed "if O then T"; it is equivalent to "not (O & not T)." This compound sentence is false if "O" is true but "T" false (if she told you once but did not tell you a thousand times), and it is true otherwise. Construed in this way, the sentence is truth-functional; its truth or falsity is strictly determined by the truth or falsity of its parts.

Let us take another similar example and see exactly what the truth function "if . . . then # # #" expresses. Suppose someone says "If the Cavaliers win today, then I'm a monkey's uncle." What he is saying can be reworded as "It's not the case both that the Cavaliers win today and that I'm not a monkey's uncle." We can draw up a table for this:

C	M	−M	C & −M	−(C & −M) If C then M
True	True	False	False	True
False	True	False	False	True
True	False	True	True	False
False	False	True	False	True

The four horizontal lines of this truth table represent the four possible combinations of truth and falsity for "C" and "M." (Since we are dealing with specific sentences here, just one of these combinations must represent the actual situation; but we are interested in all four possibilities, for we are studying the meaning of the conditional.) The first two columns of the table show these possibilities and form the starting point. In the first line, where "C" and "M" both are true, "−M" must be false. Hence "C & −M" has to be false too. Its negation "−(C & −M)" must therefore be true; "if C then M," which means the same, will be true too. In the second line, the reasoning is just the same. In the third line, since "M" is false, "−M" will be true, and "C & −M" will be true too. Thus "−(C & −M)" will be false. In the fourth line, since "C" is false, "C & −M" must be false too, and so "−(C & −M)" must be true.

What has been said in this particular case holds good in general. The rule is: A truth-functional "if . . . then # # #" sentence is false when its antecedent is true and its consequent false, and is true otherwise. We represent the truth-functional sense of "if . . . then # # #" by means of the horseshoe symbol. Thus "$p \supset q$" will be our way of writing a truth-functional conditional. It is a consequence of all this that "$p \supset q$" is equivalent to "$-(p \& -q)$."

p	q	$p \supset q$
T	T	T
F	T	T
T	F	F
F	F	T

Notice that if we want to express the negation of "$p \supset q$" we must look for a sentence whose truth and falsity are always just the opposite of that of "$p \supset q$." The negation of "$p \supset q$" can be expressed as "$p \& -q$." The form "$p \supset -q$" is not equivalent to the negation of "$p \supset q$," because "$p \supset q$" and "$p \supset -q$" do not contradict one another. They might both be true, as will happen if "p" is false.

p	q	$p \supset q$	$p \& -q$	$p \supset -q$
T	T	T	F	F
F	T	T	F	T
T	F	F	T	T
F	F	T	F	T

However, the words "if . . . then # # #" are often (perhaps much more often) used in ways that are not truth-functional. Someone might say "If you drop this vase, then it will break." He means to assert *more* than merely that it is not the case that you will drop it without its breaking. He means to assert also that dropping it *would cause* it to break. Here we may know the truth and falsity of the component sentences "You will drop this vase" and "it will break" (perhaps we agree that you are not going to drop it and that it is not going to break), yet still we may disagree or be in doubt about the truth or falsity of "If you drop it, it will break." A conditional sentence understood in this way is not truth-functional, and we lose part of its meaning (that is, we are replacing it by a weaker sentence) if we symbolize it "$D \supset B$."

However, if we make it a practice to use the truth-functional horseshoe to symbolize conditional sentences, we can usually test arguments very adequately, for the truth-functional horse-shoe expresses that part of the meaning of conditional sentences which normally is important as regards the validity or invalidity of arguments in which conditional sentences occur.

This is usually but not invariably so. Here is an example where we would be led astray by this procedure. The argument "The vase will not be dropped; therefore, if the vase is dropped, it will break" is a silly and invalid argument; but it we blindly symbolized it in the form "$-D$, therefore $D \supset B$" and then tested its validity by the truth-table method presented later in this chapter, we would get the incorrect answer that the argument is valid. When we replace non-truth-functional sentences by the corresponding truth-functional sentences that they imply, we should keep in mind the following principles: If an argument is valid, any argument exactly like it except for having one or more stronger premises must be valid too; and if an argument is invalid, then any argument exactly like it except for having a stronger conclusion must be invalid too. Replacing non-truth-functional sentences by the corresponding truth-functional sentences that they imply can be counted on to yield correct answers only when the procedure can be justified by appeal to these principles.

Biconditionals

A compound sentence is called a *biconditional* if it consists of two simpler sentences linked by the words "if and only if." When these words are understood in a truth-functional sense, "p if and only if q" is symbolized "$p \equiv q$." Of course "p if and only if q" is equivalent to "p if q, and p only if q"; that is, "$p \equiv q$" is equivalent to "$(q \supset p) \& (p \supset q)$." Let us draw up a truth table for the latter expression in order to see what the truth table for the former should be.

p	q	$(q \supset p)$	$(p \supset q)$	$(q \supset p) \& (p \supset q)$	$p \equiv q$
T	T	T	T	T	T
F	T	F	T	F	F
T	F	T	F	F	F
F	F	T	T	T	T

The third and fourth columns of this table are obtained from the first two columns, in light of the rule that a conditional is always true except when its antecedent is true and its consequent false. The fifth column is obtained from the third and fourth, in light of the rule that a conjunction is true when and only when both its parts are true. The last column is copied from the fifth; it shows us that the biconditional is true whenever its components are alike as regards truth and falsity, and it is false whenever they differ.

A biconditional says something stronger than does a single conditional. Thus "You'll pass the course if and only if you pass the examination" promises that passing the examination is necessary *and* sufficient for passing the course. In contrast, the conditional sentence "If you pass the examination, then you'll pass the course" merely says that passing the examination is sufficient, and the other conditional "You'll pass the course only if you pass the examination" merely says that passing the examination is necessary.

Grouping

When we deal with expressions containing several symbols, it is important to pay careful attention to the grouping of the parts. Changing the grouping of its parts sometimes can entirely alter the meaning of an expression. Therefore, to avoid misunderstanding, whenever we write something that is truth-functionally compound, we should be clear about the intended grouping. We shall use parentheses for this purpose.

Notice, for instance, the difference between "p & ($q \lor r$)" and "(p & q) $\lor r$." The former is a conjunction, one part of which is a disjunction; the latter is a disjunction, one part of which is a conjunction. They are not equivalent, for a sentence of the first form would not necessarily agree as regards truth or falsity with a corresponding sentence of the second form.

To see that this is so, suppose we replace "p" by the sentence "I'm going to Paris," replace "q" by the sentence "I'm going to Quebec," and replace "r" by "I'm going to Rome." Suppose that in fact I am not going to Paris or Quebec but am going to Rome. Then the compound sentence "I'm going to Paris and either I'm going to Quebec or I'm going to Rome," which is of the form "p & ($q \lor r$)," is false (since I'm not going to Paris). But the corresponding sentence "Either I'm going both to Paris and to Quebec or I'm going to Rome," which is of the form "(p & q) $\lor r$," is true (since I am going to Rome).

Our example shows that "p & ($q \lor r$)" is not equivalent to "(p & q) ∨ r." For this reason it would be improper to write the expression "p & q ∨ r" without parentheses. This expression is ambiguous, because it might have two quite different meanings. One cannot tell whether it is supposed to be a conjunction, one part of which is a disjunction, or a disjunction, one part of which is a conjunction.

Carelessly written sentences in ordinary language, such as "I'm going to Paris and to Quebec or to Rome," are ambiguous in just the same confusing way. But if we are careful to use a comma, the meaning can be made clear. Thus, "I'm going to Paris, and I'm going to Quebec or to Rome" has the logical structure "p & (q ∨ r)," while "I'm going to Paris and Quebec, or to Rome" has the logical structure "(p & q) ∨ r." The comma is one of the devices used in ordinary language to indicate groupings which in our symbolism we indicate by means of parentheses. Another device of ordinary language is the use of pairs of words such as "both . . . and . . ." and "either . . . or . . . ," for these can prevent ambiguity of grouping even when no punctuation is present.

EXERCISE 13

A Let "R" mean "it rains," let "C" mean "it gets colder," and let "B" mean "the barometer falls." Match each numbered sentence of the second group with the symbolized sentence from the first group that is equivalent to it. (Hint: Each has exactly one natural mate.)

F (a) $R \supset C$	T (b) $-R \supset C$	$R = T$
T (c) $R \supset -C$	F (d) $-R \vee C$	$C = F$
F (e) $-(R \vee C)$	T (f) $-(R \supset C)$	$B = F$
T (g) $-(R \& C)$	F (h) $-R \& -C$	
T (i) $-R \equiv C$	F (j) $R \equiv C$	
T (k) $-(R \equiv C)$	F (l) $R \equiv (C \& B)$	
T (m) $(R \& C) \equiv B$	T (n) $R \& (C \equiv B)$	
T (o) $R \supset (C \equiv B)$	T (p) $(R \equiv C) \supset B$	
F (q) $(-R \vee -C) \supset B$	F (r) $R \supset (C \& B)$	
T (s) $R \supset (C \supset B)$	T (t) $(R \& C) \supset B$	
T (u) $(R \supset C) \supset B$	F (v) $(R \supset C) \& B$	

1 Unless it doesn't rain, it doesn't get colder. C

2 It rains only if it gets colder. a

3 It neither rains nor gets colder. e

NEITHER -NOR IS THE SAME AS IT IS NOT THE CASE

UNLESS = IF NOT
PROVIDED = IF
BUT = AND

4 It doesn't both rain and get colder. *g*
5 It gets colder unless it rains. *b*
6 It rains if and only if it gets colder. *J*
7 That it gets colder if it rains is not the case. *F*
8 It doesn't rain or it gets colder. *d*
9 It is not the case that it rains if and only if it gets colder. *k*
10 If and only if it doesn't rain, it gets colder. *I*
11 It doesn't rain and doesn't get colder. *h*
12 If it rains it gets colder, and the barometer falls. *V*
13 It rains, and it gets colder if and only if the barometer falls. *N*
14 If it rains, then it gets colder only if the barometer falls. *S*
15 It rains if and only if both it gets colder and the barometer falls. *L*

COMMAS MEAN PART SENTENCE IS HANDLED SEPARATELY

16 If it rains, then it gets colder and the barometer falls. *r*
17 The barometer falls, ~~provided~~ it rains if and only if it gets colder. *P*
18 If it rains and gets colder, then the barometer falls. *t*
19 If it rains, then it gets colder if and only if the barometer falls. *O*
20 It rains and gets colder, if and only if the barometer falls. *m*
21 If it doesn't rain or doesn't get colder, the barometer falls. *q*
22 The barometer falls, provided that it rains only if it gets colder. *u*

* **B** Let "A" be short for "Arizona is a western state," let "B" be short for "Bermuda is an island," let "J" be short for "Jordan is a European country," and let "K" be short for "Kalamazoo is the capital of France." Determine whether each of the following is true.

$A \& B = T$ $J \& K = F$

1	$-A$ **F**		2	$-(-J)$ **F** *IT IS NOT THE CASE THAT JORDAN IS NOT A EUROPEAN COUNTRY*
3	$A \& K$ **F**		4	$A \& (K \& B)$ **f**
5	$B \vee J$ **T**		6	$K \vee (J \vee A)$ **T**
7	$-B \& J$ **F**		8	$-A \vee -B$ **F**
T 9	$-(J \vee K)$ *IT IS NOT THE CASE THAT J OR K*		10	$-(J \& -A)$ **T**
11	$A \supset K$ **F**		12	$-A \supset K$ **T**
13	$B \supset -J$		14	$A \supset -J$
15	$A \equiv J$ **F**		16	$-K \equiv -J$
17	$(B \& J) \equiv (K \vee -A)$ **F**		18	$(A \& B) \supset (J \vee K)$
19	$(B \equiv J) \supset -K$ **T**		20	$(J \supset A) \equiv (A \supset J)$

F   **T**

TRUTH TABLES

Looking back over what we have learned about the various types of compound sentences, we can formulate these rules:

    A *negation* always is opposite to the sentence negated, as regards truth and falsity.

    A *conjunction* is true if and only if both parts are true.

    A *disjunction* is true if and only if at least one part is true.

    A *conditional* is false when its antecedent is true and its consequent false; otherwise it is true.

    A *biconditional* is true if and only if its parts are alike as regards truth or falsity.

In the light of these rules, we shall be able to construct truth tables for more complex sentences, truth tables that will enable us to answer several kinds of logical questions.

If a truth table for a compound sentence is a complete truth table, it must show whether the sentence is true or false in every possible case, that is, in every possible situation as regards the truth and falsity of its component sentences. The number of possible situations that must be considered (the number of horizontal lines required in the truth table) depends upon the number of distinct simple components.

In the second section of this chapter we wrote a truth table for "$-p$," which needed just two lines. Similarly a truth table for "$(p \vee -p) \,\&\, p$" would have just two lines. Where only the letter "p" is present, the only possibilities to be considered are the truth of "p" and the falsity of "p." A truth table for "$p \vee q$" has to have four lines, and so does a truth table for "$(q \,\&\, p) \vee (q \vee p)$." Here "$p$" may be true or false when "q" is true and either true or false when "q" is false, making four possibilities. If we were dealing with a compound containing three different letters, there would be eight possibilities to consider and so eight lines in the truth table. In general, each additional letter doubles the number of lines required in the truth table.

In constructing a truth table, it is important to be sure that the lines are arranged so as to take account of just the proper possibilities; using a systematic procedure will help. In drawing up the initial columns, let us follow the practice of alternating the entries in the first column ("T" in the first line, "F" in the second line, etc.), pairing the entries in the second column ("T" in the first and second lines, "F" in the third and fourth lines, etc.), alternating by fours the entries in the third initial column ("T" in the first four lines, "F" in the next four lines, etc.), and so on.

When we are dealing with complicated compounds, it often helps to use auxiliary columns, working step by step to reach the final column in which we are interested. For instance, suppose we want a truth table for "$(r \mathbin{\&} q) \supset (p \equiv r)$." Since this contains three letters, we require eight lines. The compound as a whole is a conditional, one part of which is a conjunction and the other part a biconditional. Here it will be wise to use two auxiliary columns, one for the conjunction and one for the biconditional. Then it will be easy to draw up the final column for the conditional as a whole. The table will look like this:

p	q	r	r & q	p ≡ r	(r & q) ⊃ (p ≡ r)
T	T	T	T	T	T
F	T	T	T	F	F
T	F	T	F	T	T
F	F	T	F	F	T
T	T	F	F	F	T
F	T	F	F	T	T
T	F	F	F	F	T
F	F	F	F	T	T

Here the three initial columns have been drawn up in a systematic fashion so as to take account of exactly the right possibilities. The fourth and fifth columns are auxiliary columns drawn up by looking at columns 1, 2, and 3. Then from the fourth and fifth columns we get the sixth column, the one in which we are interested. The sixth column tells us whether the compound is true or false in each of the eight possible cases. From the table we obtain the information that our compound is false only if "p" is false and "q" and "r" are both true.

Logicians have also devised various other ways in which

truth functions can be handled, some of them methods that yield the desired types of information more quickly and with less writing. But our truth-table method has the advantage of being easiest to explain and to understand.

Truth-Functional Implication and Validity

A relation of implication that depends solely upon the truth-funtional forms of the sentences concerned is called a *truth-functional implication*. Thus to say that a sentence is truth-functionally implied by one or more other sentences is to say that, in virtue of their truth-functional forms, it is logically impossible for the latter all to be true without the former being true also. An argument whose premises truth-functionally imply its conclusion is said to be *truth-functionally valid*.

Truth tables provide a method for telling whether truth-functional implications hold and whether arguments are truth-functionally valid. The method is this: We construct a truth table containing a column for each sentence involved in the implication, or for each premise and the conclusion of the argument. Then we inspect the table line by line to see whether there is any line in which the supposedly implying sentences are all true and the supposedly implied sentence false, or whether there is any line in which all the premises of the argument are true and its conclusion false. If there is such a line, then the implication does not hold, or the argument is not truth-functionally valid. If there is no such line, then the implication holds, or the argument is truth-functionally valid.

All valid arguments of the forms discussed in the first section of this chapter are truth-functionally valid. Each of them can be shown to be truth-functionally valid by means of a truth table. As an example, let us consider modus ponens. A truth table for a particular argument of this form would contain columns for the two premises, say, "$A \supset B$" and "A," and a column for the conclusion "B." Or we can make the headings more general in style by expressing the premises as "$p \supset q$" and "p" and the conclusion as "q." When we do it the latter way, the understanding is that the truth table represents *any* argument of the modus ponens form.

Premise p	Conclusion q	Premise $p \supset q$
T	T	T
F	T	T
T	F	F
F	F	T

Since there are just two letters occurring in the argument, we need four lines in the table; we have a column for each premise and one for the conclusion. Now, what does the table show? We see that the first line is the only line in which both premises are true, and in the first line the conclusion is true too. There is no possibility of having the premises all true and the conclusion false. This demonstrates that the premises truth-functionally imply the conclusion, that is, that modus ponens is truth-functionally valid.

As another example, let us consider arguments of the form "p, therefore p ∨ q." This is a simple type of disjunctive argument which we have not discussed so far; it is called *disjunctive addition*.

Premise p	q	Conclusion p ∨ q
T	T	T
F	T	T
T	F	T
F	F	F

Here the table shows that whenever "p" is true, "p ∨ q" must be true also, so this form of argument is valid. Of course, it is a very trivial form of argument. Someone who argued "It is raining; therefore it is raining or snowing" would not be offering us interesting food for thought. However, his logical step is strictly valid, and it might be of value as one step in the middle of some longer chain of reasoning.

Let us treat one more example, the simple destructive dilemma. Can we show by means of a truth table that this form of argument is valid? Here we need columns for the premises "p ⊃ q," "p ⊃ r," and "−q ∨ −r," and we need a column for the conclusion "−p." Since there are three letters, the table must have eight lines. The work is easier if we use some auxiliary columns to help us reach the final ones.

p	q	r	Premise $p \supset q$	Premise $p \supset r$	$-q$	$-r$	Premise $-q \lor -r$	Concl. $-p$
T	T	T	T	T	F	F	F	F
F	T	T	T	T	F	F	F	T
T	F	T	F	T	T	F	T	F
F	F	T	T	T	T	F	T	T
T	T	F	T	F	F	T	T	F
F	T	F	T	T	F	T	T	T
T	F	F	F	F	T	T	T	F
F	F	F	T	T	T	T	T	T

Here the fourth and fifth columns are for the first two premises, and we get them from the three initial columns by using the rule for the conditional. The sixth and seventh columns are auxiliary ones taken from the initial columns by using the rule for negation. The eighth column is for the third premise, and we derive it from the sixth and seventh. Then we add a column for the conclusion. Inspection of the completed table shows that only in the fourth, sixth, and eighth lines are all premises true, and in each of these lines the conclusion is true. Hence the table shows this form of argument to be truth-functionally valid.

As a final example of this procedure, let us consider the particular argument:

If matter exists, Berkeley was mistaken.
If my hand exists, matter exists.
Therefore, either my hand exists or Berkeley was mistaken.

We may symbolize it:

$M \supset B$
$H \supset M$
$\therefore H \lor B$

Let us test the validity of this argument by means of a truth table.

M	B	H	Premise M ⊃ B	Premise H ⊃ M	Conclusion H ∨ B
T	T	T	T	T	T
F	T	T	T	F	
T	F	T	F		
F	F	T	T	F	
T	T	F	T	T	T
F	T	F	T	T	T
T	F	F	F		
F	F	F	T	T	F

We are concerned only with the question whether it is possible for the premises both to be true and the conclusion false, and so any parts of the table that do not help to answer that question may be left blank. Thus we leave the fifth column blank in the third and seventh lines, for we are interested only in lines where both premises are true. We leave the last column blank in the second, third, fourth, and seventh lines for the same reason. The eighth line finally gives a definite answer to our question, for in that line both premises are true and the conclusion is false. This demonstrates that the argument is not truth-functionally valid.

Truth-Functional Equivalence

To say that two sentences are equivalent to one another is to say that they necessarily are alike as regards truth and falsity; to say that they are *truth-functionally equivalent* is to say that they are equivalent simply because of their truth-functional form. Truth tables provide a method for determining whether sentences are truth-functionally equivalent. Does a sentence of the form "$-(p \& q)$" necessarily agree with a corresponding sentence of the form "$-p \& -q$" as regards truth or falsity? We can establish the answer by constructing a truth table containing a column for each compound. Then we compare these columns line by line; if they are alike in every line, the equivalence holds, while if the columns differ in any line, the equivalence does not hold. (Notice that it would be nonsense to say that two compounds are equivalent in some lines but not in others, because being equivalent means being alike as regards truth and falsity in *all* possible cases.)

Let us draw up a table with a column for each of these compounds; let us also include a column for "$-p \lor -q$" so that it can be compared with the others.

p	q	p & q	−(p & q)	−p	−q	−p & −q	−p ∨ −q
T	T	T	F	F	F	F	F
F	T	F	T	T	F	F	T
T	F	F	T	F	T	F	T
F	F	F	T	T	T	T	T

Here the third column is obtained from the first two and serves as an auxiliary column from which we get the fourth column. The fifth and sixth columns come from the first and second; from them we obtain the seventh and eighth. With the table complete, we look at it line by line, and we observe that in the second and third lines "$-(p \& q)$" differs from "$-p \& -q$," the former being true and the latter false. Thus a pair of corresponding sentences of these forms would not be equivalent. However, "$-(p \& q)$" and "$-p \lor -q$" are just alike in each line, which shows that any pair of corresponding sentences of these forms would be equivalent. Speaking more concisely, we shall say that "$-(p \& q)$" and "$-p \& -q$" are not equivalent, while "$-(p \& q)$" and "$-p \lor -q$" are.

Not only is "$-(p \& q)$" equivalent to "$-p \lor -q$," but also "$-(p \lor q)$" is equivalent to "$-p \& -q$," as could be shown by another truth table. These two equivalences are known as *De Morgan's laws*, after the nineteenth-century logician De Morgan. All the various equivalences mentioned earlier in this chapter can be demonstrated by means of truth tables. We can show by truth tables that "p" and "$-(-p)$" are equivalent, that "$p \& q$" and "$q \& p$" are equivalent, that "$p \supset q$" and "$-q \supset -p$" are equivalent, and so on. The notion of truth-functional equivalence will be useful in connection with reasoning, for when two sentences are truth-functionally equivalent either one may validly be inferred from the other, since if one is true the other must be true too.

Another slightly more complicated principle concerning truth-functional equivalence also is useful in connection with reasoning. This principle may be illustrated as follows: A sentence of the form "$r \supset -(p \& q)$" has to be equivalent to a corresponding sentence of the form "$r \supset (-p \lor -q)$" because these two compounds are exactly alike except that where the first contains the component "$-(p\ \&\ q)$" the second contains something equivalent to it. The reasoning behind this is that, since the two short compounds are necessarily alike as regards truth and falsity, replacing one by the other in the longer expression cannot alter the truth table for the longer expression; hence the altered longer expression is necessarily the same as the original longer one as regards truth or falsity. This principle holds in general: Any two longer truth-functional compounds are bound to be equivalent if they are exactly alike except that in one of them a component present in the other has been replaced by something equivalent to that component.

Tautology and Contradiction

When we draw up a truth table for a compound sentence or formula, usually we find that it is true in some lines and false in other lines. But occasionally we meet extreme cases; occasionally a compound sentence or formula is true in every line of its truth table. Such a compound sentence or formula is called a *tautology*. Also we occasionally meet a compound sentence or formula that is false in every line of its truth table. Such a compound sentence or formula is a truth-functional *contradiction*. (Note the difference between a contradiction, an expression that is bound to be false, and contradictories, sentences that are negations of each other and are bound to be opposite in truth and falsity.)

Sentences that are tautologies are a special type of necessarily true sentences; they are sentences whose necessary truth results from their truth-functional form. Sentences that are truth-functional contradictions are a special type of necessarily false sentences. A few examples of forms of sentences that are contradictions are "$p\ \&\ -p$," "$-(p \vee -p)$," and "$p \equiv -p$." Some examples of tautologies are these: "$p \vee -p$" (sometimes described as "the law of excluded middle," because it reflects the fact that any given sentence must be either true or false, there being no third alternative), "$-(p\ \&\ -p)$" (which is sometimes described as "the law of contradiction" because it reflects the fact that a sentence cannot be both true and false), "$p \supset p$," and "$p \equiv p$."

To every valid truth-functional argument there corresponds

a tautology; the tautology is a conditional whose antecedent is the conjunction of the premises of the argument and whose consequent is the conclusion of the argument. For example, the tautology "$[(p \supset q) \,\&\, p] \supset q$" corresponds to modus ponens. To say that a form of argument is valid is to say that if its premises are true, then its conclusion must be true. Under such circumstances the corresponding conditional cannot have a true antecedent and a false consequent, and so will necessarily be true, a tautology. Thus we can say that a truth-functional argument is valid if and only if its corresponding conditional is a tautology. Hence, another way of testing the validity of a truth-functional argument would be to form a conditional whose antecedent is the conjunction of the premises and whose consequent is the conclusion, and draw up a truth table for this conditional. If the conditional is a tautology, this shows that the argument is valid; if not, the argument is not valid. However, the method described in the preceding section is slightly simpler.

EXERCISE 14

* **A** *Determine whether each argument is valid by constructing a truth table for it.*

1   He's a lawyer only if he hasn't been disbarred. It's not the case that he hasn't been disbarred. So he isn't a lawyer. (*L, D*)

2   The engine will run if and only if the fuel line isn't clogged. The engine won't run. So the fuel line is clogged. (*E, F*)

3   It's a Seville or it's a Cadillac. But it's a Cadillac if and only if it's a Seville. So it's a Seville and it's a Cadillac. (*S, C*)

4   These are debentures or these are bonds. If these are debentures, then they are bonds. So they are debentures. (*D, B*)

5   It's not the case that the ship will dock safely and dock without the aid of a tug. The ship will dock safely or it will dock without the aid of a tug. So either the ship won't dock safely or it won't dock without the aid of a tug. (*S, T*)

6   The painting is not genuine, or it was stolen. If it was stolen, then it is genuine. So it is genuine. (*G, S*)

7   If he passed the bar exam, he has graduated from law school. He's a lawyer if and only if he passed the bar exam

and graduated from law school. So either he isn't a lawyer, or he passed the bar exam. (*P, G, L*)

8 The varnish won't adhere unless the surface is clean and dry. The surface is clean and dry if and only if it has been prepared thoroughly. The surface has been prepared thoroughly. So the varnish will adhere. (*V, S, P*)

9 Descartes and Leibniz were French, or Bergson was. But Leibniz wasn't French. If Descartes was French, Bergson was. So Bergson was French. (*D, L, B*)

10 If Mr. Midas doesn't contribute, the fund won't reach its goal. If the canvassers work hard, half the people will contribute. If Mr. Midas contributes, then not half the people will. Therefore, it's not the case both that the fund will reach its goal and that the canvassers will work hard. (*M, F, C, H,*)

B *Use truth tables to answer the following questions.*

1 Is "If costs rise, then either prices and costs both rise or costs rise but prices do not" a tautology?

2 Is "This tree is not both a beech and a sycamore" equivalent to "Either this tree is not a beech or it is not a sycamore"?

3 Which of the following are tautologies, which are contradictions, and which are neither?

(a) $p \supset (p \lor p)$ **(b)** $p \supset (p \lor q)$
(c) $p \supset -p$ **(d)** $p \,\&\, (q \,\&\, -p)$
(e) $(p \,\&\, q) \equiv (q \supset -q)$ **(f)** $(p \supset q) \lor (q \supset q)$
(g) $(p \,\&\, q) \supset (p \lor q)$ **(h)** $p \lor q$
(i) p

4 Does "$p \supset q$" imply "$p \supset (q \lor r)$"?

5 Does a sentence that is a contradiction imply every sentence? Is a sentence that is a tautology implied by every sentence?

6 Is the disjunction of a sentence with itself always equivalent to the given sentence?

† **C** *To protect investors, the Securities and Exchange Commission imposed this requirement on the sale of shares in a speculative oil investment partnership: "The purchaser must represent that he either has a net worth of $50,000 or more and had during his last tax year, or estimates that he will have during his current tax year, taxable income, some portion of which was or will be*

subject to federal income tax at a rate of 50% or more, or has a net worth of $200,000 or more." Use truth-functional symbolism to express what the purchaser is to represent. Which of the following customers could purchase shares without impropriety?

1   Mr. Green paid federal income tax last year at the rate of 14 percent. He estimates that he will be in the 16 percent bracket this year. His debts exceed his assets.
2   Miss Smith has a net worth of $500,000, which she keeps in cash in a shoebox. She had no income last year and expects none this year.
3   Last year Mrs. Brown had a salary of $1,000,000 and paid federal income tax of $600,000. Her net worth is $2000.
4   Mr. Gray's net worth was $300,000 last year and is $100,000 now. For both years he has been in the 42 percent tax bracket.
5   Mrs. Jones had a net worth last year of $100,000 and was in the 55 percent tax bracket; this year her net worth is $195,000 and she is in the 45 percent tax bracket.
6   Mr. Robinson has assets of $350,000 and liabilities of $130,000. His income this year is $60,000, on which he expects to pay federal income tax of $32,000.

FORMAL DEDUCTIONS

Truth tables provide a perfectly general method for testing the validity of truth-functional arguments. However, if the argument is a lengthy one, and especially if it contains many distinct constituent sentences, the truth-table method may be tedious and long. It is valuable to have a short-cut method to deal more efficiently with involved arguments. We shall now develop a method that involves breaking up long arguments into simpler steps. If we can show how it is possible to pass, by means of simple valid steps, from the premises to other sentences that follow from them, and then from these to the conclusion, we shall have succeeded in showing that the conclusion follows validly from the premises.

Suppose we have this argument: "If he is both vacationing at Sun Valley and buying an Alfa-Romeo, then he has inherited money. He will have inherited money only if his rich grand-mother has died. He is buying an Alfa-Romeo, but his grand-mother is hale and hearty. Therefore, he is not vacationing at Sun Valley." Since this argument contains four different basic component sentences, its truth table would require sixteen lines and would be rather tedious. Let us try to pass to the conclusion from the premises by familiar steps. Writing "S" for "He vaca-tions at Sun Valley," "A" for "He buys an Alfa-Romeo," "I" for "He inherits money," and "G" for "His rich grandmother has died," we can symbolize our starting point as follows:

1. $(S \& A) \supset I$ Premise
2. $I \supset G$ Premise
3. $A \& -G$ Premise

We can make a useful first move by separating one part of the conjunction of line 3:

4. $-G$ *From 3 by conjunctive simplification*

Next we can put together lines 4 and 2 by using modus tollens:

5. $-I$ *From 2, 4 by modus tollens*

Then we can use modus tollens again:

6. $-(S \& A)$ *From 5, 1 by modus tollens*

And from this we can get the desired conclusion:

7. A *From 3 by conjunctive simplification*
8. $-S$ *From 6, 7 by conjunctive argument*

Here we have broken up the involved argument into a particular sequence of simple valid steps. Thus we succeed in showing that the conclusion follows from the premises. When arranged in a coherent order like this, the steps are said to constitute a *deduction*. Each line in the deduction must either be a premise or be clearly justified by means of some standard principle.

In more advanced studies of symbolic logic, it is usual to se-lect some very small group of standard principles for justifying steps and then to insist upon using no others. In that way, greater elegance and economy are achieved, thereby enhancing the theoretical interest of the deductions that are constructed. For our elementary purposes, however, that sort of elegance is not so important. Let us therefore include among our principles for use in deduction all those principles with which we have so far become acquainted, and also a few new ones. This broad though inelegant approach will mean that our deductions will be comparatively easy to construct; it will spare us some of the irritation sometimes felt by beginners using elegantly economical deductive rules when they find that certain moves, which they see to be perfectly valid, nevertheless are not directly sanctioned by the rules.

Let us arrange our principles under three headings. First are our standard elementary forms of valid argument; we always may write any new line in a deduction if that new line follows from earlier lines by one of these forms of argument. Next are equivalences; we always are justified in adding a new line if it is equivalent to some preceding line. Finally, we shall allow ourselves to add any tautology as a new line; tautologies have to be true, and cannot lead us astray (the underlying idea is that adding a tautology to your set of premises cannot ever change the set of conclusions that are implied by those premises).

Truth-Functional Principles for Use in Deduction

Elementary forms of valid argument

Modus ponens:	$p \supset q$, p; therefore q
Modus tollens:	$p \supset q$, $-q$; therefore $-p$
Chain argument:	$p \supset q$, $q \supset r$; therefore $p \supset r$
Disjunctive arguments:	$p \vee q$, $-p$; therefore q
	$p \vee q$, $-q$; therefore p
	p; therefore $p \vee q$ (*disjunctive addition*)
	q; therefore $p \vee q$ (*disjunctive addition*)
Conjunctive arguments:	$-(p \,\&\, q)$, p; therefore $-q$

$-(p \mathbin{\&} q)$, q; therefore $-p$
$p \mathbin{\&} q$; therefore p (*simplification*)
$p \mathbin{\&} q$; therefore q (*simplification*)
p, q; therefore $p \mathbin{\&} q$ (*adjunction*)

Reductio ad
absurdum: $p \supset -p$; therefore $-p$
        $p \supset (q \mathbin{\&} -q)$; therefore $-p$

Dilemmas: $p \supset q$, $r \supset q$, $p \lor r$; therefore q

(*simple constructive*)

$p \supset q$, $p \supset r$, $-q \lor -r$; therefore $-p$

(*simple destructive*)

$p \supset q$, $r \supset s$, $p \lor r$; therefore $q \lor s$

(*complex constructive*)

$p \supset q$, $r \supset s$, $-q \lor -s$; therefore $-p \lor -r$

(*complex destructive*)

Equivalences

Any expression may validly be inferred from any other that is equivalent to it, according to the following principles:

"p" and "$p \lor p$" and "$p \mathbin{\&} p$" all are equivalent.
"$p \supset q$" and "$-p \lor q$" and "$-(p \mathbin{\&} -q)$" all are equivalent.
"$p \equiv q$" and "$(q \supset p) \mathbin{\&} (p \supset q)$" are equivalent.

Double negation: "p" and "$-(-p)$" are equivalent.
Contraposition: "$p \supset q$" and "$-q \supset -p$" are equivalent.
Commutation: "$p \lor q$" and "$q \lor p$" are equivalent.
        "$p \mathbin{\&} q$" and "$q \mathbin{\&} p$" are equivalent.
Association: "$p \lor (q \lor r)$" and "$(p \lor q) \lor r$" are equivalent.
        "$p \mathbin{\&} (q \mathbin{\&} r)$" and "$(p \mathbin{\&} q) \mathbin{\&} r$" are equivalent.
Distribution: "$p \mathbin{\&} (q \lor r)$" and "$(p \mathbin{\&} q) \lor (p \mathbin{\&} r)$" are equivalent.
        "$p \lor (q \mathbin{\&} r)$" and "$(p \lor q) \mathbin{\&} (p \lor r)$" are equivalent.
De Morgan's laws: "$-(p \lor q)$" and "$-p \mathbin{\&} -q$" are equivalent.
        "$-(p \mathbin{\&} q)$" and "$-p \lor -q$" are equivalent.
Exportation: "$(p \mathbin{\&} q) \supset r$" and "$p \supset (q \supset r)$" are equivalent.

Tautologies

We may add any tautology we please as a line in a deduction, provided we are prepared to show by a truth table that it is a tautology. Some examples of tautologies are:

$p \lor -p$	$p \equiv p$	$(p \mathbin{\&} q) \supset (p \lor q)$
$-(p \mathbin{\&} -p)$	$p \supset (p \lor q)$	$\cdot$
$p \supset p$	$(p \mathbin{\&} q) \supset p$	$\cdot$
		$\cdot$

This list of principles perhaps looks tediously long, but the advantage of having a good many principles is that they make deductions easier to construct; all the principles in this list are standard logical principles worth being acquainted with. We have already met the elementary valid forms of argument; if any of them seem strange or dubious, their validity can be proved by means of truth tables. Under the heading of equivalences are some principles that we have met and also some new ones. If any of these seems strange or dubious, again truth tables can be used. (It is also illuminating to invent sentences illustrating these principles.) With regard to tautologies, if there is any doubt about whether a given expression is a tautology, its truth table should be constructed to settle the question.*

Notice that our forms of valid argument are to be used only for deriving one whole line from other whole lines in the deduction, not from parts of lines. For example, by disjunctive addition from "p" we may derive "$p \lor q$," where these occupy whole lines. But suppose we have a line which is of the form "$p \supset r$." It would be a misuse of the rules to rewrite this, replacing "p" in

---

* It may be objected that this rule permitting the use of tautologies is too liberal, in that it would allow deductions to be trivially simple. For instance, any deduction having a single premise could be completed just by adding a second line which would be a conditional whose antecedent would be the premise and whose consequent would be the conclusion (this conditional could be justified by saying that it is a tautology); then the conclusion could be obtained as the third line by modus ponens. Such a deduction would indeed be rather silly. But the person who handles his problem this way is not really getting away with anything, for he must justify the tautology, if it is not a simple and obvious one. That is, he must construct a truth table to show that it is a tautology, and doing this will probably be a tougher job than it would have been to construct the deduction in a less trivial style.

it by "$p \lor q$," thus obtaining a new line of the form "$(p \lor q) \supset r$." This does not follow and is not the right way to apply the rule.

The situation is different with regard to principles of equivalence, however. These may be applied to whole lines or to parts of lines. For instance, if we have a line of the form "$p \lor q$," we may use the principle of commutation to derive "$q \lor p$," thus dealing with the line as a whole. But also from a line of the form "$r \supset (p \lor q)$" we may obtain "$r \supset (q \lor p)$" by commutation, dealing with only part of the line. The underlying justification of this is that two longer truth-functional compounds have to be equivalent if they are alike except that where one contains a certain part the other contains something else equivalent to it. Equivalence of the parts to each other guarantees that the entire compounds will be equivalent to each other.

In constructing our deductions, let us try to proceed with meticulous strictness, always using one and only one of our principles to justify each line that we write down. In considering whether a particular move is or is not an exact instance of one of our principles, we have to ask whether there is some way of getting the instance from the principle by replacing each letter in the principle ("p," "q," "r," etc.) wherever it occurs by some sentence or other, simple or compound. It is permissible to put the same sentence for more than one letter; thus, from "$(A \& B) \supset (C \lor D)$" and "$(C \lor D) \supset (A \& B)$" it would be all right to derive "$(A \& B) \supset (A \& B)$" by the principle of the chain argument—here the same thing has replaced both "p" and "r" in the principle of the chain argument, but this is permissible.

Now let us examine another example of a deduction in which more of these principles are employed. Let us suppose that we are given an argument having three premises, which we shall symbolize as lines 1, 2, and 3, and a conclusion, "C," to be derived through a deduction (we do not know at first that the conclusion will be the twelfth line; we know that only after finishing the deduction).

1. $A \lor (B \& C)$ Premise
2. $A \supset D$ Premise
3. $D \supset C$ Premise
4. $A \supset C$ From 2, 3 by chain argument

5. $-(-A) \vee (B \& C)$ *From 1 by equivalence of "p"*
                                to "−(−p)"

6. $-A \supset (B \& C)$ *From 5 by equivalence of "−p ∨ q"*
                                to "p ⊃ q"

7. $-C \supset -A$ *From 4 by contrapostion*

8. $-C \supset (B \& C)$ *From 7, 6 by chain argument*

9. $(B \& C) \supset -(-C)$ *Tautology*

10. $-C \supset -(-C)$ *From 8, 9 by chain argument*

11. $-(-C)$ *From 10 by reductio ad absurdum*

12. C *From 11 by double negation*

In constructing the deduction, our strategy could have been the following: Looking at the premises, we see that the second and third can be put together to form a chain argument, yielding line 4. Wondering how to combine line 4 with anything else, we notice that line 1 might possibly combine with line 4. If line 1 is rewritten as a conditional instead of a disjunction, it will be more likely to combine with line 4, and so we make use of the fact that "−p ∨ q" is equivalent to "p ⊃ q." Now, if line 4 is replaced by its contrapositive, we obtain a standard chain argument whose conclusion is line 8. This is close to what we want, but we still need to separate out the "C" which is contained in the consequent of line 8. If we choose an appropriate tautology, we can do this; and so we write line 9 and then get line 10 by another chain argument. Line 10 gives the desired conclusion by way of *reductio ad absurdum*. However, this is not the only way of getting from these premises to this conclusion (for instance, a shorter, more elegant deduction can be constructed using a simple constructive dilemma).

In order to construct a proof such as this, we must use a little ingenuity; we have not mastered any mechanical method that will automatically tell us what steps we should take to get from premises to conclusion. But if we are familiar with the main types of elementary forms of valid argument, with the main types of equivalences, and with simple sorts of tautologies, we find that only a very little ingenuity is required to proceed step by step.

Some tactics that often are useful are these: Try working backwards from the conclusion, seeking lines that the conclusion could be derived from. Always be alert for opportunities to apply modus ponens, modus tollens, disjunctive arguments, or the chain argument. Often when you have a conjunction, it is helpful to break it up by conjunctive simplification. When you have a negated conditional, it usually is wise to rewrite it as a conjunction making use of the fact that "$-(p \supset q)$" is equivalent to "$-[-(p \& -q)]$" and hence to "$p \& -q$."

EXERCISE 15

* **A** State the justification for each step that is not a premise in each of the following deductions. Mention what specific principle is used and what earlier lines, if any, are involved at each step.

1
1. $D \& E$ Premise
2. $D \supset F$ Premise
3. D
4. F

2
1. $J \supset K$ Premise
2. $-(K \& L)$ Premise
3. $-K \vee -L$
4. $K \supset -L$
5. $J \supset -L$

3
1. $(A \supset B) \vee C$ Premise
2. $-C \& -B$ Premise
3. $-C$
4. $A \supset B$
5. $-B$
6. $-A$

4
1. $(A \supset B)$ Premise
    $\supset (-C \supset D)$
2. $-B \supset D$ Premise
3. $A \supset -D$ Premise
4. $-(-D) \supset -A$
5. $D \supset -A$
6. $-B \supset -A$
7. $A \supset B$
8. $-C \supset D$
9. $-(-C) \vee D$
10. $C \vee D$

* **B** Construct the following deductions.

1 From the premises "$-(F \& G)$" and "G" and "$H \supset F$" deduce the conclusion "$-H$."

2 From the premises "$-(N \vee P)$" and "$N \supset P$" deduce the conclusion "$-N$."

3 From "$M \equiv N$," "$K \supset J$," and "$-M \supset -J$" deduce "$K \supset N$."

4 From "$-S$," "$R \supset T$," "$T \equiv S$," and "$P \supset (Q \supset R)$" deduce "$-(P \& Q)$."

5 From "$-(B \vee -A) \supset -D$" and "D" deduce "$A \supset (B \vee C)$."

6 From "$-(C \& B) \equiv (C \supset D)$" and "$C \& [D \equiv (B \& -B)]$" deduce "$A \lor B$."

7 From "$S \equiv (T \lor U)$" and "$-(T \lor U)$" and "$U \supset (T \& W)$" deduce "$-(S \& W)$."

8 From "$A \supset B$" and "$(B \& C) \supset D$" deduce "$C \supset (A \supset D)$."

C *Symbolize each argument, using the suggested letters. Then construct a deduction to show that it is valid.*

1 If the patient had no fever, then malaria was not the cause of his illness. But malaria or food poisoning was the cause of his illness. The patient had no fever. Therefore, food poisoning must have caused his illness. (*F, M, P*)

2 The centrifuge is to be started if the specimen remains homogenous. Either the specimen remains homogeneous or a white solid is precipitated. A white solid is not being precipitated. So the centrifuge is to be started. (*C, S, W*)

3 Had Franklin D. Roosevelt been a socialist, he would have been willing to nationalize industries. Had he been willing to nationalize industries, this would have been done during the Depression. But no industries were nationalized during the Depression. Hence Roosevelt must not have been a socialist. (*R, W, D*)

4 If either the husband or the wife paid the premium that was due, then the policy was in force and the cost of the accident was covered. If the cost of the accident was covered, they were not forced into bankruptcy. But they were forced into bankruptcy. Therefore, the husband did not pay the premium that was due. (*H, W, P, C, B*)

THE INDIRECT METHOD;
SHOWING INVALIDITY

The method of formal deduction which we have been considering is a 'direct' method: in establishing the validity of an argument, the deduction starts from the premises and moves directly toward the conclusion. However, there is another way of organizing deductions which also is worth noticing. This is the 'indirect,' or *reductio ad absurdum*, approach. It proceeds by showing that a contradiction can be deduced from the combination of the premises with the negation of the conclusion. Let us see how this would work. Suppose we have the argument "$A, A \equiv B, C \supset -B$, therefore $-C$." Let us construct a deduction whose premises are the premises of the original argument plus the negation of its conclusion. Then let us try to deduce an outright contradiction from this set of assumptions. Such a deduction can be drawn up as follows:

1.	A	Premise
2.	$A \equiv B$	Premise
3.	$C \supset -B$	Premise
4.	$-(-C)$	Premise
5.	C	From 4 by double negation
6.	$-B$	From 5 and 3 by modus ponens
7.	$(B \supset A) \& (A \supset B)$	From 2 by equivalence
8.	$A \supset B$	From 7 by simplification
9.	$-A$	From 8 and 6 by modus tollens
10.	$A \& -A$	From 1 and 9 by adjunction

What this deduction shows is that an obvious contradiction of the form "$p \& -p$" follows from the combined four premises of the deduction. This means that those four premises cannot all be true; if the first three are true, then the fourth cannot be. But the fourth was the negation of the conclusion of our original argument, while the first three were the premises of our original argument. So what we have shown is that if the premises of the original argument are true, then the conclusion of the original argument cannot be false. This establishes that the original argument is valid.

In general, then, if we want to set up a deduction using this *reductio ad absurdum* method, we proceed as follows. Suppose that what we want to show is that a certain sentence q follows validly from certain other sentences $r_1 \ldots r_n$. We take as our premises $r_1 \ldots r_n$ together with the negation of q. And the conclusion of this deduction should be some outright contradiction, preferably of the most obvious form, "$p \& -p$." If we can construct such a deduction, getting by valid steps from such premises to such a conclusion, then we shall have succeeded in showing that q does follow validly from $r_1 \ldots r_n$.

This indirect method is usually no better or quicker for

handling truth-functional arguments than is the direct method. However, if you have trouble figuring out how to complete a direct deduction, it may be worthwhile to try constructing your deduction in this indirect style instead; sometimes an indirect deduction is easier to put together.

Naturally, the method of formal deduction, whether direct or indirect, will work only for arguments that are deductively valid. If an argument is not valid, of course it will not be possible to construct a deduction that moves step by step from the premises to the conclusion. But the fact that we have failed to construct a deduction for an argument by no means demonstrates that it is invalid; perhaps we have not worked intelligently enough. Suppose we work on an argument, trying unsuccessfully to construct a deduction for it; we may eventually suspect that perhaps the argument is not valid. In such a situation we could resort to a truth table. But it is valuable also to have a short-cut method of demonstrating that an argument is invalid.

To say that an argument is invalid is to say that it is possible for the premises all to be true yet the conclusion false. This gives us the clue to a short-cut method of demonstrating invalidity. If we can find a way of assigning truth and falsity to the constituent letters so that the premises all will be true but the conclusion false, this will demonstrate that the argument is invalid.

Suppose we have an argument whose three premises are symbolized "$A \supset (B \lor C)$," "$(C \& D) \supset E$," and "$-E$," and whose conclusion is symbolized "$-A$." We shall not be able to pass, by valid steps, from these premises to this conclusion. Let us try instead to show that the argument is invalid. We want to see whether it is logically possible for the premises all to be true and the conclusion false. If the conclusion is false, "A" must be true; if "A" is true, then either "B" or "C" (or both) must be true in order that the first premise be true. Also, in order that the third premise be true, "E" must be false; if "E" is false, "C" and "D" cannot both be true, in order that the second premise be true. Let us try letting "A" be true, "E" false, "B" and "C" both true, and "D" false. This proves to be one satisfactory way of assigning truth and falsity to the constituent letters, for this is a way of making the premises all true and the conclusion false. Thus we have shown that there is a logically possible way for the premises all to be true while the conclusion is false; hence the argument is shown to be invalid. This method is like finding in the truth table for the argument one single line that suffices to show that the argument is invalid.

EXERCISE 16

* **A** Use the short-cut method to show that each of the following arguments is invalid.

1 $A \supset B$
$\quad C \supset D$
$\quad \therefore A \supset C$

2 $R \supset S$
$\quad T \supset -S$
$\quad S \vee -S$
$\quad \therefore R \vee T$

3 $A \supset B$
$\quad C \supset D$
$\quad -A \vee -C$
$\quad \therefore -B \vee -D$

4 $F \vee G$
$\quad F \supset H$
$\quad G \supset J$
$\quad \therefore H \& J$

5 $A \supset (B \vee C)$
$\quad B \supset (D \& E)$
$\quad D \supset (E \supset F)$
$\quad -(A \& F)$
$\quad \therefore A \equiv C$

6 $J \supset -K$
$\quad -J \equiv K$
$\quad -J$
$\quad \therefore -K$

B Go back to part B of Exercise 15 and rework those formal deductions, using the indirect method instead of the direct method.

C For each argument, choose an appropriate method, and show that the argument is valid or that it is invalid.

1 If the seal has not been broken and the routine servicing has been performed, the guarantee is in effect. The owner is responsible for the damage only if the routine servicing has not been performed or the seal has been broken. Hence, the guarantee is in effect unless the owner is responsible for the damage.
2 Either Thales said that nothing moves and Parmenides didn't say it, or else Parmenides said it and Heraclitus denied it. If Thales said it, his thought didn't conform to the Milesian pattern. Thales' thought did conform to the Milesian pattern. Therefore, Heraclitus denied that nothing moves.
3 If either revenues increase or debt and costs decrease, the firm's profitability will improve. Costs won't decrease unless debt decreases. It's not the case both that revenues will increase and that profitability will improve. There-

fore, either debts won't decrease or profitability will improve.

4 If Locke had denied the existence of spiritual substance, he would have been a materialist; if he had denied the existence of physical substance, he would have been an idealist. If he had been either an idealist or a materialist, he would not have been a dualist. But Locke was a dualist. Therefore, he did not deny the existence of either spiritual or physical substance.

5 If Moses and Abraham were patriarchs, then Samuel and Jeremiah were prophets. If Abraham was a patriarch, Samuel was a prophet. Therefore, either Moses was not a patriarch or Jeremiah was not a prophet.

D *A set of sentences is called* consistent *if and only if it is possible that all of them may be true together. You can show that a set of sentences is consistent by finding a way of assigning truth and falsity to the letters so as to make all the compound sentences true together. You can show that a set of sentences is inconsistent by deducing from them a contradiction. Discover whether each of these sets of sentences is consistent or inconsistent.*

1 If Jones is telling the truth, then Smith is not guilty. If Brown is telling the truth, then Jones is not doing so. Brown is telling the truth, and Smith is not guilty. (J, S, B)

2 The company earns more profit if and only if its domestic sales increase or its export sales increase. Its export sales increase if and only if its domestic sales do not increase. (P, D, E)

3 If there is water vapor on Saturn, there must be hydrogen and oxygen. And if there is carbon dioxide there, there must be carbon and oxygen. There is carbon dioxide there if and only if there is not water vapor. But there is not oxygen there. (W, H, O, D, C)

† E *Analyze the structure of each of the following truth-functional arguments. Watch for unstated premises.*

1 "I hope, Marianne," continued Elinor, "you do not consider Edward as deficient in general taste. Indeed, I think I may say that you cannot, for your behavior to him is perfectly

cordial, and if *that* were your opinion, I am sure you could never be civil to him."   JANE AUSTEN, *Sense and Sensibility*

2   Murder and treachery cannot be good without regret being bad: regret cannot be good without treachery and murder being bad. Both, however, are supposed to have been fore-doomed; so something must be fatally unreasonable, absurd, and wrong in the world. It must be a place of which either sin or error forms a necessary part. From this dilemma there seems at first sight no escape.

WILLIAM JAMES, "The Dilemma of Determinism"

3   With respect to every reality external to myself, I can get hold of it only through thinking it. In order to get hold of it really, I should have to be able to make myself into the other, the acting individual, and make the foreign reality my own reality, which is impossible. For if I make the foreign reality my own, this does not mean that I become the other through knowing his reality, but it means that I acquire a new reality, which belongs to me as opposed to him.

SÖREN KIERKEGAARD, *Concluding Unscientific Postscript*

4   Either to disinthrone the Kind of Heav'n
We war, if war be best, or to regain
Our own right lost: him to unthrone we then
May hope, when everlasting Fate shall yield
To fickle Chance, and *Chaos* judge the strife:
The former vain to hope argues as vain
The latter: for what place can be for us
Within Heav'n's bound, unless Heav'n's Lord supreme
We overpower?   JOHN MILTON, *Paradise Lost*

5   If man lacked free judgment of will, how would that be good for which justice itself is commended when it condemns sins and honors deeds rightly done? For that which was not done by the will would be neither sinfully nor rightly done. And according to this if man did not have free will, both punishment and reward would be unjust. However, there must have been justice in both punishment and reward, since it is one of the goods which are from God. Therefore, God must have given man free will.

ST. AUGUSTINE, *De Libero Arbitrio*

6 The universe, then, has no circumference, for, if it had a center and a circumference, it would thus have in itself its beginning and its end, and the universe itself would be terminated by relation to something else; there would be outside the universe another thing and a place—but all this contains no truth.

NICHOLAS OF CUSA, Of Learned Ignorance

CHAPTER 4

THE LOGIC
OF QUANTIFICATION

In Chapter 2 we met the quantifiers "all" and "some" in categorical sentences. Now we shall see how to use symbols in place of quantifier words. We shall also see how these quantifier symbols can be combined with truth-functional symbols to provide a very powerful symbolic language by means of which a much wider range of sentences and arguments can be analyzed. The development of this general theory of quantification is one of the central achievements of modern symbolic logic.

THE SYMBOLISM
OF QUANTIFICATION

Let us begin with a sentence in ordinary language and see how it can be expressed in the symbolism of quantification. Consider the sentence:

> There exists at least one unclimbed mountain. (1)

We can reword this as:

> There exists at least one thing such that it is
> unclimbed and it is a mountain. (2)

and as:

> There exists at least one thing x such that x is
> unclimbed and x is a mountain. (3)

The letter "x" in (3) is called a *variable*. There is nothing mysterious about its significance, however, for it functions as a pronoun, the way "it" did in (2), enabling us to see that in the different parts of the sentence the speaker is talking about the same thing rather than about different things. Now we introduce the symbol "($\exists$x)," which is called an *existential quantifier* and which correspond to the words "There exists at least one thing x such that." This enables us to rewrite (3) in the form:

$$(\exists x) \ (x \text{ is unclimbed \& } x \text{ is a mountain}) \tag{4}$$

This sentence is called an *existential quantification*, because it starts with an existential quantifier which is attached to the whole of the rest of the sentence. Sentence (4) can be read in various equivalent ways besides (1), (2), and (3). All the following readings are also permissible:

There is something such that it is unclimbed and is a mountain.
Something is unclimbed and is a mountain.
Some unclimbed things are mountains.
There are unclimbed mountains.
Unclimbed mountains exist.

Next let us consider another sentence in ordinary language and see how it can be expressed using another quantificational symbol. Consider the sentence:

$$\text{Each thing is either solid or not solid.} \tag{5}$$

We can reword this as:

$$\text{Each thing is such that either it is solid or it is not solid.} \tag{6}$$

and as:

Each thing x is such that either x is solid
$$\text{or } x \text{ is not solid.} \tag{7}$$

Again the variable "x" is merely doing the job of a pronoun. Now we introduce the symbol "(x)," which is called a *universal quantifier* and which corresponds to the words "Each thing x is such that." This enables us to rewrite (7) in the form:

(x) (x is a solid ∨ x is not solid)   (8)

This sentence is called a *universal quantification*, because it starts with a universal quantifier which is attached to the whole of the rest of the sentence. Sentence (8) can be read in various equivalent ways; besides (5), (6), and (7), all the following readings are possible:

> Each thing is solid or not solid.
> Anything is solid or not solid.
> Everything is either solid or not solid.
> All things are either solid or not solid.

So far, we have used just the letter "x" as a variable. But other variables, such as "y" and "z," can equally well be used in quantifications. The sentence "(∃y) (y is unclimbed & y is a mountain)" is equivalent to (4). Both say that there is something such that *it* is an unclimbed mountain. The sentence "(z) (z is solid ∨ z is not solid)" is equivalent to (8). Both of them say that each thing is such that *it* is solid or *it* is not solid. When the quantifier is "(∃x)" or "(x)," we say that "x" is the *variable of quantification*; when the quantifier is "(∃y)" or "(y)," we say that "y" is the variable of quantification; and so on.

In the cases that we have considered thus far, the quantifier has been attached to the whole of the rest of the sentence. In these cases we put parentheses around all the rest of the sentence to show that it all falls within what we call the *scope* of the quantifier. Attaching the quantifier to the whole remainder of the sentence means that every occurrence of the variable of quantification within the rest of the sentence has to be thought of as a pronoun referring back to that quantifier.

However, quantifiers are not always attached in this way; sometimes we have a quantifier that is attached only to a portion of the sentence. For example, the sentence:

> Either something is solid or everything is liquid.

can be reworded:

> Either there is something x such that x is solid or each thing x is such that x is liquid.

and can be put into quantificational symbolism as:

$$(\exists x)\ (x \text{ is solid}) \lor (x)\ (x \text{ is liquid}) \tag{9}$$

Here sentence (9) considered as a whole is not a quantification; rather it is a disjunction whose components are quantifications. The parentheses show us that the "x" within "(x is solid)" is to be thought of as a pronoun referring to the first quantifier, while the "x" in "(x is liquid)" is to be thought of as a pronoun referring to the second quantifier. Thus the scope of the first quantifier does not overlap that of the second quantifier, and the two quantifications that form parts of the disjunction are completely separate. Therefore it would be equally correct to write sentence (9) in the following equivalent form:

$$(\exists y)\ (y \text{ is solid}) \lor (z)\ (z \text{ is liquid}) \tag{10}$$

Because each quantification is self-contained, we get equivalent results whether we use different variables in the two quantifications, as in (10), or use the same variable throughout, as in (9).

All the variables we have considered so far have been functioning as pronouns referring back to quantifiers. Variables are said to be *bound* by their quantifiers when they occur in this way; a variable can be bound by (or 'governed by') only one quantifier at a time. A variable that does not refer back to any quantifier is said to be *free*. Consider the expressions:

> x is solid ∨ x is liquid
> (∃x) (x is solid) ∨ x is liquid
> (y) (y is solid ∨ x is liquid)

There are two free occurrences of "x" in the first expression, and there is one free "x" in each of the others. Expressions like these are neither true nor false, for nothing has been decided about what these free occurrences of "x" are supposed to refer to; "x" here is like a pronoun without an antecedent. An expression is not a true or false sentence so long as it contains any free occurrences of variables.

Now let us consider some basic relations of equivalence and nonequivalence that hold between certain kinds of quantificational sentences. This will help us understand better how quantifiers work. Here we shall be concerned especially with how much of what follows the quantifier falls within the scope of the quantifier.

To say that two sentences are equivalent is to say that they are necessarily alike as regards truth and falsity. Consider the sentences:

Something is liquid and is solid. (1)
Something is liquid and something is solid. (2)

These are definitely not equivalent, as is shown by the fact that (1) is false but (2) is true. In the symbolism of quantification, we use parentheses to indicate the distinction:

$(\exists x)$ (x is liquid & x is solid) (3)
$(\exists x)$ (x is liquid) & $(\exists x)$ (x is solid) (4)

Here (3) is a way of symbolizing (1), and (4) is a way of symbolizing (2). Each of these quantifiers governs just what is enclosed within the parentheses that immediately follow it. In (3) the quantifier embraces within its scope all that follows, and the whole expression is the existential quantification of a conjunction. In (4) we have two separate quantifiers each with a briefer scope; here the whole thing is a conjunction of two existential quantifications.

Similarly, with universal quantifiers we must distinguish between:

(x) (x is solid ∨ x is not solid) (5)
(x) (x is solid) ∨ (x) (x is not solid) (6)

These sentences are not equivalent. Sentence (5) is the universal quantification of a disjunction, and it truly says that each thing is solid or not solid; sentence (6) is the disjunction of two universal quantifications, and it falsely says that either everything is solid or everything is nonsolid.

We must also pay attention to the positions of negation signs. It makes a difference whether a negation sign occurs outside or within the scope of a quantifier, and we must distinguish between:

$$-(x) \ (x \text{ is solid}) \tag{7}$$
$$(x)-(x \text{ is solid}) \tag{8}$$

Sentence (7) is the negation of a universal quantification, and thus it truly says that not everything is solid. Sentence (8) is the universal quantification of a negation, and it falsely says that everything is nonsolid.*

Furthermore, we must beware of assuming that negation signs flanking a quantifier will merely cancel out; we must distinguish between:

$$-(\exists x)-(x \text{ is solid} \lor x \text{ is liquid}) \tag{9}$$
$$(\exists x) \ (x \text{ is solid} \lor x \text{ is liquid}) \tag{10}$$

These are not equivalent. Sentence (9) falsely says that nothing is neither solid nor liquid, while sentence (10) truly says that something is either solid or liquid.

However, some simple and important equivalences involve pairs of negation signs. Consider the existential quantification "$(\exists x) \ (x \text{ is liquid})$." Is there any equivalent way in which this thought can be expressed? To say that there is at least one liquid amounts to denying that everything is such as not to be liquid. Thus "$(\exists x) \ (x \text{ is liquid})$" is equivalent to "$-(x)-(x \text{ is liquid})$." And the underlying principle is perfectly general: If an existential quantifier is replaced by a universal quantifier flanked with negation signs, the new sentence is equivalent to the old one.

Next consider the sentence "$(x) \ (x \text{ is solid})$." Is there any

---

* Whenever there would be ambiguity without them, we use parentheses or brackets to enclose all that falls within the scope of a quantifier. But instead of writing "$(x) \ [-(x \text{ is solid})]$" we write simply "$(x)-(x \text{ is solid})$," as there is no danger of misunderstanding here. In the absence of parentheses or brackets, we always interpret the scope of the quantifier as being as short as would make sense.

equivalent way in which this can be expressed? To say that each thing is solid amounts to denying that there exists even one thing that is not solid. Thus "(x) (x is solid)" is equivalent to "$-(\exists x)-(x$ is solid)." The underlying principle is perfectly general: Whenever a universal quantifier is replaced by an existential quantifier flanked with negation signs, the new sentence is equivalent to the old one.

By similar reflection, we can see that "$-(x)$ (x is solid)" is equivalent to "$(\exists x)-(x$ is solid)" and that "$-(\exists x)$ (x is liquid)" is equivalent to "$(x)-(x$ is liquid)." Here too the principles involved are perfectly general. When a negation sign immediately followed by a universal quantifier is replaced by an existential quantifier immediately followed by a negation sign, the new sentence is equivalent to the old. And when a negation sign immediately followed by an existential quantifier is replaced by a universal quantifier immediately followed by a negation sign, again the new sentence is equivalent to the old. These two principles of equivalence can be summarized by saying that a negation sign may be 'passed through' a quantifier, either forward or backward, provided that the type of quantifier is changed (i.e., from universal to existential, or vice versa).

These various kinds of elementary quantificational equivalence also have some further consequences. We remember that it is a basic fact about truth-functionally compound sentences that any two such sentences have to be equivalent if they are exactly alike except that in one of them a component present in the other has been replaced by something equivalent to it. This means that, for instance, we can employ our knowledge of the equivalence of "$-(x)$ (x is liquid)" to "$(\exists x)-(x$ is liquid)" in order to conclude that a longer sentence such as "$(\exists y)$ (y is solid) $\supset -(x)$ (x is liquid)" must be equivalent to "$(\exists y)$ (y is solid) $\supset (\exists x)-(x$ is liquid)." Here the latter two sentences are truth-functional compounds (both are conditionals) and are exactly alike except that a component of one has been replaced in the other by something equivalent to it. Since the two longer sentences are exactly alike in overall form and since each component of the former necessarily agrees with the corresponding component of the latter as regards truth or falsity, the two longer sentences must agree as regards truth or falsity (i.e., they are equivalent). We shall make use of these principles of equivalence in a later section.

EXERCISE 17

* **A** *Match each sentence in the first group with its translation in the second group.*

(a) (∃x) (x is liquid)
(b) (x) (x is liquid)
(c) (x) (x is solid)
(d) (∃y) (y is solid)
(e) (x) (x is liquid & x is solid)
(f) (x) (x is liquid) & −(x) (x is solid)
(g) (∃x) (x is liquid & x is solid)
(h) (∃y) (y is liquid) & (∃z) (z is solid)
(i) (x) (x is liquid) & (∃y) (y is solid)
(j) (∃y) (y is liquid) & (z) (z is solid)

1   Everything is solid.
2   Everything is liquid.
3   Everything is both liquid and solid.
4   Everything is liquid and not everything is solid.
5   Something is liquid.
6   Something is solid.
7   Something is both liquid and solid.
8   Something is liquid and something is solid.
9   Something is liquid and everything is solid.
10 Everything is liquid and something is solid.

* **B** *Translate each of the following sentences into the symbolism of quantification.*

1   Something is a pig and can fly.
2   Everything is either physical or mental.
3   There is nothing mental.
4   There is something such that it is mental and it is immortal.
5   It is not the case that something mental is immortal.
6   Anything is physical if and only if it is not immortal.

C *Which of the following expressions are true-or-false sentences? Which of the variables are free and which are bound?*

1   (x) (x is male ∨ x is female)
2   (x) (x is male) ∨ y is female
3   x is male ∨ y is female
4   (x) (x is male) ∨ x is female

5 $(\exists y)$ $(y$ is mental$)$ & z is immortal
6 $(\exists y)$ $(y$ is mental$)$ & y is immortal
7 $(\exists y)$ $(y$ is mental & y is immortal$)$

D *Which of the following sentences are equivalent to one another?* (Hint: *They form at most four groups.*) *Try to translate each sentence into good English.*

 1 (x) $(x$ is mental $\vee x$ is physical$)$
 2 (x) $(x$ is mental$)$ $\vee$ (x) $(x$ is physical$)$
 3 $(\exists x)$ $(x$ is mental $\vee x$ is physical$)$
 4 $-(\exists x)-(x$ is mental $\vee x$ is physical$)$
 5 $(\exists x)$ $(x$ is mental$)$ $\vee$ $(\exists x)$ $(x$ is physical$)$
 6 $-(\exists x)-(x$ is mental$)$ $\vee$ (x) $(x$ is physical$)$
 7 $-(x)-(x$ is mental $\vee x$ is physical$)$
 8 $-(\exists x)$ $(x$ is mental$)$ $\supset$ $(\exists x)$ $(x$ is physical$)$
 9 (x) $(x$ is mental$)$ $\vee$ $-(\exists x)-(x$ is physical$)$
10 $(x)-(x$ is mental$)$ $\supset$ $-(x)-(x$ is physical$)$

SYMBOLIZING CATEGORICAL SENTENCES

The four traditional forms of categorical sentence can each be translated into quantificational symbolism. Practicing this will help us develop skill at using this symbolism.

Consider the **A** sentence "All Swedes are Protestants." This can be understood as a sentence concerning *each thing*, and it can be written as a universal quantification. What does it say about each thing? It says of each thing that *if* it is a Swede, *then* it is a Protestant. So the **A** sentence can be expressed in symbols as:

$$(x)\ (Sx \supset Px) \tag{A}$$

Here we write "Sx" as short for "x is a Swede." ("Sx" can also be read "x is Swedish" or "x comes from Sweden"; we get equivalent results whether we use noun, adjective, or verb here.) And we write "Px" as short for "x is a Protestant." ("Px" can also be read "x is Protestant" or "x accepts Protestantism.")

The **E** sentence "No Swedes are Protestants" can also be understood as speaking about *each thing*. What it says concerning each thing is that *if* it is a Swede then it is *not* a Protestant. So it can be written in symbols as:

$$(x) (Sx \supset -Px) \tag{E}$$

The **I** sentence "Some Swedes are Protestants" can be understood as saying that *there exists at least one thing* of a certain kind, so it can be symbolized as an existential quantification. It says that there exists at least one thing which is *both* a Swede *and* a Protestant. So it can be symbolized as:

$$(\exists x) (Sx \& Px) \tag{I}$$

The **O** sentence "Some Swedes are not Protestants" also can be understood as an existential quantification. It says that there exists at least one thing which is both a Swede and *not* a Protestant. So it may be written as:

$$(\exists x) (Sx \& -Px) \tag{O}$$

Thus, for each of the four categorical forms, we have found one way—the most straightforward way—to put it into quantificational symbolism.

However, we remember that the **A** and **O** sentences are contradictories, as are the **E** and **I**. This indicates that an alternative way of symbolizing the **A** sentence would be to write the **O** preceded by a negation sign; that is, "$(x) (Sx \supset Px)$" and "$-(\exists x) (Sx \& -Px)$" are equivalent. If you think about what the symbols mean, you can see that this makes sense, for "$(Sx \supset Px)$" means the same as "$-(Sx \& -Px)$" in virtue of the definition of the horseshoe, and so "$(x) (Sx \supset Px)$" will be equivalent to "$(x)-(Sx \& -Px)$"; and the latter in turn is equivalent to "$-(\exists x) (Sx \& -Px)$" in virtue of the principle about passing a negation sign through a quantifier. Similarly, an alternative way of symbolizing the **E** would be to write the **I** preceded by a negation sign; that is, "$(x) (Sx \supset -Px)$" is equivalent to "$-(\exists x) (Sx \& Px)$."

It is necessary to avoid the mistake of supposing that "Some S are P" could be rendered as "$(\exists x) (Sx \supset Px)$." Remembering how the conditional is related to disjunction, we can see that "$(Sx \supset Px)$" means the same as "$(-Sx \lor Px)$"; the existential quantification of either of these says merely that there exists at least one thing that is either a non-Swede or a Protestant. But this is a very weak statement; the existence of at least one stone would be enough to make it true (for stones are non-Swedes). This shows that "$(\exists x)(-Sx \vee Px)$," and with it "$(\exists x)(Sx \supset Px)$," mean something far weaker than what "Some S are P" means.

A kindred mistake would be to suppose that "No S are P" can be rendered as "$(x)-(Sx \supset Px)$." To see that this is a mistake, let us rewrite "$-(Sx \supset Px)$" in terms of disjunction, getting "$-(-Sx \vee Px)$." By De Morgan's law, this becomes "$Sx \& -Px$." The universal quantification of this says that each thing is both an S and a nonP. This is a very strong statement, far stronger than what "No S are P" says. Thus "$(x)-(Sx \supset Px)$" is not equivalent to "No S are P."

So far in our treatment of quantificational symbolism, we have been taking for granted that our 'universe of discourse' is not limited. That is, we have been taking for granted that when we talk about 'each thing' or about 'at least one thing,' the *range* of things under discussion (our 'universe of discourse') comprises everything there is, without limit or restriction. Thus the universal quantification "$(x)(x$ is physical)" is understood to mean that among all the things there are, each one is physical; the existential quantification "$(\exists y)(y$ is mental)" is understood to mean that among all things there are, at least one is mental.*

However, it sometimes is desirable to limit our universe of

---

* In more advanced discussions of quantification, the variables of quantification are said to 'range over' or to 'take as their values' all the things in the universe of discourse. To understand this way of speaking, let us introduce a new way of regarding free variables. Consider the free variable "x" in the expression "x is physical." Let us think of this "x" as a name for some particular thing selected from the universe of discourse. Suppose that on any particular occasion we allow this "x" to name only one thing, but on different occasions we allow this "x" to name different things, and any thing in the universe of discourse may at some time be selected for this "x" to name. In this sense, we are making the variable 'range over' all the things in the universe of discourse; we are allowing this "x" to 'take as its value' any one of these things. Now, the meaning of the universal quantification "$(x)(x$ is physical)" can be explained thus: It means that "x is physical" becomes a true statement whatever thing from the universe of discourse "x" is regarded as naming (or 'taking as its value'). And the existential quantification "$(\exists x)(x$ is mental)" can be explained as meaning that "x is mental" becomes a true statement for at least one choice of thing from the universe of discourse for "x" to name (that is, for at least one 'value' of "x").

discourse, and we may do so if we choose. To accomplish this, we merely stipulate how the universe of discourse is to be restricted, and then we interpret all our quantifications accordingly—that is, we interpret a universal quantification as speaking of each thing in our limited universe of discourse; and we interpret an existential quantification as speaking of at least one thing in our limited universe of discourse.

Sometimes a restriction of the universe of discourse is helpful in preventing unclarity. Suppose someone asserts that there are no carnivorous marsupials, and symbolizes his assertion as "(x) (x is carnivorous ⊃ x is not a marsupial)." This may leave us puzzled; perhaps we think of the Tasmanian tiger, but we do not know whether this is a counterexample, for it is extinct. The trouble is that we cannot tell whether the speaker intends to assert that among things at present there are no carnivorous marsupials; or that among things of past and present there are none; or that among things of past, present, and future there are none. One way of removing this unclarity would be for the speaker to stipulate what universe of discourse he intends. Suppose he stipulates that his universe of discourse consists of things existing at present. Then his quantification is to be understood as saying that among things existing at present, each thing is such that if it is carnivorous then it is not a marsupial. This will remove the unclarity that troubled us.

Another reason why it can be helpful to restrict the universe of discourse is that doing so sometimes enables us to shorten and simplify our symbolic formulas. For example, suppose we are told to symbolize the argument:

> Anyone over 7 feet tall is a giant.
> No one who is an Eskimo is a giant.
> Therefore no one who is an Eskimo is over 7 feet tall.

And suppose we are told to use "S" as short for "is over 7 feet tall," "G" for "is a giant," and "E" for "is an Eskimo." Let us consider two ways of symbolizing this, first without limiting the universe of discourse, then doing so. If we do not limit our universe of discourse, we shall need to introduce an additional letter, say "P," as short for "is a person." Then the argument may be symbolized:

(x) [Px ⊃ (Sx ⊃ Gx)]
−(∃x) [Px & (Ex & Gx)]
∴−(∃x) [Px & (Ex & Sx)]

Here the first formula says that each thing is such that if it is a person, then if it is over 7 feet tall it is a giant. The second formula says that nothing is both a person and both an Eskimo and a giant. And the third formula says that nothing is both a person and both an Eskimo and over 7 feet tall. We get a simpler symbolization, however, if we explicitly limit the universe of discourse to *persons*; then the argument can be formulated:

(x)(Sx ⊃ Gx)
−(∃x) (Ex & Gx)
∴ −(∃x) (Ex & Sx)

Here the first formula tells us that, among persons, each that is over 7 feet tall is a giant. The second formula tells us that, among persons, none is both an Eskimo and a giant. And the third formula tells us that, among persons, none is both an Eskimo and over 7 feet tall. This second way of symbolizing the argument is more convenient, and will be slightly easier to test for validity.*

EXERCISE 18

A *For each sentence, which ways of symbolizing it are correct and which are incorrect? Let "C" mean "is a conifer," and let "D" mean "is a deciduous tree."*

1 No conifers are deciduous trees.
   (a) −(x) (Cx & Dx)
   (b) (x) Cx & −Dx
   (c) (x) (Cx ⊃ −Dx)

---

* A third way of handling this argument would be to leave the universe of discourse unlimited, but to alter the meanings of the capital letters, so that the simpler set of formulas can express the argument. To do this, we would have to build the notion of being a person into the meanings of the other letters. Suppose we reinterpret "S" so that now it will be short for "is a person over 7 feet tall," and we reinterpret "E" to mean "is an Eskimo person." With the capital letters understood in this way, the second set of formulas serves as a satisfactory translation of the original argument.

2 Not all conifers are deciduous trees.
  (a) $(y) (Cy \supset -Dy)$
  (b) $-(y) (Cy \supset Dy)$
  (c) $(\exists y) (Cy \ \& \ -Dy)$
3 Some nonconifers are deciduous trees.
  (a) $(\exists x) (-Cx \ \& \ Dx)$
  (b) $(\exists y) (-Cy \supset Dy)$
  (c) $(\exists z) - Cz \ \& \ (\exists z) \ Dz$
4 Some conifers are deciduous trees and some aren't.
  (a) $(\exists x) [(Cx \ \& \ Dx) \ \& \ (Cx \ \& \ -Dx)]$
  (b) $(\exists y) \ Cy \ \& \ Dy \ \& - Dy$
  (c) $(\exists x) (Cx \ \& \ Dx) \ \& \ (\exists z) (Cz \ \& \ -Dz)$

B *Translate the following formulas into English, letting "B" mean "is a bird," letting "F" mean "can fly," and letting "M" mean "is a mammal."*

1 $(\exists x) (Bx \ \& \ Fx)$ **2** $(\exists y) (By \ \& \ -Fy)$
3 $(z) (Bz \supset Fz)$ **4** $(x) (Bx \supset -Mx)$
5 $-(y) (My \supset Fy)$ **6** $(\exists x) (Mx \ \& \ Fx)$
7 $(\exists y) (-Fy \ \& \ My)$ **8** $(\exists x) [(Bx \ \& \ Fx) \ \& \ -Mx]$
9 $(z) [Bz \supset -(Fz \ \& \ Mz)]$ **10** $(x) [(Fx \ \& \ Mx) \supset -Bx]$

C *Translate the following sentences into quantificational symbolism. Use "S" as short for "thinks scientifically," use "A" as short for "is an astrologer," and use "P" as short for "is a physicist."*

  1 Some scientific thinkers are not astrologers.
  2 Some astrologers are not scientific thinkers.
  3 No astrologers are scientific thinkers.
  4 Some physicists are scientific thinkers.
  5 All physicists are scientific thinkers.
  6 No physicists are astrologers.
  7 Some physicists are not astrologers.
  8 No physicists who are scientific thinkers are astrologers.
  9 Some astrologers who are nonphysicists are not scientific thinkers.
10 All physicists who are astrologers are nonscientific thinkers.

D *Translate the first six formulas into English, limiting the universe of discourse to chemical elements. Then translate the* second six formulas into English, letting the universe of discourse be unlimited. Finally, say which examples among the first six are equivalent to which examples among the second six. Interpret "A" as "is an acid," "R" as "is radioactive," "I" as "has isotopes," and "C" as "is a chemical element."

1	$(\exists x)\ Rx$	**2**	$-(\exists x)\ (Ax\ \&\ Rx)$
3	$(x)\ (Rx \supset Ix)$	**4**	$(\exists x)\ (Ix\ \&\ -Rx)$
5	$(x)\ (Ix \supset -Ax)$	**6**	$-(\exists x)\ Ax$
7	$-(\exists y)\ (Cy\ \&\ Ay)$	**8**	$(\exists y)\ (Cy\ \&\ Ry)$
9	$(\exists y)\ [Cy\ \&\ (Iy\ \&\ -Ry)]$	**10**	$-(\exists y)\ [Cy\ \&\ (Ay\ \&\ Ry)]$
11	$(y)\ [(Cy\ \&\ Ry) \supset Iy]$	**12**	$(y)\ [(Cy\ \&\ Iy) \supset -Ay]$

E Symbolize each of the following arguments. Consider in each case whether it is appropriate to limit the universe of discourse. Explain the meanings you are assigning to the capital letters you use.

1 Not all whole numbers are even. Every whole number is either odd or even. Hence some whole numbers are odd.

2 No Marxists are Zoroastrians. All Eurocommunists are Marxists. Hence, no Zoroastrians are Eurocommunists.

3 All germs are either viruses or bacteria. No germs that are viruses can be fought with antibiotics. So some germs cannot be fought with antibiotics.

4 Square roots of negative numbers are not real numbers. There are numbers that are square roots of negative numbers. So not all numbers are real numbers.

5 All cycads are gymnosperms. Angiosperms are either dicots or monocots. Gymnosperms are not angiosperms. So no cycads are monocots.

6 Kiwis are toothless, solitary, nocturnal, and flightless. So there are nocturnal toothless birds.

SYMBOLIZING WITH MORE THAN ONE VARIABLE

So far, we have been symbolizing relatively simple sentences. We can handle a much richer variety of sentences if we extend our symbolism in two ways. For one thing, we shall use capital letters followed by more than one variable to symbolize relations between things.   Thus we can write "Ixy," for example, to mean "x influences y."   Here it is important to notice that the order of the variables "x" and "y" in the expression "Ixy" is in one respect of no significance: "Ixy" can be put into words either as "x influences y" or as "y is influenced by x."   But in another respect the order makes an essential difference: "Ixy" is not interchangeable with "Iyx," for the former means "x influences y" whereas the latter means "y influences x."   Also, we shall allow one quantifier to occur within the scope of another.   Thus we can write such symbolized sentences as the following:

$(\exists x)\,(\exists y)\,Ixy$ (1)
$(x)\,(y)\,Ixy$ (2)
$(\exists x)\,Ixx$ (3)
$(x)\,Ixx$ (4)

Here (1) means that there is something such that there is something it influences; in other words, something influences something.   Example (2) means that each thing is such that each thing is influenced by it; that is, everything influences everything.   Notice that (2) does not mean merely that everything influences everything *else*; it means that everything influences everything, including itself.   Example (3) means that something influences itself.   Example (4) means that everything influences itself.

Now that we are allowing one quantifier to occur within the scope of another, we must notice that sometimes the order of the quantifiers can affect the meaning of the sentence. Thus "$(x)\,(\exists y)\,Ixy$" means that everything influences something; that is, each thing is such that there is something or other it influences.   If we change the order of the quantifiers, we get "$(\exists y)\,(x)\,Ixy$," which means that there is some one thing that everything influences.   These two sentences are not equivalent, for the first says that whatever we select, there is always at least one thing that it influences, whereas the second says that there is at least one thing such that whatever we pick influences it. The second sentence says more and logically implies the first; the first sentence says less and could be true even if the second is not.

Let us now get some practice in translating words into

quantificational symbols. In dealing with examples, it is usually best to proceed step by step, moving gradually toward the symbolic formulation. Let "P" mean "is a person," and let "R" mean "resembles" (so that "Rxy" means "x resembles y," "Ryx" means "y resembles x," and so on). We shall now symbolize four sentences; working downward from each original sentence, we move step by step toward a symbolization of it.

Everyone resembles someone.
Each person resembles someone.
Each x is such that if x is a person, x resembles someone.
$(x) (Px \supset x$ resembles someone$)$
$(x) (Px \supset$ there is someone x resembles$)$
$(x) [Px \supset (\exists y) (y$ is a person & x resembles $y)]$
$(x) [Px \supset (\exists y) (Py \& Rxy)]$

Someone resembles everyone.
There is a person who resembles every person.
$(\exists x) (x$ is a person & x resembles every person$)$
$(\exists x) (Px \&$ each person is resembled by $x)$
$(\exists x) [Px \& (y) (Py \supset Rxy)]$

Someone resembles someone.
There is a person who resembles someone.
$(\exists x) (Px \& x$ resembles someone$)$
$(\exists x) [Px \& (\exists y) (Py \& Rxy)]$

Everyone resembles everyone.
$(x) (Px \supset x$ resembles everyone$)$
$(x) (Px \supset$ everyone is resembled by $x)$
$(x) (Px \supset$ each person is resembled by $x)$
$(x) [Px \supset (y) (Py \supset Rxy)]$

These are not the only correct ways of symbolizing the original sentences, but they are the easiest ways. When a true-or-false sentence is properly symbolized, every occurrence of a variable in it must fall within the scope of the proper quantifier. Free variables never occur in the symbolization of sentences like these.

The following is an argument of medieval vintage and is an

example of a valid argument whose validity cannot be established either by syllogistic or by truth-functional methods:

> All circles are figures.
> Therefore, whoever draws a circle draws a figure.

We are not yet in a position to show that the argument is valid, but we can now symbolize its premise and conclusion. The premise becomes:

> $(x) (Cx \supset Fx)$

Symbolizing the conclusion is more difficult and is best done step by step. Two initial steps can be:

> Each thing is such that if it is a person who draws a circle then it is a person who draws a figure.
> $(x) (x$ is a person who draws a circle $\supset x$ is a person who draws a figure)

In order to exhibit the connection between the premise and the conclusion of the argument, we must introduce into our version of the conclusion the letters "C" and "F" that we used in the premise. Otherwise we would not bring out those aspects of the logical structure which are germane to the validity of the argument. We can do this as follows:

> (x) [(x is a person who draws something that is a circle) $\supset$ (x is a person who draws something that is a figure)]
> (x) [(something is a circle & x is a person who draws it) $\supset$ (something is a figure & x is a person who draws it)]
> (x) [$(\exists y) (Cy$ & x is a person who draws $y) \supset (\exists y) (Fy$ & x is a person who draws $y)$]

Now if we use "D" to express "is a person who draws," we have:

> (x) [$(\exists y) (Cy$ & $Dxy) \supset (\exists y) (Fy$ & $Dxy)$]

Thus we have symbolized both the premise and the conclusion of the argument in such a way as to exhibit the logical structure involved in the reasoning.   In the next section we shall develop a method by means of which the validity of an argument like this can be established.

EXERCISE 19

* **A**   *Symbolize each of the following sentences.   Are any of them contradictories of each other?   Are any equivalent?*

1   There is someone whom everybody fears.
2   Everybody fears someone or other.
3   Everybody is feared by someone or other.
4   Nobody fears everybody.
5   Nobody fears no one.
6   Someone does not fear everyone.
7   Nobody fears anybody.
8   Someone does not fear anyone.

B *Let "S" mean "is a sailor," let "G" mean "is a girl," and let "L" mean "loves."   Then translate the following into English.*

1   (x) (Sx ⊃ −Gx)
2   (∃x) (Gx & −Sx)
3   (∃x) [Sx & (∃y) Lxy]
4   (∃x) [Sx & (∃y) (Gy & Lxy)]
5   (x) [Sx ⊃ (∃y) (Gy & Lxy)]
6   (∃x) [Sx & (y) (Gy ⊃ Lxy)]
7   (∃x) [Gx & (y) (Sy ⊃ Lxy)]
8   (y) [Gy ⊃ (∃x) (Sx & Lxy)]
9   (x) [Sx ⊃ (y) (Gy ⊃ Lxy)]

C   *Give a clear reason why each of the following translations is not correct.*

1   No sailors are girls.   (x) − (Sx ⊃ Gx)
2   Every sailor loves a girl.   (x) Sx ⊃ (∃y) (Gy & Lxy)
3   There is a sailor who loves   (∃x) [Sx ⊃ (y) (Gy ⊃ Lxy)]
     every girl.
4   There is a girl who is loved by   (∃x) [Gy & (x) (Sx & Lxy)]
     every sailor.
5   Every girl is loved by some   (∃x) [Sx & (y) (Gy ⊃ Lxy)]
     sailor.

D *Symbolize the following sentences.*

1 Every problem is solvable by some method or other.
2 There is a method by which every problem is solvable.
3 There is a post office in every city.
4 If anything is damaged, someone will have to pay for it.
5 Someone will have to pay for everything that is damaged.
6 If something is damaged, someone will have to pay a fine.
7 If any automobiles are solid gold, then some automobiles are expensive.
8 If all trespassers are violators of the law and only hoboes are trespassers, then if there are any trespassers some hoboes are violators of the law.
9 If all teachers are perfectionists and no students are hard-working, then some teachers will be frustrated.
10 If any student is careless, then if all teachers are perfectionists, he will be censured.
11 There is a disease that any doctor can cure; therefore, every doctor can cure some disease or other.
12 There is a politician whom everyone likes; therefore, there is a politician who likes himself.

PROVING VALIDITY OF ARGUMENTS

Neither Venn diagrams nor truth tables are sufficient for establishing the validity of quantificational arguments in general. To do this, we need a more powerful technique. Logicians have devised a variety of methods sufficient for establishing the validity of any valid quantificational argument, but many of these methods are rather difficult to explain and use. We shall employ a method that is comparatively simple. It is an extended and specialized version of the method of deduction that was developed in the preceding chapter.

Suppose we are interested in the argument "There is something that causes everything; therefore, each thing has some cause or other." This argument can be symbolized "$(\exists x)(y)Cxy$, therefore $(y)(\exists x)Cxy$." To claim that the argument is valid is to claim that it is impossible for the premise to be true but the conclusion false. This amounts to the same thing as claiming that the sentence "$(\exists x)(y)Cxy$ & $-(y)(\exists x)Cxy$" is a contradiction (that is, inconsistent, necessarily false). If we had a way of showing that the latter sentence is a contradiction, we would thereby have a way of showing that the original argument is valid.

How can we show a sentence to be a contradiction? The *reductio ad adsurdum* reasoning mentioned in Chapter 3 gives a hint. Suppose we could show that from a sentence some other sentence that is definitely a contradiction validly follows. This would mean that the former sentence could be true only if the latter was, and since the latter is a contradiction and cannot be true, the former cannot be true either and must be a contradiction also. Going back to our example, if we can show that some obvious contradiction follows validly from "$(\exists x)(y)Cxy$ & $-(y)(\exists x)Cxy$," then we shall have shown that our original argument "$(\exists x)(y)Cxy$, therefore $(y)(\exists x)Cxy$" is a valid argument.

We shall now try to develop some rules of deduction that will enable us to do this. Use of this *reductio ad absurdum* approach means that we shall need special rules only for removing quantifiers from our formulas, not for adding them. Consequently, our set of quantificational rules does not have to be as complex to explain as quantificational rules for direct proof would be.

Let us introduce the letters "a," "b," "c," etc., which we shall employ as *names* for particular things in the universe. We must regard each letter as naming just one thing, at least during the course of any one deduction (although a letter might name different things in different deductions). By a universal quantification, we mean an expression that starts with a universal quantifier whose scope is all the rest of the expression. A universal quantification such as "(x) (x is physical)," which we might write "$(x)Fx$," says that everything is physical; thus from the universal quantification we are entitled to infer "Fa," "Fb," "Fc," etc. Here we are simply making use of the idea that what is true of everything must be true of each particular thing.

Here the singular sentence "Fa" is called an *instance* of the universal sentence "$(x)Fx$." In general, an instance is anything that we get from a quantification by removing the quantifier and inserting a name in place of the variable of quantification wherever it occurred governed by the quantifier. Even if we do not know what the various letters mean, we still can tell that "$Fa \supset Ga$" is an instance of "$(z)(Fz \supset Gz)$," that "Hbc" is an instance of "(x) Hxc," that "(∃y) Rcyc" is an instance of "(z) (∃y) Rzyz," and also that "(∃y) Rcyc" is an instance of "(z) (∃y) Rzyc." However, "Fa ⊃ Gx" is not an instance of "(x) (Fx ⊃ Gx)," for the name has not replaced all occurrences of the variable of quantification.

This rule of *universal instantiation* is perfectly general: It says that from any universal quantification we may validly deduce any instance of it. Notice, however, that the rule does not entitle us to infer "Fa ⊃ P" from "(x) Fx ⊃ P." This case is improper and does not accord with the rule because the expression with which we start is not a universal quantification; the quantifier does not govern the whole of the expression. (Here "P" is to be thought of as a letter of the kind we used in the preceding chapter; it is short for some whole sentence.) To see that this case is improper, think of the sentence "If everything is physical, Plato was mistaken," which may be symbolized "(x) Fx ⊃ P," and think of the sentence "If this book is physical, Plato was mistaken," which may be symbolized "Fa ⊃ P." The first could be true even if the second is false, which shows that the second cannot follow validly from the first.

An expression is called an existential quantification if it starts with an existential quantifier whose scope is all the rest of the expression. An existential quantification "(∃x) Fx" says that there is at least one thing that is an F. Now let us take the letter "a" and arbitrarily use it as a name to refer to this thing (or to one of these things) that is supposed to be an F. If we understand "a" in this way, we may derive "Fa" from "(∃x) Fx." Here too we can employ the notion of an instance: Anything is an instance of an existential quantification if it can be derived from the quantification by dropping the initial quantifier and inserting a name in all the places where the variable of quantification occurred governed by the quantifier.

The rule of *existential instantiation* tells us that from any existential quantification we may infer any instance of it, with one qualification. If we are to avoid fallacious reasoning, this rule has to be hedged with a restriction. We shall formulate the restriction as follows: When the instance is inferred by means of existential instantiation, the name being introduced into the instance must be one that has not previously been used in the deduction. Before we discuss this restriction more fully, let us first see how the rules are used.

In order to establish the validity of the argument "$(\exists x)$ $(y)\,Cxy$, therefore $(y)\,(\exists x)\,Cxy$," which we were considering previously, we wanted to derive some obvious contradiction from "$(\exists x)\,(y)\,Cxy$ & $-(y)\,(\exists x)\,Cxy$." We now are in a position to do this. Let us draw up our work in the form of a deduction. We shall use our two quantificational rules, the quantificational equivalences from earlier in this chapter, and also the truth-functional principles from Chapter 3:

1. $(\exists x)\,(y)\,Cxy$ & $-(y)\,(\exists x)\,Cxy$	Premise
2. $(\exists x)\,(y)\,Cxy$	From 1 by conjunctive simplification (conj. simp.)
3. $(y)\,Cay$	From 2 by existential instantiation (E.I.)
4. $-(y)\,(\exists x)\,Cxy$	From 1 by conj. simp.
5. $(\exists y) - (\exists x)\,Cxy$	From 4 by quantificational equivalence (quant. equiv.)
6. $-(\exists x)\,Cxb$	From 5 by E.I.
7. Cab	From 3 by universal instantiation (U.I.)
8. $(x) -Cxb$	From 6 by quant. equiv.
9. $-Cab$	From 8 by U.I.
10. Cab & $-Cab$	From 7, 9 by conjunctive adjunction (conj. adj.)

Looking at the deduction as a whole, we see that in the last line we have derived a definite contradiction of the form "p & $-p$." Conclusions of this form are the clearest and most obvious of contradictions, and so we shall use them as the standard type of contradiction, always trying to obtain a conclusion of this form as the last line of a quantificational deduction. In this deduction the contradiction was validly derived from the first line, and so the first line must be a contradiction too. This shows that our original argument was valid. Here then is our method for showing the validity of valid quantificational arguments.

Going back now to the rule of existential instantiation, let us consider why there must be some kind of restriction upon it. A sentence such as "$(\exists x)\,Fx$" says at least one thing is F, and if we think of the letter "a" as naming such a thing, then we may infer "Fa." But clearly it is important here that "a" be a name which has not previously been assigned some other special sense elsewhere in the same deduction. Invalid reasoning can easily occur if we neglect this restriction and allow a single letter to be assigned more than one special sense in the course of a deduction. For example, the expression "$(\exists x) Fx \ \& \ (\exists x) - Fx$" is not a contradiction, but the following deduction purports to show that it is:

1.	$(\exists x) Fx \ \& \ (\exists x) -Fx$	*Premise*
2.	$(\exists x) Fx$	*From 1 by conj. simp.*
3.	Fa	*From 2 by E.I.*
4.	$(\exists x) -Fx$	*From 1 by conj. simp.*
5.	$-Fa$	*From 4 by E.I.*
6.	$Fa \ \& \ -Fa$	*From 3, 5 by conj. adj.*

This deduction claims to show that a contradiction follows from the first line and therefore that the first line is a contradiction. But that is not so, and the deduction is illegitimate. The fallacy is that in getting line 3 we have chosen to think of "a" as naming a particular thing that is F, but in line 5 we think of the same letter "a" as naming a particular thing that is non$F$. It is illegitimate to assume that the thing that was the F is the thing that is the non$F$; there is no reason why they need be the same thing. The mistake lies in line 5, where the name introduced into the instance ought to have been a name that had not occurred before in the deduction.

Here is another example to illustrate how this restriction is needed to prevent fallacious reasoning. The sentence "There is something that causes everything" does not follow from "Each thing is caused by something or other," yet here is a deduction that purports to show that it does follow:

1.	$(x) (\exists y) Cxy \ \&$ $-(\exists y) (x) Cx\dot{y}$	*Premise*
2.	$(x) (\exists y) Cxy$	*From 1 by conj. simp.*
3.	$(\exists y) Cay$	*From 2 by U.I.*
4.	Cab	*From 3 by E.I.*
5.	$-(\exists y) (x) Cxy$	*From 1 by conj. simp.*
6.	$(y) - (x) Cxy$	*From 5 by quant. equiv.*
7.	$-(x) Cxb$	*From 6 by U.I.*
8.	$(\exists x) -Cxb$	*From 7 by quant. equiv.*
9.	$-Cab$	*From 8 by E.I.*
10.	$Cab \ \& \ -Cab$	*From 4, 9 by conj. adj.*

By apparently deducing a contradiction from the conjunction of "$(x) (\exists y) Cxy$" with the negation of "$(\exists y) (x) Cxy$," this deduction purports to show that the latter validly follows from the former. This is fallacious, and so we must think over the steps in the deduction to see what is wrong. In line 3 we let the letter "a" refer to an individual object, any object we please. Then in line 4 we let the letter "b" refer to an object related to the object a. Our choice of a was completely free, but our choice of b was not; b has to be an object to which a bears the C relation. So far it is all right. Then in line 7 we chose b again; this is still all right, for line 6 is true of everything and so must be true of b. But in line 9 we chose a again, and this is the mistake. In line 9 we should have chosen a particular object not bearing the C relation to b. Line 8 guarantees us that there is at least one such object, but we have no guarantee that a is such an object. The letter "a" is not used for the first time in line 9, for "a" was previously introduced to refer to the object chosen in line 3. We have no right to assume that the sense assigned to "a" in line 9 is compatible with the sense previously assigned to "a" in line 3. We can avoid this sort of fallacy in deductions by insisting upon the restriction that the name introduced by means of existential instantiation must always be a new name that has not previously been used in the deduction.

Let us conclude this section by returning to the medieval argument symbolized at the end of the preceding section. We now are able to demonstrate its validity by means of a deduction.

1. $(x) (Cx \supset Fx) \&$ Premise
$-(x)[(\exists y) (Cy \& Dxy)$
$\supset (\exists y) (Fy \& Dxy)]$
2. $-(x) [(\exists y) (Cy \& Dxy)$ From 1 by conj. simp.
$\supset (\exists y) (Fy \& Dxy)]$
3. $(\exists x)-[(\exists y) (Cy \& Dxy)$ From 2 by quant. equiv.
$\supset (\exists y) (Fy \& Dxy)]$
4. $-[(\exists y) (Cy \& Day)$ From 3 by E.I.
$\supset (\exists y) (Fy \& Day)]$
5. $(\exists y) (Cy \& Day) \&$ From 4 by equivalence
$-(\exists y) (Fy \& Day)$
6. $(\exists y) (Cy \& Day)$ From 5 by conj. simp.
7. $Cb \& Dab$ From 6 by E.I.
8. $-(\exists y) (Fy \& Day)$ From 5 by conj. simp.
9. $(y)-(Fy \& Day)$ From 8 by quant. equiv.

10. $-(Fb \ \& \ Dab)$	*From 9 by U.I.*
11. $(x) \ (Cx \supset Fx)$	*From 1 by conj. simp.*
12. $Cb \supset Fb$	*From 11 by U.I.*
13. Cb	*From 7 by conj. simp.*
14. Fb	*From 12, 13 by modus ponens*
15. Dab	*From 7 by conj. simp.*
16. $Fb \ \& \ Dab$	*From 14, 15 by conj. adj.* ·
17. $(Fb \ \& \ Dab) \ \&$	*From 16, 10 by conj. adj.*
$\quad -(Fb \ \& \ Dab)$	

Looking back over this deduction, we see that the steps are correct and that the deduction establishes the validity of the original argument. It should be emphasized that there can also be other correct series of steps that could establish the desired result.

But you may wonder how the deduction was invented. The rules of deduction tell us many kinds of steps that we *may* perform, but they do not tell us what we *must* do to finish the deduction; for that, some trial-and-error work will be needed. The aim in constructing the deduction is to reach a last line of the form "$p \ \& \ -p$"; anything of that form will do. Now, if we are to obtain that sort of obvious contradiction here, it is likely that we shall need different instances, some of which contain the same names. (If we introduce a new name into each new instance, we are not likely to obtain any contradiction.) For this reason, it is wise, insofar as possible, to perform E.I. before we perform U.I. Doing so allows us to introduce into the U.I. instance the same name that previously we introduced into the E.I. instance, thus improving the chances of obtaining a contradiction. This is why in the earlier lines of the deduction we elect to deal first with the right-hand part of line 1, upon which we can perform E.I., rather than with the left-hand component, upon which we would have to perform U.I. Then in lines 10 and 12, when we finally perform U.I., we choose the previously used name "b," which seems to offer the most promise of yielding a contradiction.

Our principles for use in quantificational deductions follow.

Principles for Use in Quantificational Deductions

I. *Truth-functional inference (T.F.)*
We may use any of the principles of truth-functional deduction that were listed in Chapter 3.

II. Quantificational rules of inference

Universal instantiation (U.I.): From any universal quantification we may validly infer any instance of it.

Existential instantiation (E.I.): From an existential quantification we may validly infer any instance of it, provided that the name being introduced into the instance is new to the deduction.

III. Quantificational equivalences (quant. equiv.)

From a sentence we may validly infer any sentence that is equivalent to it according to these rules:

1   Two sentences are equivalent if they are exactly alike except that where the first contains a negation sign immediately followed by a universal quantifier, the other contains an existential quantifier immediately followed by a negation sign; e.g., "$-(x)Fx$" is equivalent to "$(\exists x)-Fx$."
2   Two sentences always are equivalent if they are exactly alike except that where the first contains a negation sign immediately followed by an existential quantifier, the second contains a universal quantifier immediately followed by a negation sign; e.g., "$-(\exists x)Fx$" is equivalent to "$(x)-Fx$."

Two more quantificational equivalences will be added later.

A word of explanation about truth-functional inference. We are entitled to write down any new line that can be justified by the purely truth-functional rules of Chapter 3. For instance, if we have previous lines that read "$(\exists x)Fx \supset (y)Gy$" and "$(\exists x)Fx$," then by modus ponens we may derive "$(y)Gy$." Although these lines contain quantifiers, their overall structure is exactly that of modus ponens, and the move is purely truth-functional. However, the principles of Chapter 3 do not justify us in making changes within the scope of a quantifier. Suppose we tried to go from "$(x)(Fx \supset Gx)$" and "$(x)Fx$" to "$(x)Gx$." It would be a mistake to suppose that mere modus ponens justifies this move; here the move does not have the exact structure required by modus ponens, for the first line is not a conditional (instead, it is a universal quantification). Nor would it be correct to go from "$(x)[(Fx \supset Gx) \& Fx]$" to "$(x)Gx$" merely by modus ponens. Such a move may be valid, but it is not justified by modus ponens as such. In constructing our deductions, we want to keep strictly to those moves which we know are justified by the standard rules we have become familiar with; that is the whole point of the game. Were we to start relying upon our special intuitions as to what is valid, our deductions would cease to be reliable.

In connection with the quantificational rules of inference, it is important to keep in mind that one has to start with a universal quantification or an existential quantification before one can use these rules. That is, for U.I. one must start with a line that has a universal quantifier at the very beginning, and the scope of the quantifier must be all the rest of the line. And for E.I. one must start with a line having an existential quantifier at the very beginning, and the scope of the quantifier must be all the rest of the line. It would be a misuse of U.I. to try to use it to justify a move from "$-(x) Fx$" to "$-Fa$," because here the first is not a universal quantification; it is the negation of one. Also, it would be a mistake to try to go by E.I. from "$(\exists x) Gx \supset Fy$" to "$Ga \supset Fy$"; the first one is not an existential quantification.

Also, we must take care that the final line in a deduction is really a contradiction of the form "$p \ \& \ -p$." It would be inappropriate to terminate a deduction with "$(Fa \ \& \ Ga) \ \& \ (-Fa \ \& \ -Ga)$"; this is a contradiction, but not as obvious and clear-cut a specimen as we want. It would be much worse to try to end a deduction with "$(Fa \supset Ga) \ \& \ (Fa \supset -Ga)$," which is not a contradiction at all.

EXERCISE 20

A *Each of the following is a correct deduction. Explain the justification for each step, and state what the deduction shows.*

1
1. $(x) (Sx \supset Px)$
   $\& \ (\exists x) (Sx \ \& \ -Px)$
2. $(\exists x) (Sx \ \& \ -Px)$
3. $Sa \ \& \ -Pa$
4. $(x) (Sx \supset Px)$
5. $Sa \supset Pa$
6. Sa
7. Pa
8. $-Pa$
9. $Pa \ \& \ -Pa$

2
1. $(x) Fx \ \& \ -(y) Fy$
2. $-(y) Fy$
3. $(\exists x) -Fy$
4. $-Fa$
5. $(x) Fx$
6. Fa
7. $Fa \ \& \ -Fa$

3
1. [(x) (Mx ⊃ −Px)
& (x) (Sx ⊃ Mx)]
& −(x) (Sx ⊃ −Px)
2. −(x) (Sx ⊃ −Px)
3. (∃x) −(Sx ⊃ −Px)
4. −(Sa ⊃ −Pa)
5. (x) (Mx ⊃ −Px) &
(x) (Sx ⊃ Mx)
6. (x) (Mx ⊃ −Px)
7. Ma ⊃ −Pa
8. (x) (Sx ⊃ Mx)
9. Sa ⊃ Ma
10. Sa & Pa
11. Sa
12. Ma
13. −Pa
14. Pa
15. Pa & −Pa

4
1. (∃x) [Gx & (y) (Gy ⊃
Hxy)] & −(∃x)
(Gx & Hxx)
2. (∃x) [Gx & (y) (Gy ⊃
Hxy)]
3. Gb & (y) (Gy ⊃ Hby)
4. (y) (Gy ⊃ Hby)
5. Gb ⊃ Hbb
6. −(∃x) (Gx & Hxx)
7. (x)−(Gx & Hxx)
8. −(Gb & Hbb)
9. Gb
10. Hbb
11. −Hbb
12. Hbb & −Hbb

5
1. (∃z) [−Rzz & (y) Rzy]
2. −Rcc & (y) Rcy
3. (y) Rcy
4. Rcc
5. −Rcc
6. Rcc & −Rcc

6
1. −(x) [(y) Fy ⊃ Fx]
2. (∃x) − [(y) Fy ⊃ Fx]
3. −[(y) Fy ⊃ Fa]
4. (y) Fy & −Fa
5. (y) Fy
6. Fa
7. −Fa
8. Fa & −Fa

B *Explain the justification of each legitimate step. If any step is illegitimate, explain why and consider whether the deduction could be rearranged so as to demonstrate the desired result legitimately according to our rules.*

1
1. [(x) (Mx ⊃ Px) & (∃x) (Sx & −Mx)] & −(∃x) (Sx & Px)		Premise
2. (x) (Mx ⊃ Px) & (∃x) (Sx & −Mx)		From 1
3. (x) (Mx ⊃ Px)		From 2
4. (∃x) (Sx & −Mx)		From 2
5. −(∃x) (Sx & Px)		From 1
6. −(Sa & Pa)		From 5
7. (∃x) Sx		From 4

8.	Sb	From 7
9.	−Sa	From 6
10.	Sb & −Sa	From 8, 9

2

1.	[(x) (Mx ⊃ −Px) & (∃x) (Mx & Sx)] & −(∃x) (Sx & −Px)	Premise
2.	(x) (Mx ⊃ −Px) & (∃x) (Mx & Sx)	From 1
3.	(x) (Mx ⊃ −Px)	From 2
4.	(∃x) (Mx & Sx)	From 2
5.	−(∃x) (Sx & −Px)	From 1
6.	Mx ⊃ −Px	From 3
7.	(∃x) Mx	From 4
8.	−(∃x) −Px	From 5
9.	−(−Pa)	From 8
10.	Pa	From 9
11.	Ma ⊃ −Pa	From 6
12.	−Ma	From 10, 11
13.	(∃x) Mx & −Ma	From 7, 12

USING THE METHOD

When a quantificational sentence is a contradiction, our method of quantificational deduction enables us to demonstrate this by showing that from the given sentence a truth-functional contradiction of the form "p & −p" validly follows. As we have already seen, this method can be used to answer questions about the validity of arguments because any question about the validity of an argument (or about an implication) can be rephrased as a question about whether some sentence is a contradiction.

If we want to test the validity of a quantificational argument, we put the premise into conjunction with the negation of the conclusion, and we try to show that this conjunction is a contradiction. When we have an argument with more than one premise, we can also use this method. However, now we must form a conjunction of all the premises, put this into conjunction with the negation of the conclusion, and see whether this is a contradiction. If it is, that shows that it is impossible for the conclusion to be false, provided that all the premises are true; that is, it shows that the premises imply the conclusion and the argument is valid.

Another question we can handle is whether a quantificational sentence is necessarily true in virtue of its quantificational form. This question can be rephrased as a question about a contradiction. That is because a given sentence is necessarily true if and only if its negation is a contradiction. For instance, a sentence of the form "$(x) (Fx \supset Fx)$" is necessarily true if and only if the corresponding sentence of the form "$-(x) (Fx \supset Fx)$" is a contradiction. This provides a method of demonstrating the necessary truth of a quantificational sentence: We form the negation of the given sentence and then show that this negation is a contradiction.

Also, our method can be used to show that two quantificational sentences are equivalent. To say that two sentences are equivalent is to say that each follows from the other. So to establish the equivalence of two sentences A and B, we first construct a deduction to show that A follows from B, and then construct another deduction to show that B follows from A.

When we use our method of quantificational deduction to answer questions of these various kinds, we sometimes may need to construct fairly complex deductions. In figuring out how to finish them, it will be helpful to keep in mind certain points of strategy.

One point has to do with how to avoid being balked by the restriction on the rule of existential instantiation. The restriction requires that any name introduced by means of E.I. must be a new name. We should not let this restriction prevent us from getting the legitimate results that we want. For example, suppose we are trying to show by deduction that a syllogism of the type **AII** in the first figure is valid. Symbolizing the premises and putting them into conjunction with the negation of the conclusion, we have the following:

1. $[(x) (Mx \supset Px) \ \& \ (\exists x) (Sx \ \& \ Mx)] \ \& \ -(\exists x) (Sx \ \& \ Px)$

We might then attempt to deduce a contradiction from this by proceeding as follows:

2. $(x) (Mx \supset Px)$ *From 1 by conj. simp.*
      $\& \ (\exists x) (Sx \ \& \ Mx)$

3. $(x) (Mx \supset Px)$　　　　　From 2 by conj. simp.
4. $Ma \supset Pa$　　　　　　　From 3 by U.I.
5. $(\exists x) (Sx \ \& \ Mx)$　　　　From 2 by conj. simp.

But now we are in trouble. We cannot properly obtain "$Sa \ \& \ Ma$" from line 5 by E.I., for the name "a" already has been used in the deduction, and no other instance would yield a contradiction. Here the solution is to take our steps in a different order. We perform E.I. first, and then U.I.

1. $[(x) (Mx \supset Px)$
　　$\& \ (\exists x) (Sx \ \& \ Mx)] \ \&$
　　$-(\exists x) (Sx \ \& \ Px)$
2. $(x) (Mx \supset Px)$　　　　　From 1 by conj. simp.
　　$\& \ (\exists x) (Sx \ \& \ Mx)$
3. $(\exists x) (Sx \ \& \ Mx)$　　　　From 2 by conj. simp.
4. $Sa \ \& \ Ma$　　　　　　　From 3 by E.I.
5. $(x) (Mx \supset Px)$　　　　　From 2 by conj. simp.
6. $Ma \supset Pa$　　　　　　　From 5 by U.I.
7. $-(\exists x) (Sx \ \& \ Px)$　　　From 1 by conj. simp.
8. $(x)-(Sx \ \& \ Px)$　　　　From 7 by quant. equiv.
9. $-(Sa \ \& \ Pa)$　　　　　　From 8 by U.I.
10. Ma　　　　　　　　　From 4 by conj. simp.
11. Pa　　　　　　　　　From 6, 10 by modus ponens
12. Sa　　　　　　　　　From 4 by conj. simp.
13. $Sa \ \& \ Pa$　　　　　　From 11, 12 by conj. adj.
14. $(Sa \ \& \ Pa) \ \& \ -(Sa \ \& \ Pa)$　　From 9, 13 by conj. adj.

Here we get the contradiction we want, because we have arranged the sequence of steps so that we do not violate the restriction. As was mentioned at the end of the preceding section, it always is wise to perform E.I. before U.I., insofar as that is possible.

As another example of strategy, let us consider how we could show that the sentence "There is something such that if something is physical then it is physical" is necessarily true. We may symbolize it "$(\exists x) [(\exists y) Fy \supset Fx]$." To show that it is necessarily true, we must derive a contradiction from its negation.

1. $-(\exists x) [(\exists y) Fy \supset Fx]$
2. $(x) - [(\exists y) Fy \supset Fx]$　　From 1 by quant. equiv.

3. $-[(\exists y) Fy \supset Fa]$ *From 2 by U.I.*
4. $(\exists y) Fy \,\&\, -Fa$ *From 3 by equivalence*
5. $(\exists y) Fy$ *From 4 by conj. simp.*

At this point in the deduction we are prevented from reaching "*Fa*" as the next line, for that would violate the restriction. And here we cannot perform the existential instantiation first, because the existential quantifier is buried within the scope of the universal quantifier. (The rule of existential instantiation allows removal of an existential quantifier only when it stands at the beginning of the expression and governs the whole.) Here the problem of strategy is momentarily puzzling. The solution is to use another name and then go back and obtain a second instance from the universal quantification so as to produce the contradiction.

6. Fb *From 5 by E.I.*
7. $-[(\exists y) Fy \supset Fb]$ *From 2 by U.I.*
8. $(\exists y) Fy \,\&\, -Fb$ *From 7 by equivalence*
9. $-Fb$ *From 8 by conj. simp.*
10. $Fb \,\&\, -Fb$ *From 6, 9 by conj. adj.*

In general, when we instantiate, we want to select names in ways that will improve our chances of obtaining a contradiction quickly. This means that our strategy should be to carry out all our instantiation steps, using as few different names as possible. With deductions that involve no relations (that is, where each of the capital letters occurs followed by only one variable at a time), we should try to carry out all instantiation steps, using just one single name. When the deduction contains one or more relations, we ordinarily have to use two or more distinct names in order to obtain a contradiction; but we should select names to occur in our instances in such a way as to make it likely that we can obtain a contradiction. Suppose we are considering the argument "$(x) (y) Cxy$, therefore $(\exists x) (y) Cxy$." We start the deduction as follows:

1. $(x) (y) Cxy \,\&\, -(\exists x) (y) Cxy$ *Premise*
2. $(x) (y) Cxy$ *1, conj. simp.*
3. $-(\exists x) (y) Cxy$ *1, conj. simp.*
4. $(x)-(y) Cxy$ *3, quant. equiv.*
5. $(x) (\exists y)-Cxy$ *4, quant. equiv.*

6. $(\exists y) -Cay$	5, U.I.
7. $-Cab$	6, E.I.

From this point, we might be inclined to continue as follows:

8. $(y) Cby$	2, U.I.
9. Cba	8, U.I.
10. $Cba \ \& \ -Cab$	7, 9, conj. adj.

But this will not do. What we have reached is not a contradiction at all, and we have no way to go on from line 10 toward any contradiction. Bad strategy has been followed. We should go back and replace the last three lines by others, making a different selection of names.

8. $(y) Cay$	2, U.I.
9. Cab	8, U.I.
10. $Cab \ \& \ -Cab$	9, 7, conj. adj.

In inventing deductions like these, we have to use trial and error, experimenting with various possibilities until we find a combination of steps that will yield the needed result.

There is a further slight extension of our symbolism which will be useful to us in handling some kinds of arguments that contain singular terms. A sentence containing a proper name or other phrase that purports to apply to exactly one individual is called a singular sentence. Such sentences can be translated into categorical form, as we saw in Chapter 2. But quantificational symbolism offers a better way of treating them, for we can use the letters "a," "b," "c," etc., as names. Thus, for instance, "All philosophers are wise; Socrates is a philosopher; therefore Socrates is wise" can be symbolized as "$(x) (Px \supset Wx), Pa$, therefore Wa." Here "a" refers to Socrates. We can demonstrate the validity of the syllogism thus:

1. $[(x) (Px \supset Wx)$ $\& \ Pa] \ \& \ -Wa$	
2. $(x) (Px \supset Wx) \ \& \ Pa$	From 1 by conj. simp.
3. $(x) (Px \supset Wx)$	From 2 by conj. simp.
4. $Pa \supset Wa$	From 3 by U.I.
5. Pa	From 2 by conj. simp.

6. Wa *From 4, 5 by modus ponens*
7. $-Wa$ *From 1 by conj. simp.*
8. Wa & $-Wa$ *From 6, 7 by conj. adj.*

EXERCISE 21

A *Do these deductions conform to our rules? If not, can the desired results be obtained in some other way that does conform to the rules?*

1
1. $(x) Fx$ & $-(y) Fy$
2. $(x) Fx$
3. Fa
4. $-(y) Fy$
5. $(\exists y) -Fy$
6. $-Fa$
7. Fa & $-Fa$

2
1. $(\exists x)(\exists y) Rxy$ & $-(\exists x) Rxx$
2. $(\exists x)(\exists y) Rxy$
3. $(\exists y) Ray$
4. $-(\exists x) Rxx$
5. $(x)-Rxx$
6. $-Raa$
7. Raa
8. Raa & $-Raa$

B *In each case, construct a quantificational deduction to show that the example is logically correct.*

1 "Something is bigger than something" validly follows from "Everything is bigger than something."

2 If there is something such that everything is bigger than it, then for each thing there is something than which it is bigger.

3 "Each thing is such as not to be bigger than anything" contradicts "Something is bigger than something."

4 All these jewels are valuable. Whatever gets lost will have to be paid for. Therefore, if everything valuable gets lost, then all these jewels will have to be paid for.

5 There is a subject that is liked by any student who likes any subject at all. Every student likes some subject or other. Therefore, there is a subject that is liked by all students.

6 No cities of any size lie in Antarctic regions. Capetown is a sizable city. So Capetown does not lie in Antarctic regions.

7 Every Scandinavian nation is democratic. Some kings rule Scandinavian nations. So some kings rule democratic nations.

8 The regulations of a certain ship state that any barber aboard that ship must shave all and only those aboard the ship who do not shave themselves. Show that according to these regulations there can be no barber aboard the ship.

9　No human person is a parent of himself. Therefore, a person who is a parent of every human person is not human.

10　Infinity is larger than every countable number. No number is larger than itself. Therefore, infinity is not a countable number.

EXTENDING THE METHOD

Although our method of quantificational deduction already enables us to handle many examples, it is not yet complete. There are many other kinds of examples with which we are not yet in a position to deal. The difficulty is this. In using the method to derive a contradiction, we need to be able to obtain instances of the various quantifications that occur in the first line. The rules of U.I. and E.I. allow us to obtain an instance from a quantification only when the quantifier is at the very beginning and governs the whole expression. Hence we have to derive from the first line new lines that will have quantifiers at the beginning governing the whole lines; from these lines we in turn obtain our instances. When the first line is a conjunction of quantifications or their negations, the truth-functional rule of conjunctive simplification together with the quantificational equivalences suffices to enable us to derive the new lines needed, each having at its beginning a quantifier that governs the whole. But where the first line contains quantifications that are linked together in ways other than mere conjunction, the rule of conjunctive simplification is powerless.

Consider the quantificational sentence "Either everything is solid and not solid or everything is liquid and not liquid," which may be symbolized "$(x) (Sx \& -Sx) \vee (y) (Ly \& -Ly)$." This sentence is a contradiction, but so far we do not have any way of showing it to be a contradiction. If we write this as the first line of a deduction, there is no rule permitting us to take any useful step beyond the first line. We shall now extend our method by adding to it a pair of further principles of equivalence that will enable us in cases like this to obtain the needed further lines, each having at the beginning a quantifier governing all the rest.

Consider the two sentences:

Either each thing is mental, or Berkeley's philosophy is mistaken.
Each thing is such that either it is mental or Berkeley's philosophy is mistaken.

Writing "M" for "is mental" and "B" for the whole sentence "Berkeley's philosophy is mistaken," we can symbolize the two sentences thus:

$(x) Mx \lor B$
$(x) (Mx \lor B)$

The first sentence is a disjunction one component of which is a universal quantification, while the second sentence is a universal quantification of a disjunction. The two sentences are equivalent, however, for each is true if and only if either everything is mental or Berkeley's philosophy is mistaken. The underlying principle of equivalence here can be stated in more general terms: Any disjunction, one part of which is a universal quantification, may be rewritten in the equivalent form of a universal quantification of a disjunction.*

This principle of equivalence can itself be justified in terms of the principles we already have. To show that "$(x) (Mx \lor B)$" is equivalent to "$(x) Mx \lor B$," we show that each implies the other. This requires two deductions.

1.	$[(x) Mx \lor B] \& -(x) (Mx \lor B)$	Premise
2.	$-(x) (Mx \lor B)$	1, conj. simp.
3.	$(\exists x)-(Mx \lor B)$	2, quant. equiv.
4.	$-(Ma \lor B)$	3, E.I.
5.	$-Ma \& -B$	4, De Morgan
6.	$-B$	5, conj. simp.
7.	$(x) Mx \lor B$	1, conj. simp.
8.	$(x) Mx$	7, 6, disj. arg.

* It might seem that there are exceptions to this rule. Consider "$(x) Fx \lor (x) Gx$"; can this be rewritten as "$(x) [Fx \lor (x) Gx]$"? This is not an exception, however. The new universal quantification looks odd, but it is perfectly acceptable; in it, the inner quantifier governs the second occurrence of "x," while the outer quantifuer governs only the first occurrence of "x." The formula goes into words as "Each thing is such that either it's an F or everything is G."

9. Ma	8, U.I.
10. $-Ma$	5, conj. simp.
11. Ma & $-Ma$	9, 10, conj. adj.

1. $(x) (Mx \lor B)$ & $-[(x) Mx \lor B]$	Premise
2. $-[(x) Mx \lor B]$	1, conj. simp.
3. $-(x) Mx$ & $-B$	2, De Morgan
4. $-(x) Mx$	3, conj. simp.
5. $(\exists x) -Mx$	4, quant. equiv.
6. $-Ma$	5, E.I.
7. $(x) (Mx \lor B)$	1, conj. simp.
8. $Ma \lor B$	7, U.I.
9. B	6, 8, disjunctive arg.
10. $-B$	3, conj. simp.
11. B & $-B$	9, 10, conj. adj.

Since each can be shown to follow from the other, the sentences are equivalent. Thus our new principle of equivalence has been justified in terms of principles that we already had. We need this new principle, as our method was incomplete without it, but we can see that the idea involved in this principle is derivable from our earlier principles.

Returning now to the example we were considering in the second paragraph of this section, we can carry out the desired deduction fairly easily.

1. $(x) (Sx$ & $-Sx) \lor (y) (Ly$ & $-Ly)$	
2. $(x) [(Sx$ & $-Sx) \lor (y) (Ly$ & $-Ly)]$	From 1 by quant. equiv.
3. $(Sa$ & $-Sa) \lor (y) (Ly$ & $-Ly)$	From 2 by U.I.
4. $(y) [(Sa$ & $-Sa) \lor (Ly$ & $-Ly)]$	From 3 by quant. equiv.
5. $(Sa$ & $-Sa) \lor (La$ & $-La)$	From 4 by U.I.
6. $(Sa$ & $-Sa) \supset (Sa$ & $-Sa)$	Tautology
7. $(La$ & $-La) \supset (Sa$ & $-Sa)$	Tautology
8. Sa & $-Sa$	From 5, 6, 7; dilemma

Here we twice make use of our new principle of quantificational equivalence, first in line 2 and again in line 4. In each case we take a universal quantifier that governed only one component of a disjunction and move it so that it governs the whole disjunction.

Still another kind of example that our method does not yet enable us to handle is illustrated by the sentence "Either something is liquid and is not liquid or something is solid and is not solid," which may be symbolized "$(\exists x) (Lx$ & $-Lx) \lor$

($\exists y$) (Sy & $-Sy$).'' This sentence is a contradiction, but here again we cannot show that it is so, for our rules do not yet enable us to take any useful step beyond the first line. We need one more principle of equivalence.

To understand this last principle of equivalence, consider these sentences:

Either something moves or Zeno's philosophy is correct.
Something is such that either it moves or Zeno's philosophy
   is correct.

Writing "M" for "moves" and "Z" for the whole sentence "Zeno's philosophy is correct," we can symbolize these as follows:

($\exists x$) $Mx \lor Z$
($\exists x$) ($Mx \lor Z$)

The first sentence is a disjunction one component of which is an existential quantification, while the second sentence is an existential quantification of a disjunction. They are equivalent, however, for each is true if and only if either at least one thing moves or Zeno's philosophy is correct. The underlying principle of equivalence here can be stated in general terms: Any disjunction, one part of which is an existential quantification, may be rewritten in the equivalent form of an existential quantification of a disjunction. This principle of equivalence could also be justified in terms of the principles we already have, but we shall not pause to present the two deductions that would be required.

Returning to our example, we now can complete the desired deduction.

1. ($\exists x$) (Lx & $-Lx$) $\lor$
   ($\exists y$) (Sy & $-Sy$)
2. ($\exists x$) [(Lx & $-Lx$) $\lor$ *From 1 by quant. equiv.*
   ($\exists y$) (Sy & $-Sy$)]
3. (La & $-La$) $\lor$ *From 2 by E.I.*
   ($\exists y$) (Sy & $-Sy$)
4. ($\exists y$) [(La & $-La$) $\lor$ *From 3 by quant. equiv.*
   (Sy & $-Sy$)]

5. $(La \& -La) \lor$ *From 4 by E.I.*
 $(Sb \& -Sb)$
6. $(La \& -La) \supset$ *Tautology*
 $(La \& -La)$
7. $(Sb \& -Sb) \supset$ *Tautology*
 $(La \& -La)$
8. $La \& -La$ *From 5, 6, 7; dilemma*

Here we twice make use of our newest principle of quantificational equivalence, first in line 2 and again in line 4. In each case we take an existential quantifier that governed only one component of a disjunction and move it so that it governs the whole disjunction.

These principles of quantificational equivalence for use in deductions involve negation and disjunction, and so by themselves they do not tell us how to deal with lines in which quantifications are linked by the conditional or other truth-functional compounds. However, the conditional or any other truth-functional compound can be equivalently expressed using nothing but conjunction, negation, and disjunction; thus we are able to take the steps we need. For example, the sentence "If everything is liquid or not liquid, then something is solid and not solid" is shown to be a contradiction in the following manner:

1. $(x) (Lx \lor -Lx) \supset$
 $(\exists x) (Sy \& -Sy)$
2. $-(x) (Lx \lor -Lx) \lor$ *From 1 by equivalence*
 $(\exists y) (Sy \& -Sy)$
3. $(\exists y) [-(x) (Lx \lor -Lx) \lor$ *From 2 by quant. equiv.*
 $(Sy \& -Sy)]$
4. $-(x) (Lx \lor -Lx) \lor$ *From 3 by E.I.*
 $(Sa \& -Sa)$
5. $(\exists x) -(Lx \lor -Lx) \lor$ *From 4 by quant. equiv.*
 $(Sa \& -Sa)$
6. $(\exists x) [-(Lx \lor -Lx) \lor$ *From 5 by quant. equiv.*
 $(Sa \& -Sa)]$
7. $-(Lb \lor -Lb) \lor$ *From 6 by E.I.*
 $(Sa \& -Sa)$
8. $(-Lb \& Lb) \lor$ *From 7 by equivalence*
 $(Sa \& -Sa)$

9. $(Sa \ \& -Sa) \supset$ *Tautology*
     $(Sa \ \& -Sa)$
10. $(-Lb \ \& Lb) \supset$ *Tautology*
      $(Sa \ \& -Sa)$
11. $Sa \ \& -Sa$ *From 8, 9, 10; dilemma*

Here we make use of a truth-functional equivalence to obtain line 2 and start the deduction.

In light of what has been said in this section, we can now add two further principles of quantificational equivalence to the list on page 165. These additional principles belong under heading III of the list. It is necessary to mention, however, that in discussing these two principles of equivalence we have taken it for granted that the sentences with which we are concerned do not contain any free variables. These principles would have to be restated in narrower form if they were to hold good for sentences containing free variables, but we are not concerned with that sort of sentence.

Additional principles of quantificational equivalence
3 Any disjunction, one component of which is a universal quantification, may be rewritten in the equivalent form of a universal quantification of a disjunction; e.g., "$(x) Mx \lor B$" is equivalent to "$(x) (Mx \lor B)$."
4 Any disjunction, one component of which is an existential quantification, may be rewritten in the equivalent form of an existential quantification of a disjunction; e.g., "$(\exists x) Mx \lor Z$" is equivalent to "$(\exists x) (Mx \lor Z)$."

A further refinement of our method that could be introduced would streamline our truth-functional steps. Instead of principle I on page 164, we could adopt the principle that we may infer *any* sentence that is truth-functionally implied by one or more preceding sentences. If one decides to use this streamlined rule of truth-functional inference, one must always stand ready to *justify* one's claim that a certain sentence is truth-functionally implied by preceding ones (this can be done by constructing a truth table).

Also, now that we have become fully familiar with the idea underlying the *reductio ad absurdum* approach to deduction, we might allow ourselves to adopt a further slight short cut.

Where we are constructing a deduction to show that a set of two
or more sentences is inconsistent, we may write these sentences
as separate premises at the beginning of the deduction—instead
of always using a single premise that is formed by putting the
sentences into conjunction. This can make our deduction one
or more lines shorter, and will spare us monotonous use of
conjunctive simplification.

EXERCISE 22

A *In each case, construct a deduction showing that a sentence
symbolized in the given way would be a contradiction.*

1 $-[-(x) Ax \lor (y) Ay]$
2 $-[(\exists x) Bx \supset (\exists z) Bz]$
3 $(\exists x) (Ax \supset Ax) \supset (y)-(By \supset By)$
4 $(\exists x) (Ax \lor Bx) \& -(\exists x) (-Bx \supset Ax)$
5 $[(x) (Gx \supset Kx) \supset (\exists x) (Gx \& -Kx)] \& (x) (-Kx \supset -Gx)$

B *Show that these would be contradictions.*

1 $(\exists x)-(Ax \lor -Ax) \equiv (y) (Ay \equiv Ay)$
2 $[(x) (Ax \supset Bx) \& (x) (Cx \supset Ax)] \& (\exists x) (Cx \& -Bx)$
3 $[(\exists y) (Ky \& -Jy) \& (z) (Kz \supset Hz)] \& -(\exists x) (Hx \& -Jx)$
4 $(\exists x) (y) Dxy \& -(y) (\exists x) Dxy$
5 $(\exists x) (y) Kxy \& -(\exists z) Kzz$

† C *Show that these would be contradictions.*

1 $\{(x) (Ax \supset Bx) \& (\exists x) [Ax \& (y) Cyx]\} \& -(\exists z) (Bz \& Czz)$
2 $(\exists x) (y) (z) Dxyz \& -(\exists x) Dxxx$
3 $-\{(x) (\exists y) (Bx \supset Cxy) \lor (\exists x) [Bx \& -(\exists y) Cxy]\}$
4 $(x) [Ax \supset (\exists y) Cxy] \equiv (\exists z) [Az \& (y) -Czy]$
5 $(\exists x) [Bx \& (y) -By] \lor (z) [Bz \& -(\exists y) By]$

NEGATIVE DEMONSTRATIONS

The method of quantificational deduction that we have been
using is basically a method for bringing out contradictions. We
have been using it also to establish the validity of quantificational
arguments and to detect necessarily true quantificational sentences. But can this method be used to demonstrate that a

quantificational sentence is *not* a contradiction (and thereby that an argument is not valid or a sentence not necessarily true in virtue of its quantificational form)? In one special kind of case it is possible to do so: Specifically, if it can be shown that the negation of a sentence is a contradiction, this will suffice to demonstrate that the given sentence is not a contradiction. However, suppose we start with a sentence that is not a contradiction and whose negation is not a contradiction either. Can we demonstrate that a sentence of this kind is not a contradiction? The mere fact that we have tried to deduce a truth-functional contradiction from it and have not been successful does not prove that there is no contradiction; perhaps we have not worked intelligently enough. Our method of deduction simply does not offer a general way of demonstrating the negative fact that a quantificational sentence is not a contradiction.

Consider the sentence "There is something that is a unicorn only if it is herbivorous, and all unicorns are nonherbivorous." It may be symbolized "$(\exists x)(Ux \supset Hx)$ & $(x)(Ux \supset -Hx)$." Suppose we want to learn whether it is a contradiction. If we try to use our method of deduction, we find that even after working long and hard we do not deduce a truth-functional contradiction. But this lack of success means merely that we have established nothing. Can we show more definitely that the sentence is not a contradiction?

If a sentence of the form "$(\exists x)(Ux \supset Hx)$ & $(x)(Ux \supset -Hx)$" is not a contradiction, this means that some sentences of this form are true. If we find at least one sentence of this form that is definitely true, we shall thereby demonstrate that our original sentence is not a contradiction. Or, to put it more accurately, we shall have demonstrated that our original sentence is not a contradiction on account of having this quantificational form; we have not dealt with and have not removed the possibility that it might be a contradiction for some other reason, although in this example there is no other reason that merits consideration.*

---

* Being a contradiction on account of its quantificational form is a sufficient though not a necessary condition for a sentence's being a contradiction. A sentence like "Some wealthy persons are not rich" is a contradiction even though its quantificational form—presumably, "$(\exists x)(Wx \& -Rx)$"—is not what makes it so.

Let us try then to discover a sentence of this same form that is very clearly true. This can best be done if we seek a sentence dealing with things concerning which very clear and definite assertions can be made. Numbers are probably the best subject matter for this purpose. Let us see whether we can discover a way of *reinterpreting* the letters "U" and "H" so that "$(\exists x)(Ux \supset Hx) \,\&\, (x)(Ux \supset -Hx)$" becomes a true sentence about numbers. Let us reinterpret "U" to mean "odd" and "H" to mean "even," and limit our universe of discourse to numbers. Under this reinterpretation, "$(\exists x)(Ux \supset Hx) \,\&\, (x)(Ux \supset -Hx)$" turns into the sentence "There is at least one number such that if it is odd then it is even, and every number is such that if it is odd then it is not even." (Here we are thinking of numbers as being the only objects under discussion; we are limiting our 'universe of discourse' to numbers.) This sentence is a conjunction, and its first component is definitely true since there is at least one number, for instance 2, such that if it is odd then it is even. (Remember that this is the truth-functional sense of "if-then.") The second component of the conjunction is definitely true too, since no odd numbers are even. Thus the sentence as a whole is definitely true. This shows that our original sentence is not a contradiction (at least, not on account of its quantificational form).

So far, we have discussed a procedure for showing that a quantificational sentence is not a contradiction. This same procedure can be employed to show that an argument is not valid in virtue of its quantificational form. For example, suppose the question is whether the argument "Everything attracts something; therefore something is attracted by everything," symbolized as "$(x)(\exists y)\,Axy$, therefore $(\exists y)(x)\,Axy$," is valid. We can show that it is an invalid argument if a reinterpretation of "A" can turn the premise into a definitely true sentence and turn the conclusion into a definitely false one.

To do this, let us again talk about numbers, and let us think of numbers as being the only things to which we shall refer for the moment. (We limit our 'universe of discourse' to numbers.) Let us reinterpret "A" to mean "is smaller than." Then "$(x)(\exists y)\,Axy$" comes to mean "Each number is smaller than some number," while "$(\exists y)(x)\,Axy$" becomes "There is a number than which every number is smaller." The former sentence is definitely true whereas the latter is definitely false, thus showing the invalidity of the original argument, or, more accurately, showing that the original argument is not valid on account of its quantificational form.

Finally, we shall note one further sort of negative result that can be established by this procedure of reinterpreting quantificational sentences. Suppose the question now is whether two quantificational sentences are equivalent. Consider, for example, the sentences:

> If something is not for the best, then Leibniz's philosophy is mistaken.
> Something is such that if it is not for the best then Leibniz's philosophy is mistaken.

Writing "B" for "is for the best" and "L" for the sentence "Leibniz's philosophy is mistaken," we can symbolize these:

> $(\exists x) - Bx \supset L$
> $(\exists x) (-Bx \supset L)$

Perhaps we can start by trying to demonstrate that the two sentences are equivalent. To say that two sentences are equivalent is to say that they are necessarily alike as regards truth and falsity. This means that each must validly follow from the other. We could attempt to construct two deductions, one showing that the first sentence validly follows from the second, and another showing that the second sentence validly follows from the first. In this case, however, we would be unable to complete both deductions. Encountering difficulty, we could change our approach and seek to show instead that the two sentences are not equivalent. How can we do this?

One way of showing that they are not equivalent is to reinterpret the letters "B" and "L" so that we obtain two new sentences having the very same forms but definitely differing as regards truth and falsity. In doing this, let us again work with numbers. Reinterpret "B" to mean "is even" and reinterpret "L" to mean "2 is smaller than 1." Then we obtain two new sentences:

> If something is not an even number, then 2 is smaller than 1.
> Something is such that if it is not an even number then 2 is smaller than 1.

The first sentence is definitely false because it is a conditional with true antecedent and false consequent. The second sentence is definitely true because there is at least one thing, say the number 4, such that if it is not an even number then 2 is smaller than 1. (Here again we recall the truth-functional sense of "if-then.") Thus we have found two sentences definitely different as regards truth and falsity but having the very same forms as the original two sentences. This shows that our original two sentences are not equivalent; at any rate, they are not equivalent in virtue of their quantificational form.

In trying to work out a negative demonstration like this, it is usually good strategy to try to interpret the conclusion first, and then the premises, when dealing with an argument.

EXERCISE 23

* **A** *Show that sentences of each of the following forms are not contradictions on account of their quantificational form.*

1 (x) (Fx ⊃ Gx)
2 (∃x) Fx & (∃x) −Fx
3 (∃x) (Fx & Gx) & (∃x) (Fx & −Gx)
4 (x) (−Gx ⊃ Gx)
5 (∃x) (Fx ⊃ −Fx)
6 (∃x) (∃y) Rxy & −(x) (∃y) Rxy

B *Show that arguments of the following forms are not valid on account of their quantificational form.*

1 (∃x) (∃y) Rxy; therefore (∃x) (y) Rxy
2 (x) [(Fx & Gx) ⊃ Hx]; therefore (x) [(Fx ∨ Gx) ⊃ Hx]
3 (x) Fx ⊃ (∃y) Gy; therefore (x) [Fx ⊃ (∃y) Gy]
4 (x) Fx ⊃ (∃y) Gy; therefore Fa ⊃ (∃y) Gy
5 [(x) (Dx ⊃ Kx) & (x) (Dx ⊃ Jx)]; therefore (∃x) (Jx & Kx)
6 (x) [Ax ⊃ (∃y) Bxy]; therefore (∃x)[Ax & (y)Bxy]

C *Show that each of the following statements is correct.*

1 Sentences of the forms "(x) (∃y) Rxy" and "(x)−(∃y) Rxy" are not contradictories of each other.
2 Sentences of the form "(x) (∃y) Rxy ∨ (x) (∃y) − Rxy" are not necessarily true.
3 The following regulations of Warren G. Harding University do not involve a contradiction:

Students who study the same subject must not room together. Every student who is a dormitory resident must have a roommate.

No law student may have a roommate who is studying a different subject than he is.

4 Even if each thing has a purpose, it does not follow that there is a purpose which all things have.

5 Even if each road leads to some places, it does not follow that each place is reached by a road.

6 Even if everyone prefers some persons to others, it does not follow that there is anyone whom everyone prefers to anyone.

† **D** *Determine whether each argument is valid.*

1 Every type of rock is either igneous, sedimentary, or metamorphic. Each geologist investigates some type of rock. Therefore, some geologist investigates rocks of the sedimentary type.

2 Every idealist is more interested in metaphysics than is any positivist. Schopenhauer was an idealist and Comte was a positivist. So Schopenhauer was more interested in metaphysics than was Comte.

3 Any railway unit that carries a payload must be propelled by something. A railway unit is a locomotive if and only if it propels itself and does not carry a payload. Therefore, every railway unit that carries a payload must be propelled by a locomotive.

4 If one hospital has a lower rate of occupancy than another, its costs per patient will be higher. If one hospital has higher costs per patient than another, its charges will have to be higher. So if one hospital has a lower rate of occupancy than another, its charges will have to be higher.

5 A man who does not respect himself is not respected by anyone. No woman loves a man she does not respect. Therefore, no woman loves a man who does not respect himself.

6 Whatever is, cannot be permanent if that in which it exists is not permanent. . . . Truth remains [i.e., is permanent] even when true things perish. Truth, therefore, does not exist in mortal things. But it must exist somewhere. There are, therefore, immortal things. But nothing is true in which Truth does not exist. Therefore, only immortal things are true. AUGUSTINE, *Soliloquies*

CHAPTER 5

FALLACIES

Logicians normally give their attention to logically correct types of reasoning and do not devote much effort to cataloguing the myriad forms of logical error, for the former prove to be of much greater theoretical interest than the latter. When we are concerned with the practical aspect of logic, however, some discussion of logical errors is very worthwhile. The efficient way of improving one's ability to tell the difference between good and bad reasoning is to look at tempting examples of the bad as well as the good.

INCONSISTENCY, PETITIO, AND THE PURE NON SEQUITUR

A *fallacy* is a logical mistake in reasoning. The term "fallacy" is often loosely applied to any sort of mistaken belief or untrue sentence. "It's a fallacy to believe that handling a toad causes warts," people say; here the thing being called a fallacy is just a belief, not an inference. In logic the term "fallacy" is restricted to mistakes in reasoning. When there are premises and a conclusion that through some logical error is mistakenly thought to be proved by them, then and only then is there a fallacy in the logical sense. Innumerable kinds of logical mistakes can be made in reasoning. Some kinds are more tempting and more likely to deceive than others, and many of these have specific names.

The great advantage of a name for something is that it enables us to keep the thing clearly in mind and helps us recognize it when we meet it. In this sense, knowing the name gives us a sort of power over the thing. By learning the names of some of the commoner kinds of fallacies and by having a general scheme for classifying them, we are able to recognize fallacies more readily and think more clearly about them.

Classification of Fallacies

In order to have a definite scheme for thinking about fallacies, we shall classify them in terms of the headings shown in the following table. It embodies some of the traditional terminology for fallacies, but in reorganized form. This classification covers fallacies in both deductive and inductive reasoning, although for the present we shall limit our examples to fallacies that arise in deductive reasoning.

In thinking about the classification of fallacies, let us recall that the purpose of constructing arguments is to prove conclusions that are in some way unknown or doubtful or that have been challenged and called into question. A speaker can have a chance of proving his conclusion only if his argument employs premises that (1) are logically capable of all being true, (2) are such that the speaker and his hearers can know them to be true without being aware of whether the conclusion is true, and (3) support the conclusion to the required degree—with deductive arguments the premises must strictly guarantee the conclusion. The neglect of any one of these three requirements for a successful proof gives rise to a separate category of fallacies.

Neglect of the third requirement gives rise to the fallacies of *non sequitur* (Latin: "it does not follow"). These fallacious arguments are fallacies in the most obvious sense of the term, for their logical defect is that they have an insufficient link between premises and conclusion.

Neglect of the second requirement gives rise to reasoning that is fallacious in a more subtle sense. If the premises are related to the conclusion in such an intimate way that the speaker and his hearers could not have less reason to doubt the premises than they have to doubt the conclusion, then the argument is worthless as a proof, even though the link between premises and

Classification of Fallacies

General type			Some specific forms
Inconsistency			⋮
Petitio principii			Fallacy of complex question ⋮
Non sequitur	*Pure fallacies*	*Formal fallacies in deduction*	Undistributed middle Illicit process Affirming the consequent Denying the antecedent ⋮
		Pure inductive fallacies	Forgetful induction Hasty induction Slothful induction
	Fallacies of ambiguity	*Equivocation*	Fallacy of four terms Composition, division ⋮
		Amphiboly	⋮
	Fallacies of irrelevance (ignoratio elenchi)		ad hominem abusive circumstantial tu quoque ad baculum ad verecundiam ad misericordiam black-and-white thinking ⋮

conclusion may have the most cast-iron rigor. Fallacies of this second category are called fallacies of *petitio principii* (Latin: "begging of the question").

Finally, neglect of the first requirement gives rise to the remaining category of fallacies. If someone uses as premises sentences that are logically related in such a way that they necessarily could not all be true at once, then his reasoning certainly cannot establish his conclusion, even though the link between premises and conclusion is as rigorous as can be. When someone reasons from such a set of premises, he is committing a fallacy of *inconsistency*.

Using our scheme for classifying fallacies, we shall have to keep in mind that sometimes a fallacious argument may allow of being interpreted in more than one way so that its fallacy can be classified in more than one way. Perhaps when interpreted in one fashion it commits one fallacy, while under some other legitimate interpretation it would be regarded as committing some different fallacy. (We shall meet examples of this sort presently.) But every fallacious argument should admit of being classified in at least one place in our scheme. Also we should note that an argument may fall under some general heading without being an example of any specifically named form of fallacy under that heading; the dots at various places in the table indicate where there are further specific types of fallacies, many of them without special names.

Although we have been concentrating so far on deductive reasoning, it should be noted that inductive reasoning can be subject to fallacies of inconsistency, of begging the question, of ambiguity, and of irrelevance, just as deductive reasoning can. Only with regard to the pure fallacies do we need to treat induction and deduction separately, as we shall see.

Inconsistency

Suppose someone reasons in the following way: "Franklin is 20 miles due north of Jefferson. There is a straight road that starts at Franklin and goes through Adamston to Sperryville. Jefferson is 20 miles due west of Adamston. Sperryville is northeast of Adamston. Therefore, Jefferson is nearer to Adamston than to Sperryville."

There is something wrong with this argument, even though the speaker may not have noticed it. The trouble here is not that there is any insufficiency about the link between premises and conclusion; instead, the trouble is with the premises themselves. They cannot all be true. Now, to use premises that are not all true is always a mistake, but it is not always a logical mistake. In this case, however, the premises do not merely happen to be not all true; they necessarily cannot all be true, so we may say that here a logical error is being committed and thus a fallacy is occurring. In this example, one can see that something is logically wrong if one notices that the stated premises imply pairs of consequences that are contradictories; for example, they imply both "Sperryville is southeast of Adamston" and "Sperryville is not southeast of Adamston." Thus one would be contradicting oneself if one accepted all four of these premises. To use this argument is to commit a logical error, a fallacy of inconsistency. In general, anyone commits a fallacy of inconsistency if he reasons from premises that necessarily could not all be true because they logically imply contradictory consequences.

Sometimes inconsistency in the premises of an argument is brought about by the logical forms of the premises. For example, if you have one premise of the form "p" and another of the form "$-p$," you have a formal inconsistency; if you have one premise of the form "$p \ \& \ q$" and another of the form "$p \equiv -q$," again you have a formal inconsistency; and so on. However, not all inconsistency results merely from logical form. In the geographical example of the first paragraph, the mere logical forms of the premises do not give rise to an inconsistency; the inconsistency results from the special meanings of particular nonlogical words ("straight," "north," "west," etc.) occurring as they do in the premises.

Should we say that arguments are invalid when their premises are inconsistent? No, for the following reason. If the premises form an inconsistent set, this means either that one premise is the negation of another, or that there is some consequence which follows from the premises but whose negation also follows from them. So either among the premises or implied by them, we have both "p" and "$-p$." If we have both "p" and "$-p$," what else can be deduced? Consider the following deduction.

1. p Premise
2. $-p$ Premise
3. $p \lor q$ From 1, by disjunctive addition
4. q From 2, 3 by disjunctive argument

Here each step is strictly legitimate, according to our principles of truth-functional deduction. The conclusion "q" can be any new sentence we please. And what this deduction illustrates is that *any* sentence deductively follows from a pair of contradictory sentences. Thus, if we have both "p" and "$-p$" either among our premises or implied by them, any conclusion whatsoever validly follows. Thus arguments which commit the fallacy of inconsistency at any rate have the virtue of being valid—although this is not enough to make them good arguments.

The Petitio Principii

An argument is called a *petitio principii* (or begging of the question) if the argument fails to prove anything because it somehow takes for granted what it is supposed to prove. Suppose someone says "Jones is insane, you know," and we reply "Really? Are you sure?" and he responds, "Certainly, I can prove it. Jones is demented; therefore he is insane." This is a valid argument in the sense that if the premise is true, the conclusion must be true too; but the argument is unsatisfactory, for it does not really prove anything. The premise is merely another statement of the conclusion, so that anyone who doubts the truth of the conclusion surely ought to be equally doubtful about the truth of the premise, and the argument would be valueless for the purpose of convincing him of the truth of the conclusion. Thus the argument takes for granted just what it is supposed to prove; it begs the question.

Consider a longer chain of reasoning:

"We must not drink liquor."
"Why do you say that?"
"Drinking is against the will of Allah."
"How do you know?"
"The Koran says so."
"But how do you know that the Koran is right?"
"Everything said in the Koran is right."
"How do you know that?"
"Why, it's all divinely inspired."
"But how do you know?"
"Why, the Koran itself declares that it is divinely inspired."
"But why believe that?"
"You've got to believe the Koran, because everything in the Koran is right."

This chain of reasoning is a more extended case of begging the question; the speaker is reasoning in a large circle, taking for granted one of the things that he professes to be proving.

One specific form of *petitio principii,* or begging of the question, has a special name of its own: the fallacy of *complex question.* This is the fallacy of framing a question so as to take for granted something controversial that ought to be proved.

Suppose Mr. White is trying to prove that Mr. Black has a bad character, and White asks Black the famous question "Have you stopped beating your wife yet?" If Black answers "Yes" to this question, White will argue that Black is admitting to having been a wife-beater; if he answers "No," then White will argue that Black is admitting to still being a wife-beater. The questioner has framed his question in such a way as to take for granted that Black has a wife whom he has been beating. The fallacy is that this is a controversial proposition that is at least as doubtful as is the conclusion (that Black has a bad character) supposedly being established. It is not proper in this debate to take for granted this controversial proposition; it needs to be proved if White is to make use of it at all.

However, it would also be legitimate to regard the fallacy of complex question as a kind of fallacy of ambiguity. In the example we could say that the answer "No" is ambiguous, for it could mean either "No, I'm still beating my wife" or "No, I haven't stopped because I never started."

An argument committing the fallacy of begging the question usually does so on account of its premises. Thus far in our discussion we have spoken as though that were the only way in which this fallacy could be committed. However, it also is possible for an argument to beg the question in a subtler way, on account of its logical form. Such arguments rarely occur in ordinary discourse, but they are of philosophical interest.

Suppose someone argues: "All syllogisms conforming to the five rules of the syllogism are valid; some syllogisms conforming to the five rules are in the mood **AII**, third figure; therefore, some syllogisms in the mood **AII**, third figure, are valid." Here there is nothing especially objectionable about the premises. But the peculiarity is that the argument itself is in the mood **AII**, third figure. Consequently anyone who has any doubt about the truth of the conclusion ought to be at least equally doubtful about the validity of this argument. Hence the argument is ineffectual for proving its conclusion and deserves to be classified as a *petitio principii*.

The Non Sequitur: Pure Fallacies

We call an argument a *non sequitur* if its conclusion does not follow from its premises. The fallacies of *non sequitur* form the largest category, which we shall subdivide into three types. First we shall consider what, for want of a better name, may be called *pure fallacies*. These are *non sequitur* fallacies in which the source of the error is purely some misunderstanding of specific logical principles themselves. The principles of deductive reasoning are distinctly different from those of inductive reasoning. Therefore, in treating this type of fallacy, we need to classify the deductive and the inductive cases separately; this is not necessary with regard to the other sorts of fallacy. For the present, we shall not discuss the inductive cases of pure fallacies but shall focus our attention upon the deductive cases.

The specific logical principles with which deductive logic deals are principles that have to do with the logical forms of sentences. Therefore, pure fallacies in deduction are *formal* fallacies. That is, they are *non sequiturs* because of defects in their logical form. The victim of such a fallacy commits a logical error because he mistakenly supposes that the form is valid. He symbolizes the argument correctly (if he is using symbols). His mistake is not that of misinterpreting what logical form the argument has (as would be the case if he symbolized the argument incorrectly)—instead, his mistake is that of believing the logical form to be deductively valid when it is not. Thus, for example, when people are taken in by the fallacy of affirming the consequent, the likeliest source of their confusion is failure to notice that this form, unlike modus ponens, is invalid.

A more complicated example occurs if someone argues: "If men are not really evil, then it is unnecessary to have police to prevent crime. And if men are really evil, then police will be ineffectual in preventing crime. Now, either men are not evil or they are evil. Therefore, police are either unnecessary or ineffectual." The argument is in the form of a valid dilemma, but even though the dilemma is valid, there is something amiss about the thinking here. The trouble is that the third premise is an absurd oversimplification; it is absurd to believe that either all men are free of evil or that all men are full of evil. But what would lead anyone to accept a premise like this? By what sort of reasoning would one arrive at the premise itself? The line of thought leading to the third premise can best be regarded as committing a formal fallacy. The fallacy lies in thinking that from the necessary truth "Every man is such that either he is evil or he is not evil" we may validly infer "Either every man is evil or every man is not evil." It is the formal fallacy of supposing that from a universal sentence whose parts are disjunctions, we may infer a corresponding disjunction both of whose parts are universal. This is a mistake arising from misunderstanding a specific principle about logical form.

Notice that fallacies of inconsistency do not ordinarily arise in this way. Ordinarily, a person who uses inconsistent premises simply has not noticed that one premise contradicts another; his mistake results from an oversight, rather than from actually employing some incorrect logical principle. Similarly, fallacies of begging the question also ordinarily result from sheer oversight, rather than from employing some incorrect logical principle.

EXERCISE 24

Identify, explain, and discuss any fallacies that are present in the following examples.

1 All chows have black tongues. Poodles are not a kind of chow. Therefore, no poodles have black tongues.
2 Shoplifting is an immoral activity. The reason why is that shoplifting is not ethically permissible.
3 Well-behaved children are welcome in this restaurant. It follows that ill-behaved children are unwelcome in this restaurant.
4 Tan ah Tiat, forty-nine years old, a native of Kuala Lumpur, Malaysia, was charged with possession of opium. Arguing for acquittal, he told the judge that his opium habit did no harm, as he was too old to work anyway. Asked how he lived, he replied that he lived on the earnings of his grandmother.
5 Of course she likes me. She told me that she does, and she wouldn't lie to me about it, for she always tells the truth to people she likes.
6 Recently we interviewed 147 local voters to find out their opinions of how the President is handling his job. Of these, 113 approved his handling of domestic affairs, 89 approved his handling of foreign affairs, and 51 approved of both. We conclude that a majority of these voters approve of the President's handling of his job.
7 I'm in favor of free enterprise in the economic area. This is

because I support individual rights to life, liberty, and property. However, I believe that there should be military conscription, because the policy of all-volunteer armed forces is unsatisfactory.

8   Railway passenger service must be further curtailed, unless larger subsidies are forthcoming. Since service must be further curtailed, we may conclude that larger subsidies have not been forthcoming.

9   Everything that is in motion must be moved by something else. If therefore the thing which causes it to move be in motion, this too must be moved by something else, and so on. But we cannot proceed to infinity in this way, because in that case there would be no first mover, and in consequence neither would there be any other mover; for secondary movers do not cause movement except they be moved by a first mover, as, for example, a stick cannot cause movement unless it is moved by the hand. Therefore it is necessary to stop at some first mover which is moved by nothing else. And this is what we all understand God to be.

ST. THOMAS AQUINAS, *Summa Theologica*

10   Now you might ask: When is the will right? The will is unimpaired and right when it is entirely free from self-seeking, and when it has forsaken itself and is formed and transformed into the will of God, indeed, the more it is so, the more the will is right and true.

MEISTER ECKHART, *Treatises and Sermons*

FALLACIES OF AMBIGUITY AND IRRELEVANCE

So far, we have considered fallacies of *non sequitur* in which the logical form is at fault. A quite different sort of *non sequitur* occurs when we make the mistake of incorrectly interpreting what logical form an argument has. The language in which the argument is expressed leads us to misunderstand the logical structure of the argument; we incorrectly translate the argument into a valid form, when actually its form is invalid. We shall distinguish between two different ways in which the language of an argument may tempt us to make this mistake.

Perhaps some one word or phrase in the argument is used in two different senses. In this case, if we do not notice these different senses, we may carelessly assume that they are the same; thus we misinterpret the logical form of the argument. It is called a fallacy of *equivocation* if some definite word or phrase is ambiguous.

Some fallacies of equivocation have special names of their own. In an argument that is intended to be a syllogism but that really contains four terms instead of three, we have the *fallacy of four terms*. For example, the argument "No designing persons are to be trusted; architects are people who make designs; therefore, architects are not to be trusted" is a crude specimen of this fallacy. Here the terms "designing person" and "person who makes designs" are used by the speaker as if they meant the same, but of course they do not have the same sense at all; the first term refers to people who hatch evil schemes, while the second refers to people who draw blueprints. The argument is intended to be a syllogism but is not really one, for it has no middle term. In this example the equivocation is very obvious and the fallacy easy to detect, but sometimes fallacies of this sort are more hidden and insidious.

Next we shall consider the fallacies of *composition* and *division*, two special forms of equivocation that involve an improper sort of reasoning from part to whole or from whole to part. This may occur in syllogisms or in other kinds of argument.

Suppose someone reasons: "No man can sing as loud as an organ plays; the glee club are men; therefore, the glee club cannot sing as loud as an organ plays." This is intended to be a syllogism of the form **EAE** in the first figure. If it really were **EAE** in the first figure, it would have to be valid. Since it certainly is not valid, something is wrong. The second premise talks about the glee club *distributively*; that is, it says something about individual members of the glee club considered singly (that each individual member is a man). The conclusion, however, talks about the members of the glee club *collectively*; that is, it says something about the members of the glee club considered as a whole unit, not about each of them considered singly.

This argument cannot correctly be translated into a syllogism, for we cannot word it so as to consist of categorical sentences containing just three terms. If we put the premises into categorical form, they become "No men are singers louder than organs" and "All groups identical to the glee club are groups consisting of men," with more than three terms; if we use just three terms, we cannot put the premises into categorical form. The equivocation between "the glee club" understood distributively and "the glee club" understood collectively causes the speaker to reason fallaciously from a fact about individual members of the group to a conclusion about the group as a unit. This is called the *fallacy of composition*.

To be sure, another possible interpretation would be to regard the fallacy of composition as a formal fallacy. It would be a formal fallacy if the speaker were clear about how to symbolize the argument correctly but thought it a valid logical principle that whatever holds true of each member of a group must hold true also of the group considered as a whole. If this is what he thinks, his mistake is caused by a pure misunderstanding of logical principles, and he is committing a pure formal fallacy rather than a fallacy of equivocation.

A kindred example is this: "Accidents are frequent; getting struck by lightning is an accident; therefore getting struck by lightning is frequent." Here again we have an argument probably intended to be a valid syllogism, but it is invalid, and the mistake is most likely a case of equivocation. The trouble is that the first premise talks about accidents collectively; it says that the whole class of accidents is a class such that at almost any moment some of its members are occurring. The second premise, however, talks about accidents distributively, for it says that each individual case of getting struck by lightning is an individual case of an accident. Here equivocation arises because the word "accidents" is used in these two senses, collective and distributive. This causes the speaker to reason fallaciously from a fact about the whole to a conclusion about a part. This is called the *fallacy of division*.* Notice, however, that it is not always fallacious to reason from part to whole or

---

* The fallacy of division also could occur in such a way as to be a formal fallacy. It would be a formal fallacy if the speaker is clear about what the premises say but thinks it a valid logical principle that whatever holds true of a group considered as a whole must hold true also of each part of that group. Then the mistake would be caused by a pure misunderstanding of logical principles.

from whole to part; normal valid syllogisms in a sense do this and do it legitimately. The fallacies of composition and division are improper because, when they do this, they confuse the collective with the distributive sense of terms.

Another fallacy of equivocation may be called *illicit obversion*. It arises when terms that are not really negations of one another are used as though they were. If someone reasons "All child-murderers are inhuman; therefore no child-murderers are human," he is guilty of this fallacy. The example purports to be obversion but it is not correct obversion, for the predicate has not really been negated. The term "human" is not the negation (or contradictory) of the term "inhuman," for "inhuman" means cruel rather than nonhuman. If we correctly obverted the sentence "All child-murderers are inhuman" we would get "No child-murderers are noninhuman." It would be the same type of fallacy if someone were to argue "No rocks are alive; therefore all rocks are dead." Here again the obversion is incorrect, for "alive" and "dead" are not contradictory terms; instead they are merely contraries.

In general, two terms are *contradictories* (or negations) of each other if and only if one or the other but not both of the terms must apply to each thing; while two terms are *contraries* of each other if and only if at most one of them applies to each thing and neither applies to some things. The terms "alive" and "dead" are contraries rather than contradictories because there are some things, such as rocks, that are neither alive nor dead. (To call a thing dead is to imply that it once was alive.) The proper contradictory of "alive" is "lifeless," and so the sentence "No rocks are alive" has as its correct obverse "All rocks are lifeless."

Another logically interesting kind of equivocation arises from confusion about the distinction between words and what they represent. Were someone to argue: "Much ancient history is contained in the Bible; the Bible is a phrase of eight letters; therefore, much ancient history is contained in a phrase of eight letters," he would be making a crude mistake of this kind. The trouble is that the first premise talks about (mentions) the Bible, a lengthy book, whereas the second premise talks about (mentions) the words "The Bible," a short phrase. The argument is confusing because it is written in such a way as to use the very same two-word expression to mention the book and to mention the name of the book. We can avoid this sort of confusion if we form the habit of using quotation marks when we want to mention words. Let us always write:

"The Bible" is a phrase of eight letters.

instead of:

The Bible is a phrase of eight letters.

If we follow this practice, we shall be less likely to confuse the name of a thing with the thing itself.

There are far too many kinds of equivocation to discuss them all, but we shall consider one more kind, which arises from confusion among the various senses of the verb "to be." The sense of "is" and "are" with which we have mainly been concerned is the sense in which these verbs are used for *predication,* that is, when the verb is followed by a general term, as in "Bread is starchy" or "Crows are raucous." Here we are simply attributing some property to something. There is a second important sense of "to be," however, in which it means *identity.* In this sense the verb is followed by a singular term, as in "Boise is Idaho's capital" or "12 is the sum of 5 and 7." Here "is" means absolute identity; Boise is the very same city as Idaho's capital, and 12 is the very same number as the sum of 5 and 7. Some famous confusions in philosophy have arisen from neglecting this distinction.

The forms of inference that are valid with the "is" of identity differ, of course, from those which hold for the "is" of predication. Three usually valid forms of inference employing the "is" of identity are the following:

Forms of identity reasoning

$x = y$	e.g., Scott is the author of *Waverly.*
Fx	Scot wrote *Ivanhoe.*
$\therefore Fy$	Therefore the author of *Waverly* wrote *Ivanhoe.*

$x = y$	e.g., Boise is Idaho's capital.
$\therefore y = x$	Therefore Idaho's capital is Boise.

$$x = y$$
$$y = z$$
$$\therefore x = z$$

e.g., Boise is Idaho's capital.
Idaho's capital is Idaho's largest city.
Therefore Boise is Idaho's largest city.

The first of these three forms involves the principle that whatever is true of a thing must also be true of anything identical to it. The second involves the principle of the symmetry of identity, the principle that an identity sentence remains true when its items are transposed. The third involves the principle of the transitivity of identity, the principle that when the identity relation holds between a first thing and a second and between a second and a third, then it must hold also between the first and the third.

For the sake of accuracy, we must notice that the first of these three forms of identity reasoning is not valid without qualification. For ordinary cases it is valid, but there are three types of exceptions.

1. One type of exception arises when the name in the second premise is mentioned rather than used. For example, it would be invalid to argue.

Boise is Idaho's capital.
"Boise" is a five-letter word.
Therefore Idaho's capital is a five-letter word.

2. Further exceptions arise when the name occurs in the second premise within a sentence saying that something is necessary, not necessary, possible, not possible, or the like. Thus it would be invalid to argue:

Nine is the number of planets.
Nine is necessarily greater than seven.
Therefore, the number of planets is necessarily greater than seven.

Also belonging to this group of exceptions are kindred cases where the second premise declares that something is provable or unprovable in a certain way, knowable or unknowable by certain means, and the like.

3. Still further exceptions can arise when the name occurs in the second premise within the scope of a verb that expresses some psychological attitude such as believing, desiring, fearing, or the like. Suppose someone argues:

Matilda is Hugo's future wife.
Hugo fears that Matilda will reject his proposal of marriage.
Therefore Hugo fears that his future wife will reject his proposal of marriage.

If the conclusion is understood as telling what it is that Hugo is fearful of (and this is the most straightforward way of understanding it), then the argument is definitely fallacious. But aside from these three types of exceptions, this form of identity reasoning is reliable.

These forms of identity reasoning are clear enough and simple enough so that fallacies are not likely to arise in connection with them except when there is misunderstanding regarding the sense of the verb "to be." But suppose someone were to reason as follows: "Time is money; time is measured in seconds; and so money is measured in seconds." This argument is intended to be a case of the first of the three forms of identity reasoning, and so it has a confusing air of correctness about it. But the fallacy arises because the first occurrence of "is" in this argument is not the true "is" of identity. When we say "Time is money," we do not mean that time is just the same thing as money; we mean only that time is as good as money or that time can be exchanged for money. Here the word "is" is used in a metaphorical sense which is strictly neither the "is" of predication nor the "is" of identity.

Again, suppose that someone argues: "God is love; love is an emotion; therefore God is an emotion." Again the argument apes our first form of identity reasoning. Here too the fallacy is one of equivocation, for the premise "God is love" probably is not meant as an identity sentences. People who say "God is love" probably mean that God personifies love or exhibits love; again the "is" is used in some metaphorical sense. The moral of this is that we must be alert against fallacies arising from confusion among the different senses of "to be."

So far in this section, we have been considering equivocation, the type of ambiguity arising when a single word or phrase is used in more than one sense. We shall conclude our discussion of ambiguity by noting that sometimes the logical form of an argument is misinterpreted not because any single word is ambiguous but because the grammar of a whole sentence is ambiguous and allows of more than one interpretation. This type of ambiguity traditionally has been called *amphiboly*. An example occurs in Shakespeare's *Henry VI* when the spirit prophesies "The Duke yet lives that Henry shall depose." Henry infers from this prophecy that he is going to depose a duke. However, a better conclusion to have inferred would have been that a duke was going to depose Henry. (It is easier for a prophet to stay in business if he makes his predictions amphibolous.)

Throughout this section we have been considering logical mistakes that can arise from ambiguity. It would be incorrect, however, to conclude that ambiguity is always bad. Ambiguous language sometimes has a vivid flavor which can be admirable, if we are not misled by it. Ambiguity, like vagueness, is objectionable only insofar as it confuses people and causes them to commit fallacies in their reasoning.

In the remainder of this section, let us turn to the third and last kind of fallacy of *non sequitur.*

The third kind of *non sequitur* arises when something about an argument tempts us simply to overlook the fact that there really is no connection between the premises and the conclusion. The argument excites us somehow, and we are misled into thinking that the premises support the conclusion, when actually they have nothing to do with the point supposedly being proved. Fallacies of this sort are called *fallacies of irrelevance,* or fallacies of *ignoratio elenchi* (Latin and Greek: "ignorance of the refutation").

One important type of fallacy of this kind is the *ad hominem* fallacy. An argument is *ad hominem* (Latin: "to the man") if it is directed at an opponent in a controversy rather than being directly relevant to proving the conclusion under discussion. Such arguments are often, but not always, fallacious. For example, suppose someone argues: "Of course Karl Marx must have been mistaken in maintaining that capitalism is an evil form of economic and social organization, bound to harm the working class. Why, he was a miserable failure of a man who couldn't even earn enough money to support his family." This is an *ad hominem* argument, for it attacks Marx the man instead of offering direct reasons why his views are incorrect. And it is a fallacy because the premise does not really establish the conclusion at all. This is the *abusive* form of the *ad hominem* argument.

Another form of the *ad hominem* argument occurs if a speaker produces reasons why his opponent might be expected to believe the conclusion, rather than reasons why the conclusion is true. Suppose members of Congress are debating whether the United States should permit localities to tax church buildings at their fair market value. Senator Brown happens to be religious but supports the proposal, while Senator Green, who is not, opposes it. Suppose Senator Green argues with Senator Brown, saying, "This proposal would harm religion, which you support, so that ought to prove to you that it's a bad proposal." Here Green is appealing to religious principles in which he himself does not believe; he has not offered any direct reason why the proposal is bad but instead has given a reason why Brown might have been expected to regard the proposal as bad. This is called the *circumstantial* form of the *ad hominem* argument.

A third form of the *ad hominem* argument occurs when a speaker, trying to show that he is not at fault, argues that his opponent has said or done things just as bad as those of which he, the speaker, is accused. For example, suppose White has accused Black of driving a car that is not safe, because it has no brakes. Black, aiming to refute the accusation, might reply "Who are you to talk? On your car the doors won't even latch, and you tie them shut with bits of string." This is the *tu quoque* (Latin: "you're another") form of the *ad hominem* argument.

Not all *ad hominem* arguments are fallacious. The abusive form of the *ad hominem* argument says that because a man has some weakness or defect, his views are incorrect. This is often but not always a worthless line of reasoning; sometimes it can be quite a good argument and not a fallacy at all. For instance, the fact that Professor Smith is a stupid, maladjusted man of paranoid tendencies increases the probability that his views on economic theory are unsound, for we know from past experience that economic theory is a difficult subject and that intelligent men of balanced judgment are more likely to have sound views about it. Perhaps we still ought to read Professor Smith's books, if we have time, before we definitely dismiss his views, but this information about his personality certainly is not irrelevant to the question whether his views are correct. We have here an inductive argument, which is not conclusive but is logically respectable (unlike the argument concerning Karl Marx, which is silly, for we have no reason to think there is a correlation between a man's earning power and the soundness of his views on social philosophy).

The circumstantial form of the *ad hominem* argument also can be of some value, though never as a direct proof of the conclusion. Pointing out to Senator Brown that his views on legislation are inconsistent with his religious principles may be worthwhile, for if his views contradict one another, they cannot both be right. To point this out does not show which view is mistaken, but it shows that Senator Brown needs to change at least one opinion or the other. Even the *tu quoque* form of *ad hominem* reasoning is not always worthless; it can be of real intellectual value in helping us form a consistent view of the comparative depravity of different individuals. It is fallacious if and only if it is supposed to be something more than that.

Another quite different fallacy of irrelevance is the appeal to unsuitable authority (the argument *ad verecundiam*). If we appeal to some admired or famous person as if he were an authority on a certain question when really he is not, we are making this fallacious appeal to authority. It is not always illogical to appeal to authorities, but we are not entitled to appeal to persons as authorities unless there are good reasons for believing them to be authorities, and we should not trust an authority outside his special proven field of competence. A famous guitarist may be an expert on her type of music, but this does not make her an authority on philosophy of life. A movie star may be an authority on how to look attractive to the opposite sex, but he is not likely to be an authority on which pain reliever is most healthful or tastes best.

The appeal to force is another fallacy of irrevelance (also called the *ad baculum* argument—"appeal to the stick"). By threatening a person we may succeed in winning him over to our point of view, but we must not think that a threat constitutes a logically valid argument. Usually a threat is not presented as an argument at all. We have the *ad baculum* fallacy only when the threat is treated as if it were a proof. A robber who says "Give me your money or I'll blow your brains out" is not committing the fallacy of appeal to force. He is not committing any fallacy at all, for he is not reasoning; he is just giving an order and stating an intention. However, a dictator who says "My opinions are right, because I'll imprison anyone who disagrees with me" perhaps would be committing the fallacy; he might be treating a threat as though it were a logical reason in favor of a conclusion.

Even if cases in which anyone really thinks that a threat can serve as a logical reason are very rare or nonexistent, the traditional phrase "*ad baculum* argument" is a good phrase to have in our vocabulary. We can use it to refer to the procedure of people who abandon reasoning and resort to force, or threats of force, in trying to get their way. In this loose sense, the *ad baculum* 'argument' is not really an argument and is not a fallacy in reasoning; instead, it is an abandonment of reasoning. (And it is often but not always wrong to abandon reasoning in favor of force.)

The appeal to pity, or appeal for mercy (*ad misericordiam* argument), is the fallacy of arguing that a certain conclusion must be true because otherwise someone whom there is reason to pity will be made more miserable. An appeal to pity or a plea for mercy is not a fallacy unless it is claimed to be a logical reason for believing some conclusion. The *ad misericordiam* fallacy is committed by the employee who argues "Please, Boss, you can see that my work is worth higher wages; I've got many hungry wives and children to feed." And a criminal would be committing this fallacy if he tried to offer evidence about his unhappy childhood as a reason why the court should believe that he did not perform the killings of which he stands accused. (However, it might be no fallacy for him to offer evidence about his unhappy childhood in trying to show that he deserves to be treated leniently.)

We conclude with what is perhaps the most common of all fallacies of irrelevance, the fallacy of *black-and-white thinking*. A wife may say to her husband "So you think the soup is too cold, do you? Well, I suppose you would like to have had it scalding hot then, instead." The second remark is presented as if it followed logically from the first, yet there is no logical connection whatever. But people find it very easy to fall into this sort of thinking in extremes, especially in the heat of controversy.

EXERCISE 25

A *Identify, explain, and discuss any fallacies which occur in the following sentences. (In some cases there may be more than one legitimate way of interpreting and classifying a fallacy.)*

1　All roads going west lead to Indiana. This road goes south, and therefore does not lead to Indiana.
2　Salesman: This car does cost 20 percent more than that other model you were considering, but it's a better buy,

because it gives greater fuel economy—10 more miles per tankful.

3   There are some real bargains listed in the advertising for a sale at Rose's department stores. But it says, "All items not available in all stores." So I guess one can't actually buy these bargains at any of their stores.

4   My father says it's antisocial of me to do all this shoplifting. Well, that criticism is pretty ridiculous—for I happen to know that he himself often pads his expense account.

5   No ex-Presidents are convicted felons. Therefore, all ex-Presidents are unconvicted felons.

6   A larger allowance? Surely you realize that money doesn't bring happiness. So if I increased your allowance it would only increase your unhappiness.

7   The *Britannica* is the finest of all encyclopedias. So you get the most for your money when you buy the *Britannica*.

8   We know that all inconsistent sentences are untrue. It follows that all consistent sentences must be true.

9   Members of the jury, you must convict the defendant, if not of murder, then of manslaughter. For when I asked him, "Did you intentionally kill the deceased?" he answered, "No." Thus he himself confesses that he killed, at least unintentionally.

10   Mice are animals. So a big mouse is a big animal.

11   All the people in New York cannot be interviewed in a year. Therefore, Green, who lives in New York, cannot be interviewed in a year.

12   Mr. Mayor, we firemen deserve a healthy pay hike now. You say that we're already better paid than the policemen, but that's not relevant. The point is that you'll face a tough strike if you don't see things our way.

13   You think that I ought to study more, instead of averaging sixty hours a week at parties? That's absurd, because one can't get an all-around education by spending one's every waking hour grinding away at those dreary textbooks.

14   Amphetamines are perfectly safe for diet control; Swami Mananda told me so, and he really knew all about hygiene. That was before he was committed, of course.

15   To call you an organism is to speak the truth. To call you a swine is to call you an organism. So to call you a swine is to speak the truth.

16 You didn't come out to join our march against repression. Why are you supporting repression?

17 Bugs are everywhere this summer. But praying mantises aren't everywhere this summer. So they aren't bugs.

18 It would be a good idea for each college student to spend every second year working at a job away from school. Thus what is now a four-year undergraduate program would require eight years to complete, which would automatically reduce the total undergraduate enrollment by 50 percent.

19 Anyone who works for the company can understand an English sentence. The instructions for operation of this computer are just English sentences. So anyone who works for the company can understand the instructions for operation of this computer.

20 We want to make education joyful, humane, responsive, and warm. Yet how can this be accomplished in a society which is racist, hierarchical, competitive, violent, repressive, narrow-minded, and selfish? It follows that the only sure way to reform education is to abolish capitalism.

B *Discuss whether fallacies occur in each of these examples.*

1 It's good politics for the mayor to brag about how he kept the tax rate low. But how much has the city suffered? The economic reality is that city workers expect increases in pay, and the city's other costs are rising too. It follows, therefore, that city expenses and taxes must continue to rise. When will the mayor stop playing politics?

2 There is a compelling logic for Rolls-Royce ownership. Of all the Rolls-Royce cars built since 1904, more than half are still cruising the world's highways. Total up the purchase prices of all the ordinary cars you have owned, or plan to own, subtracting their trade-in values. Now match this figure against the purchase price of a Rolls Silver Shadow. This remarkable value cannot go unheeded.

3 See how absurd and stupid it is to say: I should prefer non-existence to miserable existence. He who says, I prefer this to that, chooses something. Non-existence is not something; it is nothing. There can be no real choice when what you chose is nothing.   ST. AUGUSTINE, *De Libero Arbitrio*

4 If a friend of yours requests you on his deathbed to hand over his estate to his daughter, without leaving his intention anywhere in writing . . . or speaking of it to anybody, what will you do? You no doubt will hand over the money; perhaps Epicurus himself would have done the same. . . . Do you not see that . . . even you Epicureans, who profess to make your own interest and pleasure your sole standard, nevertheless perform actions that prove you to be really aiming not at pleasure but at duty . . . ? CICERO, *De Finibus*

5 From the moment when private property in movable objects developed, in all societies in which this private property existed there must be this moral law in common: Thou shalt not steal. Does this law thereby become an eternal moral law? By no means. In a society in which the motive for stealing has been done away with, in which therefore at the very most only lunatics would ever steal, how the teacher of morals would be laughed at who tried solemnly to proclaim the eternal truth: Thou shalt not steal!
FRIEDRICH ENGELS, *Anti-Dühring*

6 We are what we all abhor, *Anthropophagi* and Cannibals, devourers not onely of men but of our selves; and that not in an allegory, but a positive truth; for all this mass of flesh which we behold, came in at our mouths; this frame we look upon, hath been upon our trenchers; in brief, we have devour'd our selves. SIR THOMAS BROWNE, *Religio Medici*

7 But, say you, surely there is nothing easier than to imagine . . . books existing in a closet, and nobody by to perceive them. . . . But what is all this, I beseech you, more than framing in your mind certain ideas, which you call books . . . and at the same time omitting to frame the idea of anyone that may perceive them? But do not you yourself perceive or think of them all the while? This therefore . . . only shows you have the power of imagining or forming ideas in your mind; but it does not show that you can conceive it possible the objects of your thought may exist without the mind. To make out this, it is necessary that you conceive them existing unconceived or unthought of, which is a manifest repugnancy.
BISHOP BERKELEY, *Principles of Human Knowledge*

8 Nay, dearest Anna! why so grave?
    I said you had no soul, 'tis true!
    For what you *are*, you cannot *have*:
    'Tis I, that *have* one since I first had *you*!
SAMUEL TAYLOR COLERIDGE, "To a Lady"

AVOIDING AMBIGUITY:
DEFINITIONS

When we encounter words that cause confusion because their meanings are ambiguous, it is often helpful to define them. A traditional way of characterizing the definition of a word is to say that the definition is a verbal formulation of its meaning. However, the word "meaning" itself is ambiguous. Thus a general term may be said to mean each individual thing to which it applies (for example, the general term "man" means Socrates, Caesar, and each other man). This is called *extensional* meaning, and the totality of things to which the general term applies is called the extension of the term. But also a general term may be said to mean those characteristics which anything must possess in order that the term correctly apply to it (for example, the term "bachelor" means being a man and being unmarried). This is called *intensional* meaning, and the totality of characteristics which anything would have to possess in order that the term apply to it is called the intension of the term. A definition of a general term tries to specify the intension; the definition does not tell us what the extension is.

From another point of view, however, we can characterize definitions without employing the term "meaning." We may say that a definition of a word is a recipe for eliminating the word by paraphrasing, that is, for transforming sentences containing the word into equivalent sentences that contain other expressions instead. Recipes of this kind are of especial practical value when they tell us how to eliminate ambiguous, confusing, or unfamiliar words by paraphrasing—replacing them with clearer or more familiar words.

The most fundamental way of explaining a word is to give examples. Sometimes we do this by pointing to visible examples. When a child asks "What's a dog?" we respond by pointing to Fido, Rover, and Bruno. Some philosophers have called this procedure "ostensive definition," but it is better to call it merely ostensive teaching of words. This ostensive procedure differs from definition in that it gives no recipe for paraphrasing the word. Although explaining a word by giving examples often can be indispensably valuable, it is not the same as giving a definition. Sometimes a definition is much more helpful than a list of examples.

In ordinary discourse we often express definitions in ways that do not clearly show that they are definitions. Wishing to define the word "dormouse," a speaker may say, "A dormouse is a small hibernating European rodent resembling a squirrel." The hearer is then expected to realize that the speaker is intending to define the word "dormouse," rather than intending to make an ordinary statement about dormice (as he would be doing if he said, "Dormice are rather prolific animals"). A careful speaker can make his intention clearer by stating his definition in such a way as to leave no doubt that it is a definition. If he says "The word 'dormouse' means 'small hibernating European rodent resembling a squirrel,' " then he has made it perfectly clear that he is defining the word. Moreover, here he has given what is called an *explicit* definition, that is, a definition in which the *definiendum* (the expression being defined) is declared to be replaceable by another explicitly given expression, the *definiens* (that which does the defining).

Not all definitions are explicit ones. In a dictionary many words have to be defined not by giving one exact equivalent but by giving several partial synonyms. Thus "honesty" may be defined as "refraining from lying, cheating, or stealing; being truthful, trustworthy, upright, sincere, fair, straightforward or chaste." Here the meaning of the definiendum is adequately if not rigorously explained, but this is not an explicit definition, for we are not given some one other word or phrase that always means just the same as the definiendum.

In logic and mathematics, rigorous definitions that are not explicit definitions sometimes are used. For example, if we wish to define the biconditional symbol we can say "$p \equiv q$" is defined as "$(q \supset p) \& (p \supset q)$." This is called a *definition in context*; it supplies a rule enabling us to rewrite any expression containing the biconditional sign so that it will contain the horseshoe and ampersand instead. If we already understand the horseshoe and ampersand, this definition shows us exactly what the biconditional sign means. But this is not an explicit definition, for the whole expression containing the biconditional sign must be rearranged completely; we do not just remove one sign and put some other sign in its place.

Definitions that are useful in preventing ambiguity may be subdivided into two types. Some of them serve the purpose of describing the meaning that a word already has in language. We might call these *analytical* definitions. In giving this kind of definition of a word, the speaker does not aim to change its meaning; he aims only to characterize the meaning it already has. Dictionary definitions are of this type. When a definition has this purpose, we can properly ask whether the definition is correct or incorrect.

In order to be correct in its description of the meaning of a word, an analytical definition must not be *too broad*; that is, it must not embrace things that do not really belong. (To define "pneumonia" as "disease of the lungs" would be too broad, for there are many lung diseases besides pneumonia.) Also, in order to be correct in its description of the meaning of a word, an analytical definition must not be *too narrow*; that is, it must not exclude things that really belong. (To define "psychosis" as "schizophrenia" would be too narrow, for there are other kinds of psychoses.) Sometimes an incorrect definition errs by being too broad in one respect and also too narrow in some other respect (for instance, defining "liberalism" as "the view that the power of the federal government should be increased").

Furthermore, analytical definitions should be clear enough to be understood by those for whom they are intended; otherwise they are of little use. When in his dictionary Dr. Johnson defined a net as "any thing made with interstitial vacuities," his readers would not have understood the definiens as well as they already understood the definiendum; the definition uses murky words to explain a relatively clear one and so is not helpful.

Finally, a definition cannot serve much useful purpose if it is circular, that is, if the definiendum occurs within the definiens in such a way that no one could understand the definiens who did not already understand the definiendum. For example, to define "straight line" as "the line along which a ray of light travels when it goes straight" is circular and uninformative.

Traditional logic used to prescribe additional rules for definitions, including the rule that definitions should be given by genus and species and the rule that a definition ought not to be negative. However, these rules need not always be obeyed. To be sure, in giving a definition it often is helpful to proceed by genus and species, that is, first saying what general kind of thing the word means and then saying what the specific form is. But not all legitimate definitions follow this pattern. Also, it is often wise to avoid definitions couched in negative terms ("A lion is a big cat; not a tiger, not a leopard, not an ocelot"), for such definitions are likely to be too broad. But some negative definitions are perfectly legitimate.

A second kind of definition useful in preventing ambiguity is the *stipulative* definition, whose purpose is to declare how a speaker intends that a certain word, phrase, or symbol shall be understood ("Let 'S' means 'Samoans' "; "Let 'heavy truck' mean 'truck that can carry a load of 5 tons or more' "; etc.). Perhaps the expression being defined is one that previously had no meaning, or perhaps it had a different or a vaguer meaning. At any rate, the point of the stipulative definition is that the expression now is deliberately endowed with a particular meaning. Obviously, a stipulative definition cannot be of much use if it is unclear or circular. However, we do not have to worry about whether it is too broad or too narrow, for that sort of correctness cannot pertain to stipulative definitions. A stipulative definition is arbitrary, in the sense that it expresses only the speaker's intention to use the word in the stipulated manner, and he is, after all, entitled to use it however he pleases, so long as he does not cause confusion.

In order to avoid causing confusion, however, a stipulative definition should not assign to a word that already has an established meaning some new meaning that is likely to be confused with it. Consider the following dialogue:

Black: General Green is insane, you know. He ought to be dismissed.
White: He is? I agree that we should not have insane persons serving in the Army. But how do you know he's insane?
Black: It's obvious. He says he believes in extrasensory perception, and according to my definition—surely I'm entitled to use words as I please—anyone who does that is insane.

Here the stipulative definition is used to promote ambiguity rather than to prevent it. In the ordinary sense of the term "insane," White agrees with Black that insane persons ought not to be generals. But Black offers no evidence that General Green is insane in this sense. All that Black shows is that the general is 'insane' in a special, idiosyncratic sense of the word. From that, nothing follows about whether he ought to be dismissed. Black is causing confusion by failing to keep distinct these two very different senses of the word; this happens because he fails to recognize the difference here between a stipulative and an analytical definition.

Confusion can be caused in another way by a stipulative definition if a word or symbol that purports to name some individual thing (such a word or symbol is a singular term) is introduced even though it is not known that there is any such thing. Suppose I say "Let 'n' stand for the largest whole number." And then I go on to use this symbol "n" in making supposed assertions about this largest whole number. Here I am guilty of constructing a confused definition, for there is no largest whole number; hence, I have no right to introduce and use a symbol for this nonentity.* I may become badly confused if I assume that this definition is enough to entitle me to start talking about this largest whole number as if it existed. There is no such number, and a mere definition cannot create a number or any other object.

The two kinds of definitions mentioned so far both aim to inform us about verbal usage. The stipulative definition expresses a speaker's intention henceforth to use his definiendum in a certain way, and the analytical definition describes the way in which the definiendum already is used in language. These two kinds of definitions are valuable in helping to prevent ambiguity.

It would be a mistake, however, to suppose that everything called a definition belongs to one of these two kinds. In fact, the profoundest and most valuable definitions usually do not fit tidily into either kind. When Newton defined force as the product of mass times acceleration, when Einstein defined simultaneity of distant events in terms of the transmission of

---

* The situation is different with regard to general terms. It is all right to define the general term "unicorn" as "horse with a horn in its forehead." There are no unicorns, but the definition tells us that, if there were any horse with a horn in its forehead, it would be called a unicorn. We can use the general term "unicorn" even though there are no unicorns, but we must beware of using the singular term "n" unless we know that there is such a number.

light rays, and when Whitehead and Russell defined zero as the class of all empty classes, these important definitions expressed stipulations about how Newton, Einstein, and Whitehead and Russell proposed to use their terms. But these definitions did not merely do this; they also reflected previously established usage. What these definitions did was to propose new verbal usages growing out of the previously established usages: new usages that, it was felt, perfected tendencies of thought implicit in the old usages and thereby offered improved scope for the development of insight into the subject matter being treated.

We might give the name *revelatory* definitions to definitions like these, which do not fit into either of the two categories of stipulative and analytical. Revelatory definitions constitute a third category. Further examples of revelatory definitions can be found in other, diverse fields. For example, when a nineteenth-century writer defined architecture as frozen music, he was not trying to describe how the word "architecture" is used in our language. (He took it for granted that his readers would know what kinds of constructions are considered architecture.) Nor was he proposing some arbitrary new usage. We should not censure his definition on the ground that it is unhelpful for the purpose of preventing ambiguity; that is not the purpose of this kind of definition. This definition is a metaphor, and it suggests a new way of looking at architecture, comparing the structural organization of the parts of a building with the structural organization of the parts of a musical composition. In trying to decide whether the definition is a good one or not, we must reflect about the extent and validity of this comparison between music and buildings; the definition is a good one if and only if the comparison is revealing.

Or again, when a writer on psychoanalysis says that man is to be defined as the neurotic animal, this definition does not have the purpose of explaining the meaning of the word "man" to someone unfamiliar with it. Instead, its purpose is to call attention to something about men that the writer thinks is of fundamental importance in making men what they are and in explaining the differences between the life of men and the life of animals. The definition is a good one if it achieves this. These revelatory definitions have no relation to the elimination of ambiguity; they are mentioned only to indicate that analytical and stipulative definitions are not the only kinds of definition.

Traditional philosophers, in line with Aristotle and scholasticism, emphasized what were called *real* definitions. Like the definitions which we are calling revelatory, real definitions were not supposed to state the meanings of words but rather were supposed to describe things in a fundamental way. It was believed, however, that there must be only one proper real definition of each species of natural being. For instance, it was held that the real definition of man is that he is the rational animal. According to this traditional point of view, it would have been thought incorrect to define man as the tool-using animal or the animal with language, let alone as the neurotic animal. The weakness of this traditional view is that it fails to recognize how the same thing may be defined in different yet perhaps equally legitimate ways which reveal different aspects of its nature.

How frequently are definitions needed? People sometimes think that one always should define one's terms at the beginning of any discussion. But this idea becomes absurd if carried too far. Suppose that a speaker did undertake to define all his terms in noncircular ways. However far he proceeded, he would always still have at least one definiens containing as yet undefined terms; therefore his task is an impossible one to complete. Moreover, we do have a fairly adequate understanding of the meanings of many words that we have never bothered to define and also of many words that we would not know how to define satisfactorily even if we tried. Thus, it would be foolish to try indiscriminately to define all or even most of our terms before proceeding with our thinking. What we should do at the beginning of a discussion is seek definitions of those particular words which are especially likely to make trouble in the discussion because they are harmfully ambiguous, obscure, or vague.

This is especially true with regard to discussions in which confusion is caused by failure to notice the different meanings of a term. A *verbal dispute* is a dispute arising solely from the fact that some word is being used with different meanings; this kind of dispute can be settled merely by giving the definitions that clarify the situation (though to say this is not to say that such disputes always are *easy* to settle).

The American philosopher William James gives a classic example of such a verbal dispute.* Suppose there is a squirrel

---

* William James, *Pragmatism*, Lecture II.

on the trunk of a tree, and a man walks around the tree. The
squirrel moves around the tree trunk so as to stay out of sight,
always facing the man but keeping the tree between them. Has
the man gone around the squirrel or not? Some of James's
friends disputed hotly for a long time about this question. Here
is a purely verbal dispute; it can be settled by pointing out that
in one sense the man has gone 'around' the squirrel, for he has
moved from the north to the west and then to the south and
east of the squirrel's location, but in another sense the man has
not gone 'around' the squirrel, for the squirrel has always been
facing him. Once we have pointed out these two different
senses of the word, we have done all that can reasonably be done;
there is nothing more worth discussing (though this does not
ensure that discussion will cease). With a verbal dispute like
this, giving definitions is the way to resolve the dispute. But
it would be utterly wrong to assume that all disputes are verbal
in this way. There are many serious problems for the settling
of which definitions are not needed, and there are many other
problems where, if definitions help, they mark only the beginning of the thinking needed to resolve the issue.

EXERCISE 26

A *For each example, explain the main ambiguity and discuss
whether definitions would be helpful.*

1 This is a wild horse.
2 She lacks broad vision.
3 He got high on the mountain.
4 He is the forty-five-year-old son of a West Virginia coal
   miner and an ordained minister of the United Church.
5 They were found murdered in the blood-spattered apart-
   ment they shared in northwest Washington.
6 The grand jury issued an illegal gambling indictment.
7 A mighty fortress is our God.
8 Headline: "Life Raft Company Picks Wreck Survivor's
   Brain."
9 How did this group of adolescent mothers make out?
   Eventually, two-thirds of the sample married, and 70 percent married the fathers of their children.
10 No man can walk while sitting.
11 Nothing is too good for him.

12 Which is heavier, a quart of heavy cream or a quart of light cream?

B *Discuss the purpose and adequacy of the definition involved in each example.*

1 Theft may be defined as a reduction, without the owners's consent, of an owner's right to his property.
2 Any change by which the kind of matter is altered is called a chemical change.
3 When a price is raised or lowered, and total expenditure on the commodity changes in the opposite direction from the price, demand is elastic.
4 A sphere is a surface all points of which are equidistant from a point within called the center.
5 Intelligence may be defined as that which intelligence tests measure.
6 Purple of Cassius is finely divided gold adsorbed on a hydrosol of stannic acid.
7 Constructive notice is information or knowledge of a fact imputed by law to a person (although he may not actually have it), because he could have discovered the fact by proper diligence, and his situation was such as to cast upon him the duty of inquiring into it.
8 When we say that a certain proposition is true, we mean merely that the proposition follows logically from the assumtions upon which it is based.

C *Discuss the adequacy of the definition stated or involved in each example.*

1 A few years ago a German-born woman appeared before a federal district judge in Los Angeles, seeking to become a citizen of the United States. In order to be granted citizenship, she would have to take an oath of allegiance, the wording of which expresses belief in a supreme being. She testified that she considered herself an atheist, because she did not believe in a supreme being; however, under questioning by the judge, she agreed that she regarded the universe as ordered and not created by any human beings or animals. "That qualifies as religion," the judge said, swearing her in. "That's the same as believing in a supreme being."

2 By *Original Sin,* as the phrase has been most commonly used by divines, is meant *the innate, sinful depravity of the heart.*   JONATHAN EDWARDS, *Doctrine of Original Sin*

3 Evil, as we have said, is nothing else but *the privation of what is connatural and due to anyone;* for the term *evil* is used in this sense by all.

ST. THOMAS AQUINAS, *Summa Contra Gentiles*

4 By pleasure we mean the absence of pain in the body and of trouble in the soul.   EPICURUS

5 Time is our consciousness of the succession of ideas in our mind. . . . If a mind be conscious of a hundred ideas during one minute, by the clock, and of two hundred during another, the latter of these spaces would actually occupy so much greater extent in the mind as two exceed one in quantity. If, therefore, the human mind, by any future improvement of its sensibility, should become conscious of an infinite number of ideas in a minute, that minute would be eternity. . . . Perhaps the perishing ephemeron enjoys a longer life than the tortoise.

PERCY BYSSHE SHELLEY, *Queen Mab*

6 We were never more free than under the German Occupation. We had lost all our rights, above all the right to speak; we were insulted daily and had to remain silent. . . . Since the Nazi poison was seeping into our thinking, each accurate thought was a victory; . . . since we were hunted, each gesture had the weight of a commitment. The often frightful circumstances of our struggle enabled us finally to live, undisguised and unconcealed, that anxious, unbearable situation which is called the human predicament. Exile, captivity, death, which in happier times are skillfully hidden, were our perpetual concern. . . . The choice that each of us made of himself was authentic, because it was made in the presence of death.

JEAN-PAUL SARTRE, *Situations*

7 We must first be clear on what is meant by "the people" and what is meant by "the enemy." . . . At the present stage,

the period of building socialism, the classes, strata and social groups which favor, support and work for the cause of socialist construction all come within the category of the people, while the social forces and groups which resist the socialist revolution and are hostile to or sabotage socialist construction are all enemies of the people.

MAO-TSE-TUNG, *On the Correct Handling of Contradictions*

8   We reject the subjectivist view that to call an action right, or a thing good, is to say that it is generally approved of, because it is not self-contradictory to assert that some actions which are generally approved of are not right, or that some things which are generally approved of are not good.

A. J. AYER, *Language, Truth and Logic*

9   They are not being tried by a jury of their peers, for these two defendants are black, young, and inmates of California's penal institutions—segments of society from which jury panels are not drawn.

SOLEDAD BROTHERS LEGAL COMMITTEE

10   I hear people saying: The priest has lost his identity card. It is not so.   Let's not lose too much time in asking who we are, because it is not a question of defining our priesthood but of living it.   The example of Christ is before our eyes: meek and humble, chaste, poor and obedient.

POPE JOHN PAUL I

D   *In each case, discuss the definitions being employed and the nature of the disagreement, and explain whether there is purely verbal confusion.*

1   **Black:** The law says "No trucks over 1 ton on this street." You're driving your van on this street, and your van weighs 2 tons.   So you're violating the law.
   White: No, that's unsound reasoning.   My van has a payload of only 1 ton, so it's a 1-ton truck.
2   **Black:** The price of gold has fluctuated dreadfully in recent years.
   White: That's only the dollar price of gold.   Actually, gold is the most stable thing there is, because it is the standard of value.   It is the value of the dollar that fluctuates, not gold.

3   Black: Corporations pay heavy taxes.
White: No, they don't pay taxes. They merely collect taxes from their customers in the form of higher prices. It is the consumer who ultimately pays the taxes.

4   Brown: How dare you tell everyone that I stole this car? You know I bought it.
Green: You bought it for a ridiculously low price, and according to my definition that's stealing. So when people ask me about you I tell them you're a thief.

5   Brown: What fine, solid furniture!
Green: It's not solid at all. It consists of swarms of atoms whirling through mostly empty space. It's no more solid than a swarm of bees.

6   Gray: People are less religious than they used to be.
Brown: Religion is best defined as "ultimate concern"; whatever a man's ultimate concern is, that is his religion. Perhaps nowadays more people have television, making money, or taking drugs as their religions; but people are not less religious now.

7   Black: The universe is infinitely old.
Green: Impossible. Let e be the earliest event in the history of the universe. Now, there cannot have been any happening earlier than e, since e is by definition the earliest event. As every two points in time are separated by only a finite interval, e must have occurred only a finite length of time ago.

8   White: Brown is a barbarian. He never bathes or changes his clothes.
Gray: He's no barbarian. He reads Proust in French and plays the viola da gamba.

E *In each case discuss the soundness of Black's criticism of White's argument.*

1   White: If you were rich, you could afford a skiing holiday in Switzerland. But I see you cannot afford that. So you must not be rich.
Black: Your argument is no good, because the way you use the word "rich" is vague. How much money does a person have to have before he's rich?

2   White: You grant me that no fishes have feathers and that all sharks are fishes. Therefore, you've got to grant that no sharks have feathers.

Black: Invalid. You are committing the fallacy of division, by reasoning from whole (fishes) to part (sharks).

3 **White:** If your girl friend is mad, you can't have a pleasant evening with her. And she is mad. So if you want a pleasant evening, don't spend it with her.

Black: That's invalid thinking, because the word "mad" can have two meanings, "angry" and "insane."

4 **White:** Surely there must be something unsound about the current indeterministic theory of quantum mechanics, for Einstein himself opposed it, saying that he could not believe that God would play dice with the universe.

Black: You are appealing to authority. That is the fallacy of the argument *ad verecundiam*.

5 **White:** I define God as the basic reality of the universe, whatever that may be. The universe exists, and therefore its basic reality, whatever that may be, must exist too. Thus I prove that there is a God, in my sense at least.

Black: That definition is incorrect; lots of people don't mean that by the word "God." So your argument is unsound.

6 **White:** You tell me that my money will be just as safe and will earn a much higher return if I take it out of government bonds and put it into these Baffin Island real estate shares that you're selling. But I know that you earn a sizable commission on whatever shares you sell, so I don't think I can trust what you say about this.

Black: My friend, you accuse me of having a selfish motive instead of disproving what I said. You've committed the *ad hominem* fallacy.

CHAPTER 6

INDUCTIVE REASONING

So far, we have been concentrating on deductive arguments. But a large fraction of the arguments we encounter in ordinary thinking are inductive in character. Let us turn now to a fuller consideration of inductive reasoning.

INDUCTION AND PROBABILITY

Valid deductive arguments are demonstrative; that is, if the premises are true, the conclusion must necessarily be true also. Because of this, the conclusion cannot embody conjectures about the empirical world that go beyond what the premises say; in this sense the conclusion of a valid deductive argument must be 'contained in' its premises. However, an inductive argument (as we defined induction) has a conclusion embodying empirical conjectures about the world that do go beyond what its premises say; in an inductive argument the conclusion is not wholly 'contained in' the premises. Consequently, in an inductive argument the truth of the premises cannot absolutely ensure the truth of the conclusion, and the argument cannot be demonstrative in the way that valid deduction is. But if the premises of an inductive argument are true and the reasoning is good, then it is reasonable to believe the conclusion; the conclusion is *probably* true.*

Inductive reasoning is of great importance because so many of our beliefs about the world cannot be proved by deduction alone. If they are to be proved at all, the reasoning in support of them must include inductive reasoning; it cannot all be deductive. For example, it is a very ordinary belief that if a person eats bread for lunch it will nourish him, whereas if he eats arsenic it will poison him. What reasoning can we employ in justification of these beliefs? Fundamentally, the belief that bread will nourish and that arsenic will poison is supported by past experience, by our observation of past cases in which these effects occurred. Thus, the direct way of reasoning here is to infer that bread will nourish us if we eat it today, since bread that we know of in the past has usually nourished, and that if we eat arsenic today it will poison us, since arsenic that we know of in the past has usually poisoned. This reasoning is obviously inductive in character.

To be sure, we could reason deductively that since bread always nourishes, it will nourish us today, and that since arsenic always poisons, it will poison us if we eat it today. But this deductive reasoning depends on major premises that themselves require justification. How do we know that bread always nourishes and that arsenic always poisons (not just in the past, but always)? Here the direct answer would be that we know this, if at all, by induction; in the past this is what happened, and so probably it is what always happens. In justifying beliefs like these about how things happen in the world, we must sooner or later resort to inductive inference; deduction alone would not suffice for completing a proof. Because our actions are so largely based upon beliefs arrived at by induction, the English philosopher Bishop Butler declared, "Probability is the very guide to life."

---

* In order to emphasize the contrast between induction and deduction, we shall speak of inductive conclusions as being probable, no matter how well established they are. This is a departure from ordinary usage, for in ordinary discourse a well-established inductive conclusion, e.g., that the sun will rise tomorrow, is called certain rather than highly probable. But for purposes of logic it is convenient to conceive of probability in a broader sense, applying it to the conclusions of all arguments that are not deductive. By using the term in this way, we emphasize the difference between deductive and nondeductive reasoning.

With inductive arguments, just as with deductive ones, we have to distinguish between the truth of the conclusion and the logical validity of the reasoning. However, in inductive reasoning the situation is more complicated than in deductive reasoning, since we must allow for variations in the degree to which, according to the speaker, the premises supposedly make it reasonable to believe the conclusion. That is, we must allow for variations in the degree of probability the speaker claims that his premises confer on his conclusion.

A speaker claims a high degree of probability for his conclusion if the says "My past experience is such-and-such; therefore it is practically certain that arsenic is always poisonous." He claims a much lower degree of probability for his conclusion if he says "My past experience is such-and-such, and so it is rather likely that arsenic is always poisonous." An inductive argument that is perfectly legitimate when a moderate degree of probability is claimed for the conclusion (e.g., "He's a Hindu, and so quite likely he's a vegetarian") can become fallacious if an unduly high degree of probability is claimed for the conclusion (e.g., "He's a Hindu, and so he's sure to be a vegetarian").

What then should we mean by calling an inductive argument valid? An inductive argument is a valid argument if the degree of probability claimed for its conclusion is indeed a reasonable degree of probability to attribute to that conclusion, relative to the given premises. The argument is a *non sequitur* if it claims for its conclusion a degree of probability that it is unreasonable to attribute to the conclusion, relative to the given premises.

Keeping this in mind, we can see that an inductive argument may happen to reach a true conclusion without being a logically good argument. (In this respect, induction is like deduction.) For instance, suppose a person sees a black cat cross his path and infers that bad luck is surely imminent; soon after, he is struck by lightning. Here his conclusion happens to have been true, but his reasoning may well be invalid all the same; relative to what he knew at the time he made the inference, it may not have been very probable that he was going to have bad luck. The conclusion accidentally turned out to be true, but the reasoning was logically bad.

Also, an inductive argument may reach a false conclusion even though the reasoning involved is logically good and starts from true premises. (In this respect, induction is unlike deduc-

tion.)   For instance, suppose there has been a thunderstorm
every afternoon at five o'clock for the past week, and I infer
that there will rather likely be one tomorrow too.   Here my
data are true and my reasoning may well be perfectly logical,
yet it is possible that my conclusion is false; perhaps no storm
occurs on the morrow.   Here it is reasonable for me to make
this inference, even though the conclusion may turn out not to
be true.

To grasp this character of inductive reasoning, we must
understand the notion of probability.   When we speak of the
degree of probability of a conclusion, we are referring to the
degree to which it is reasonable to believe the conclusion;
probability here is the same thing as rational credibility.   Probabilities in this sense are sometimes, but not always, numerically
measurable, as we shall see.

This is not the only sense of the term "probability," to be
sure.   A quite different sense is involved when a physicist
speaks of the probability of decay of a uranium atom; what he
means is, roughly, the *relative frequency* with which uranium
atoms do, in fact, disintegrate.   Probability in that sense is
always numerical.   Mathematical formulations of the theory of
probability often employ the term "probability" in that relative-
frequency sense rather than in the sense of rational credibility.

But now, probability when understood as rational credibility
is a *relative* matter, in this respect: The degree to which it is
reasonable to believe something depends upon how much we
know.   The very same conjecture takes on different degrees of
probability relative to different amounts of evidence.   For example, if all we know about Hugo is that he is twenty years old,
then, relative to this evidence, the conjecture that he will be
alive next year is highly probable and very reasonable to believe
(for we know that most twenty-years-olds survive).   But if we
learn that young Hugo loves fast driving and has already had
several accidents, the probability is distinctly diminished.   And
if we learn in addition that he has just collided with a concrete
abutment at 90 miles per hour, then, relative to this augmented
evidence, the probability of his being alive next year is very
much further reduced.   Relative to our original information,
the conjecture that he will survive was highly probable; relative
to our augmented information, it has only a low degree of
probability.   This illustrates how changes in available evidence

can change the degree to which it is reasonable to believe a conclusion. And it illustrates how probability is something quite different from truth, for the conjecture could be highly probable without being true or could be true without being very probable.

Probabilities always are relative to evidence, yet often we speak of *the* probability of something, without specifically stating to what evidence this probability is related. When we speak of *the* probability of a sentence, we mean its probability relative to *all* the information that we possess. If someone asks, "What is the probability that there is life on Mars?" he means, "What is the probability, relative to all the evidence now available?" The degree of probability may have been different in times past when there was less evidence, and it will surely be different in the future when more evidence is gathered.

This brings us to another basic difference between deductive and inductive reasoning. Deductive arguments are *self-contained* as regards validity in a way that inductive arguments are not. Thus, the question whether it is deductively valid to argue "No deciduous trees are conifers; all fig trees are deciduous; therefore no fig trees are conifers" is a question whose answer depends solely upon the logical relation of the stated premises to the conclusion. No further information about botany or anything else (excepting logic, or course) is required. Indeed, there exists no other sentence (excluding sentences that express principles of logic) the truth or falsity of which has any decisive bearing upon whether this reasoning is deductively valid.

Because of this, when we are determining whether a deductive argument is valid, we may limit our attention strictly to the stated premises, except for deductive arguments having suppressed premises (which we shall discuss in Chapter 7); even with them the unstated premises always are limited in number and can, in principle, be stated in full.

Inductive arguments are not self-contained in this way. Consider the argument: "Hugo is twenty; most twenty-year-olds survive another year, and so probably Hugo will reach twenty-one." The person who presents this argument is not just claiming that the conclusion *would* be probable *were* the stated premises *all* our relevant evidence; if he were making only that very uninteresting, milksop claim, his remark would be a mere conditional sentence, not an inference at all. The arguer is claiming something more significant: He is claiming that the conclusion *is* reasonable to believe in the light of *all* that we know. He is concerned with the degree of probability of the conclusion relative to all the directly and indirectly relevant evidence that we possess. How much evidence is this? A great deal—indeed, indefinitely much, for so many of the things we know about the world have at least indirect bearings on the question of Hugo's survival. (Our knowledge of the longevity of other people, of the longevity of other animals, and of the general regularity of nature are all indirectly relevant.) If we tried to list all the empirical sentences we know to be true that are at least indirectly relevant to the question of young Hugo's survival, we would find that we had embarked upon a task that we could not complete or at any rate that we could never be sure we had completed. There are indefinitely many such sentences, and in trying to list them all we never could be certain that we had not omitted some.

In an inductive argument the explicitly stated premises are only a tiny part, although usually the most noteworthy part, of the indefinitely vast amount of information about the world upon which the conclusion depends. Each bit of this known but unstated information has a bearing upon whether the argument is inductively valid. But where reasoning involves relevant premises so rich that we cannot be sure even of stating them completely, we cannot expect to be able to impute to the premises and conclusion any specific logical form in virtue of which the argument would be valid or invalid. We cannot rely on considerations of logical form for judging the validity of inductive reasoning. Thus inductive arguments are not 'self-contained' in the way that deductive arguments are, which makes their whole logic profoundly different, for it means that formal rules cannot play the central role in inductive logic that they do in deductive logic.

EXERCISE 27
Discuss the following examples.

1 A sentence is either true or false. If it's true, then it can't be improbable, and there's no point to calling it probable. If it's false, it can't be probable, and there's no point to calling

it improbable. So probability and improbability are not notions that are of any use.

2 On Friday, all the indications were that the weather would be fair for sailing on the weekend; the barometer was high and there was no report of storm systems moving in our direction. But by Saturday afternoon a fierce squall had blown up, capsizing our boat. How wrong we had been to think that it would probably be fair.

3 To me, probability means the relative frequency with which a given characteristic occurs in a population. If nine out of ten Swedes are blue-eyed, then the probability that a Swede will be blue-eyed is 90 percent. As I see it, probabilities are objective facts about populations, not some hazy kinds of weak logical links.

INDUCTIVE GENERALIZATION

Suppose we have met some swans and observed each of them to be white. This information is not enough to enable us to prove deductively whether all swans are white, or even whether the next swan we meet will be so. But here we might construct an inductive argument of the form:

Inductive generalization
a, b, c . . . each has been observed to be S and P.
Nothing has been observed to be S without being P.

Therefore, probably, all S are P.

Here the conclusion is an "all" sentence and is called a generalization. In terms of our example, a, b, c . . . would be the individual swans that have been observed; "S" would be interpreted to mean "swans," and "P" would be interpreted to mean "white things." This is the simplest form of inductive generalization.

A kindred but slightly more complicated form of reasoning would start from evidence that a certain percentage of observed S are P, and it would pass to the conclusion (a statistical generalization) that probably approximately the same percentage of all S are P. For example, from the fact that 20 percent of the birds I have seen today were robins, I might infer that probably about 20 percent of the birds now in my part of the country are robins.

   Some arguments of this type are strong arguments; some are weak arguments. In trying to judge how strong such an argument is (that is, in trying to judge the degree of probability with which the conclusion follows from the evidence), we need to take account of various factors that determine how reasonable it is to suppose that the things observed constitute a 'fair sample' of S in general, with regard to being P. How reasonable is it to suppose that the particular swans that we have observed constitute a 'fair sample' of swans in general, with regard to color? Five factors should be considered.

1   The degree to which a, b, c . . . have been observed to be alike (besides the mere fact that each is both S and P) is important. This is called the *positive analogy*. For instance, suppose that all the observed swans were female and American. Then our argument would be relatively weak, for we would not be entitled to feel very confident that our sample is representative of the whole class of swans with regard to color; we would not have excluded the real possibility that it is only female swans, or perhaps only American swans, that are white. In general, the greater the positive analogy among the observed instances, the weaker is the argument, other things being equal.

2   Also important is the degree to which a, b, c . . . have been observed to differ one from another. This is called the *negative analogy*. For instance, if we have observed swans in winter and in summer, in the wilds and in captivity, young and fully grown, then our argument is strengthened. We have increased the probability that the sample is representative as regards color, for we have excluded the possibilities that it is only swans in winter, or only wild swans, or only young ones that are white. In general, the greater the negative analogy among the observed instances, the stronger is the argument. (Notice that the extent of the positive analogy and the extent of the negative analogy are two quite independent matters; having much positive analogy need not entail having little negative analogy.)

3   Also we should consider the *character of the conclusion*; we must take account of how much it says. The more

sweeping the generalization that we seek to establish, the less is its probability relative to our evidence, and the weaker is our argument. For example, "All swans are white" is a generalization that says more than "All American swans are nonblack." The less specific the subject term and the more specific the predicate term, the more a universal generalization says. Statistical conclusions too can differ in how much they say; that at least 10 percent of the birds in this wood are robins is a statistical generalization that says less than does the generalization that between 19 and 21 percent of birds in this wood are robins.

In addition to these three factors, there are two others, perhaps less fundamental but also deserving notice.

4 We should consider the *number of observed instances* (*a, b, c* . . .). An increase in the number of observed instances normally means an increase in the strength of the argument. Here a rather abstract question may be raised: Does an increase in the number of observed instances, just as such, necessarily increase the probability of the generalization? Or does the conclusion become more probable only because additional observed instances ordinarily mean an increase in the extent of the negative analogy among the observed instances? Suppose that the number of observed instances was increased without the negative analogy thereby being increased. Would this strengthen the argument, or would this leave the probability of the conclusion unchanged? Philosophers disagree in their views about this abstract question. Fortunately, the matter is very academic, for in actual practice whenever we increase the number of observed instances we usually also increase the extent of the negative analogy among the observed instances.

5 Finally, we should consider the *relevance* of S to P. How probable is it that there would be a connection between the property of being a swan and the property of being white? Are these properties that may reasonably be expected to be correlated? Here we must rely upon knowledge gained through previous inductions. In our example we might reasonably suppose that being a swan is relevant to being white, since we know (from previous inductions) that birds of the same species usually have the same coloring.

In practice, we should take all five of these factors into account, weighing them together, when we seek to decide whether a specific inductive argument is relatively strong or relatively weak. We need to use common sense as we ask ourselves whether we are entitled to suppose that our observed instances constitute a 'fair sample' of the whole class about which we are generalizing.

As we try to weigh the strength of an inductive argument, three main types of mistakes should be avoided. We shall call these the fallacies of forgetful induction, hasty induction, and slothful induction. All three are mistakes that can arise in inductive reasoning of any type, but we shall consider them now just in connection with inductive generalization. First there is the mistake that arises from neglecting some of the relevant empirical information that we possess. Let us call this the fallacy of *forgetful induction*. Where the conclusion is a generalization, we may speak of the fallacy of forgetful generalization.

For example, suppose someone wishes to estimate how many polo players there are in a given city. He visits a golf club there and interviews the first 500 people he meets, of whom 10 percent say that they play polo. He then concludes that it is highly probable that just about 10 percent of the people in this city are polo players. This is an example of very faulty reasoning. His mistake lies in forgetting that people met in a golf club are usually sportsmen and relatively well-to-do; sportsmen and the well-to-do play polo more than other people do, as polo is a sporty and expensive game. These are facts that we all know, if we only stop to think. Thus there is positive reason to believe that this sample is not representative of the population of the city at large, with respect to polo playing. Under the circumstances, this man's conclusion is not highly probable, as he imagines, but really has a very low degree of probability.

A second type of mistake in inductive reasoning is the fallacy of leaping to a conclusion when the evidence is too slight to make the conclusion very probable. Let us call this the fallacy of *hasty induction*. With regard to inductive generalization, this has traditionally been called the fallacy of hasty generalization. For example, suppose a young man for the first time meets a girl from Carrie Nation College; he finds her dumpy and dull, and so the next day he tells his friends that all the girls from Carrie Nation are 'pigs.' Here his reasoning is illogical, for he has based a sweeping generalization upon very slight evidence. The probability of the conclusion relative to his data really is very low, yet he states his conclusion as though it were highly probable. His mistake is that he leaps to a conclusion on the basis of very little evidence. This is somewhat different from the mistake made by the man who visited the country club; he collected a considerable amount of evidence but, in evaluating it, forgot about relevant information that was available to him.

The third type of mistake is the mistake of treating a conclusion as though it were less probable than it is. If a conclusion is something that, for one reason or another, we would prefer not to believe, all too often we refuse to accept it even after the evidence has piled up strongly; we persist in believing that the conclusion is improbable when it is not. Let us call this the fallacy of *slothful induction*. When it arises in connection with inductive generalization, it is the fallacy of slothful generalization.

Suppose the question is whether Hugo is a driver who will have relatively few accidents in the long run. In March the Buick he was driving ran into a tree. His father then bought him a Chrysler, but in April it collided with a telephone pole. His indulgent father then bought him a Pontiac, but in May it struck a stone wall. His still-indulgent father then bought him a Dodge, but in June it plunged into a river. The father, thinking back over the available evidence, begins to wonder whether it does not perhaps point toward the generalization that if young Hugo is allowed to continue driving, he will comparatively often have accidents. But Hugo insists that it is just a series of unfortunate coincidences; after all, a person can have some accidents without necessarily having a bad record in the long run. He urges his father to buy him a Cadillac so that he can show how safe a driver he really is. Here is an instance of slothful generalization. Hugo is refusing to face the facts, for the evidence is sufficient to make it very probable that he is not a safe driver; the probability, which a prudent father ought to recognize, is that if Hugo is given more cars he will smash them soon.

EXERCISE 28

A *Our first manned rocket ship to Mars has just landed. The astronauts begin to explore, and encounter ten Martians, all of whom they observe to be three-legged, insectlike creatures living underground beside the canals. They infer that probably all three-legged insectlike Martians live underground. Consider whether (and why) this inference would be made stronger or weaker by the following changes.*

1 Suppose that the observed Martians are of various colors: some purple, some pink, some green, some yellow.
2 Suppose that all the observed Martians are blue and live together in a particular spot.
3 Suppose that all the observations so far have been made during the Martian morning.
4 Suppose that 100 Martians are observed.
5 Suppose the astronauts infer that all three-legged, insectlike Martians live underground near canals and not on mountains.
6 Suppose that the observations have been made at different times of day and night, in different seasons, and over a wide area including different types of terrain.
7 Suppose they infer that all Martians live underground.
8 Suppose they infer that all three-legged, insectlike Martians go underground at least sometimes.
9 Suppose the landing took place on April Fool's Day.
10 Suppose that the landing took place during a period of especially intense sunspot activity.

B *Discuss any fallacies committed in the following examples.*

1 The writings of Edgar Rice Burroughs are all trash, by my standards. The book of his that I read was *Tarzan Triumphant*, and I thought it was awful.
2 Alaska has quite a mild climate in wintertime. I know, because I visited Juneau for Christmas and it wasn't very cold.
3 Murders are always discovered, sooner or later. Just think back: When did you ever hear of a murder that wasn't discovered?
4 We interviewed 1000 people during the lunch hour at Federal Plaza, downtown, and 987 of them agreed that budgets

for government departments should be increased. We conclude that probably most people in the city favor an increase in these budgets.

5 Using an accurate steel ruler, we measured the lengths of ninety-two iron bars on the hottest and the coldest days of the year. We found no significant changes between the hot and cold lengths. So probably changes in temperature are not associated with any significant changes in the lengths of iron objects.

6 I admit that I can hardly ever find my keys, I've lost my wallet for the tenth time, I never remember to put out the garbage, and I don't keep in mind my children's birthdays. Is it possible that I'm a tiny bit absent-minded?

7 It rained last weekend, and the weekend before. Rain is spoiling every weekend, this year.

8 The doctor took a single blood specimen, and observed that there were comparatively few white blood cells in the specimen. He concluded that the patient had comparatively few white blood cells throughout his bloodstream.

9 I see you've noticed that a few features of this house are not so good: the paint is peeling, the roof does leak, the wiring is burned out, and the plumbing pipes have burst. But don't go leaping to conclusions about its not being a very desirable house when *all* its features are considered. Let me show you the fine storage space in the attic, the new sump pump that keeps the basement dry, and the sturdy grillwork over the windows that keeps burglars out.

10 Since we learn by experience that abundance of bodies are hard, we therefore justly infer the hardness of individual undivided particles not only of bodies we feel, but of all others. For the hardness of the whole arises from the hardness of the parts.   SIR ISAAC NEWTON, *Principia*

INDUCTIVE ANALOGY

An analogy is a parallel or a resemblance between two different things. Sometimes we use literal language to talk about analogies, and when we use figurative language we nearly always employ analogies. To use language in a *figurative* way is to stretch words beyond the bounds of their normal literal uses. Figurative language often is used for description, though sometimes as a basis for argument. Simile and metaphor are the two most familiar forms of figurative language.

A *simile* is a statement that one thing is *like* something else of a very different type, or that one thing *does* something as if it were something else of a very different type. A metaphor states that one thing *is* something else of a very different type, or that it *does* something very different from what it literally does do. In Shakespeare's account of Cleopatra on the Nile we find a combination of forms of description:

The barge she sat in, like a burnished throne,
Burned on the water; the poop was beaten gold.

Here the claim that the barge was like a burnished throne is a simile; to say that it burned on the water is to use a metaphor; and to say that its poop was beaten gold is literal, nonfigurative description. A simile or metaphor says something which, if taken literally, would be false or even absurd; when we understand that it is intended to be figurative, we see that it rests upon an analogy of a kind not ordinarily noticed, an analogy that may be vivid and illuminating.

Often we use analogies in our discourse just for purposes of description, but sometimes we employ them also as a basis for reasoning. In connection with inductive generalization, we have already noted the importance of the positive and negative analogies among the observed instances; but we shall see that there are other inductive inferences in which analogy plays a still more prominent role. This happens when an arguer points out an analogy between two things for the purpose of proving something about one of them.

Suppose that the postman once met a boxer dog and found that it had a bad temper and a tendency to bite; if he now meets another boxer dog, he may reason by analogy that this dog also is likely to have a bad temper and a tendency to bite. Here his reasoning rests upon analogy, for, from the fact that the present dog resembles the past one in breed, he infers that probably it resembles it in temperament as well. Moreover, his reasoning is inductive, since the conclusion (that this new dog has a bad temper and will bite) expresses an empirical conjecture going beyond the evidence then available to the postman.

We can describe this type of reasoning in more general terms if we notice that sometimes there may be more than one past instance upon which the inductive analogy is based. For example, suppose that we have observed a number of swans in the past (call them a, b, c) and have observed each of them to be white; now we learn of another swan (call it d) whose color we have not yet had opportunity to observe. We may reason by analogy that since this new bird resembles the already observed ones in species, probably it will resemble them in color as well. Here the reasoning rests upon an analogy drawn between the present bird and a number of previously observed ones.

Inductive analogy

a, b, c each has been observed to be S and P.
d is an S.

Therefore, probably, d is P.

The form of this reasoning is closely akin to that of inductive generalization, but the difference is that here the conclusion is a singular sentence rather than a universal generalization.

> Some philosophers have held that an argument like this, which reaches a singular conclusion, ought to be interpreted as involving two steps: first, the inferring of an inductive generalization ("Since a, b, c each has been observed to be S and P, therefore probably all S and P"); and second, a deductive syllogism ("All S are P; d is an S; therefore d is P"). However, there is no reason why we must interpret the reasoning in this way. Moreover, this interpretation misleadingly suggests that the singular conclusion is no more probable than the inductive generalization, whereas actually the singular conclusion usually would be more probable than the corresponding generalization.

In judging the strength of an argument of this type, we need to take account of the five factors discussed in connection with inductive generalization and also of one additional factor:

1 We must consider the extent of the positive analogy among the observed instances, a, b, c; that is, the respects (not counting being S and being P) in which the previously observed instances are known to be alike. In the example of the post-

man, there was only one past instance; there the question of positive analogy among the previously observed instances does not arise.

2 Also we must consider the extent of the negative analogy among the observed instances, that is, the respects in which they are known to differ from one another. The greater the extent of these differences, the stronger is the argument.

3 We must consider how much the conclusion says. Does it make a very informative claim or is it comparatively vague? The more the conclusion says, the weaker is the argument. For example, the conclusion "This dog will bite" says more than does "This dog will bark or bite."

4 We should consider the number of observed instances, a, b, c, etc.; the more of them there are, the stronger is the argument.

5 We should consider what our past experience tells us about the probable relevance of S to P.

6 The additional very important factor that must be taken into account is the degree of analogy between the new thing d on the one hand and the previously observed instances a, b, c, etc., on the other hand. If it is known that d has properties that none of a, b, c, etc., possesses, or if it is known that all a, b, c, etc., possess properties that d lacks, then the argument is weaker than it would otherwise be. For example, if we know that a, b, c, etc., are all European swans but that d is an Australian swan, then our argument is weakened. But if d, to the best of our knowledge, is very like a, b, c, etc., then the argument may be quite strong.

When an argument by analogy is weak, sometimes a good way of showing that it is weak is to show that the available evidence permits us to construct other arguments by analogy that are no weaker but that reach an opposite conclusion. If I think that the postman is unduly worried about the analogy between the present boxer dog and the one he met in the past, I may try to show him the weakness of his reasoning by constructing an equally strong argument in support of the conclusion that this dog will not bite. I remind the postman that this new boxer belongs to old Mrs. Jones, who is well known for her amiable pets; the postman is forgetting that her cats are very friendly, so is her goat, and so is her pet crow. By analogy, since this dog resembles the cats, goat, and crow in being a pet of good old Mrs. Jones, probably it resembles them also in being friendly. Here I am able to use a *counteranalogy* in order to exhibit the weakness of the original argument by analogy.

EXERCISE 29

A *Coolidge College has played football against Harding University every year for the past ten years. In each of the past years, Harding has won. The odds makers predict that Harding will win again this year. How will the probability of that prediction be affected by each of the following situations?*

1 The games in past years took place in all kinds of weather: fair, rainy, snowy, cool, hot.
2 This year's game, unlike past games, will be at night under lights.
3 This year's game is the first of the season, just as all the past games were.
4 In all the past games, Harding won by at least three touchdowns.
5 The odds makers predict that Harding will win by at least three touchdowns.
6 The odds makers predict merely that Harding will not lose.
7 The Harding team has a new coach, whose previous experience has been in field hockey.
8 A professor at Coolidge has just won a Nobel prize in chemistry.
9 The team and fans at Harding have just recovered from an unprecedented epidemic of food poisoning.
10 Acting on behalf of the university, the trustees of Harding have wagered a substantial part of its endowment on the outcome of the game.

B *In each case explain what items are being compared, and in what respects. Is the analogy being used as the basis for an argument? If there is an argument, discuss its strength.*

1 As when a lion has worsted a tireless boar in conflict, when, with high hearts, they battle for some scant spring upon a mountain's peaks and both would drink, and the lion with

his might overcomes the quickly panting boar, so Hector, Priam's son, deprived Menoetius' brave son of his life with the spear, from close at hand, after he had slain many.

HOMER, *The Iliad*

2 The old couple were left alone in a home that looked suddenly shrunken and decrepit too. . . . Then Arina Vlasyevna went up to him and, laying her gray head to his, said: "It can't be helped, Vasya! A son is like a severed branch. He's like the falcon that comes when it wants and goes when it wants; and you and I are like mushrooms on a tree stump, sitting side by side forever on the same spot. Only I will remain the same to you always, and you to me."

IVAN TURGENEV, *Fathers and Sons*

3 Existential philosophy and the psycho-therapists . . . demonstrate to secure, contented, and happy mankind that it is really unhappy and desperate and simply unwilling to admit that it is in a predicament about which it knows nothing, and from which only they can rescue it. Wherever there is health, strength, security, simplicity, they scent luscious fruit to gnaw at or to lay their pernicious eggs in.

DIETRICH BONHOEFFER, *Letters and Papers from Prison*

4 Justice is the first virtue of social institutions, as truth is of systems of thought. A theory however elegant and economical must be rejected or revised if it is untrue; likewise laws and institutions no matter how efficient and well-arranged must be reformed or abolished if they are unjust. . . . The only thing that permits us to acquiesce in an erroneous theory is the lack of a better one; analogously, an injustice is tolerable only when it is necessary to avoid an even greater injustice.   JOHN RAWLS, *A Theory of Justice*

5 Mistresses are like books. If you pore upon them too much they doze you and make you unfit for company; but if used discreetly, you are the fitter for conversation by 'em.

WILLIAM WYCHERLEY, *The Country Wife*

6 Why then should the education of apes be impossible? Why might not the ape, by dint of great pains, at last imitate after the manner of deaf mutes, the motions necessary for pronunciation? I do not dare decide whether the ape's organs

of speech, however trained, would be incapable of articulation. But because of the great analogy between ape and man and because there is no known animal whose external and internal organs so strikingly resemble man's, it would surprise me if speech were absolutely impossible to the ape.

JULIEN OFFRAY DE LA METTRIE, *Man a Machine*

7 Every one who really thinks for himself is like a monarch. His position is undelegated and supreme. His judgments, like royal decrees, spring from his own sovereign power and proceed directly from himself. He acknowledges authority as little as a monarch admits a command; he subscribes to to nothing but what he has himself authorized. The multitude of common minds, laboring under all sorts of current opinions, authorities, prejudices, is like the people, which silently obeys the law and accepts orders from above.

ARTHUR SCHOPENHAUER, *The Art of Literature*

8 "Do you think," said Candide, "that men have always massacred each other, as they do today, that they have always been false, cozening, faithless, ungrateful, thieving, weak, inconstant, mean-spirited, envious, greedy, drunken, miserly, ambitious, bloody, slanderous, debauched, fanatic, hypocritical, and stupid?"

"Do you think," said Martin, "that hawks have always eaten pigeons when they could find them?"

"Of course I do," said Candide.

"Well," said Martin, "if hawks have always had the same character, why should you suppose that men have changed theirs?" VOLTAIRE, *Candide*

9 Words are like leaves; and where they most abound,
Much fruit of sense beneath is rarely found.

ALEXANDER POPE, "Essay on Criticism"

10 Johnson told me, that he went up thither without mentioning it to his servant, when he wanted to study, secure from interruption; for he would not allow his servant to say he was not at home when he really was. "A servant's strict regard for truth (said he) must be weakened by such a practice. A philosopher may know that it is merely a form of denial; but few servants are such nice distinguishers. If I

accustom a servant to tell a lie for *me*, have I not reason to apprehend that he will tell many lies for *himself*."

JAMES BOSWELL, *Life of Johnson*

HYPOTHESES ABOUT CAUSES

Next we shall consider inductive arguments that aim to establish conclusions about relations of cause and effect. Much of our thinking about the world involves questions of causes and effects; we need to know not merely what phenomena take place but also which phenomena cause which others. A sentence saying that one thing is cause of another thing (e.g., "Arsenic causes death") normally has to be an empirical sentence; it must be supported by inductive reasoning based upon observational evidence. Let us consider the sort of evidence and the sort of reasoning that are required. (To be sure, there are necessary sentences about causal relations, e.g., "Fatal wounds cause death." But these are comparatively trivial and uninteresting.)

A fallacy related to causes occurs often in political speeches and in other common kinds of careless thinking. Suppose someone argues, "There was a decrease in unemployment soon after President Smith took office. So Smith deserves credit for getting people back to work." This is an inductive argument, an argument whose conclusion is a hypothesis about cause and effect (that decreased employment was an effect caused by Smith). But it is a very bad argument. It commits the fallacy of *post hoc, ergo propter hoc* (Latin: "after this, therefore on account of it"). This fallacy is a special case of the general fallacy of hasty induction. Here the speaker has leaped from the evidence that unemployment declined soon after Smith took office to the conclusion that unemployment declined because Smith had taken office. This is too hasty a leap. To be sure, the fact that unemployment declined soon after he took office may, if there is no contrary evidence, make it faintly probable that perhaps he was the cause; but this fact is utterly insufficient to make it strongly probable that he was the cause. We would need much more evidence before we could reasonably attach any strong probability to the conclusion.

In order to know that one thing is the cause of another, we

need to know that the first thing happened or existed earlier than the second, but we need to know a great deal more besides. (In most ordinary cases a cause certainly must precede its effect; whether there are some cases in which a cause may merely be simultaneous with its effect is a point disputed by philosophers, upon which we need not enter.)

What is involved in saying that one thing causes another, beyond the claim that the former thing happens earlier? Let us consider another case: A doctor gives an experimental drug to a patient suffering from a serious disease; the next day the patient's symptoms are lessened, and he gradually recovers. What would it mean to say that taking the drug caused the cure in this particular case? We can discuss this matter without worrying about the inner biochemical processes occurring in the patient's bloodstream, for it is possible to know that x causes y without knowing the intervening steps by means of which x causes y (the Indians knew that taking quinine often causes relief from malaria, although they knew nothing about how it does so).

But what does it mean to say that taking the drug caused the cure? For one thing, it means that taking this drug was somehow *sufficient* to ensure this patient's cure. If he took the drug, then he would be cured. This still is not very clear. But it can be explained as follows: What has happened in this patient's case is an instance of some general regularity, whereby anyone whose case is appropriately similar to that of this patient will cease to have the ailment after taking the drug as he did. (Note that the claim that taking the drug cured this patient would be refuted if we discovered that other, similar patients are not cured after taking it as he did.)

For another thing, to claim that this dose cured this patient surely is to claim that in cases like his, taking the drug is *necessary* in order for the cure to occur when it does. That is, if the patient had not had the drug, he would not have been cured (at least, not when he was). Yet someone may object: What sense does it make to talk about what would have occurred if something that did happen had not happened? We cannot go back and change the past; how could we ever find out whether the patient would have recovered without the drug? We must answer this objection by pointing out that talk about what would have happened to this patient derives its sense from its implicit reference to what does happen to other, appropriately similar patients on other sufficiently similar occasions. When we say that if this patient had not had the dose, he would not have been cured, we are implicitly claiming that other patients with the same ailment, whose cases are appropriately similar to that of this patient except that they do not get the drug, are not usually cured.

Putting together these points and generalizing them, we may say that a sentence of the form "x causes y" by its very meaning normally implies not only that x occurs earlier than y but also that, in cases of some appropriate kind, x always is present if y is, and only if y is. This is a central part, though to be sure not all, of what is meant by speaking of causes.

> Some people might object to what has been said, on the ground that it is vague to speak of "cases of some certain kind" or of cases that are "appropriately similar." To this we must reply that of course it is vague, but that is not a ground for objecting. The general notion of causation is a rather vague notion, though not on that account a useless notion.
>
> Another aspect of the notion of cause is that we commonly speak about *the* cause of an event. For instance, a coroner is asked to determine *the* cause of a victim's death. There are innumerable events, each of which in a sense could be said to have caused the death: the victim died because his brain ceased to receive oxygen, because his blood stopped circulating, because his heart stopped beating, because a bullet traveled toward his body, because his enemy pulled the trigger, and so on. Each of these events is such that death in closely similar cases occurs if and only if the given event occurs. But the coroner will report as the cause of death that a bullet passed through the heart. When he calls this *the* cause of death, the coroner is not denying that many other events belonged to the chain of causes and effects that eventuated in death; the coroner is doing his duty by focusing attention upon one especially significant event in the chain. This event, which he calls *the* cause, is especially significant because it is the event upon which we can best focus our attention if we want to assign responsibility for such a death and upon which we can best focus our efforts if we want to prevent or control deaths of this type.

The nineteenth-century English philosopher John Stuart Mill described several fundamental ways of detecting causes. These are known as *Mill's methods*. When properly understood and not overrated, these methods are useful in guiding our thinking about causes. We shall consider three of these methods, discussing them first in connection with a concrete example.

Suppose that some of the students who eat in the Coolidge College cafeteria are taken ill after lunch. We investigate a few of the cases and gather the following data:

Student *a* ate soup, ate fish, ate salad, and got ptomaine.
Student *b* ate soup, ate no fish, ate salad, and got ptomaine.
Student *c* ate no soup, ate fish, ate salad, and got ptomaine.

These data will enable us to reach a conclusion about the cause of the food poisoning, provided that we may make a certain assumption. We must be entitled to assume that one and only one of the factors listed (eating of soup, eating of fish, eating of salad) is the cause of the food poisoning. If we assume that, we can use what Mill called the *method of agreement:* We reason that the cause must be present in each case where the effect is present. Here eating salad must have been the cause of the ptomaine, since it is the factor with regard to which all the cases agree.

On another occasion, students again are taken ill. This time we collect the following data:

Student *a* ate meat, ate pie, ate ice cream, and got ptomaine.
Student *b* ate no meat, ate pie, ate no ice cream, and got no ptomaine.
Student *c* ate meat, ate no pie, ate no ice cream, and got no ptomaine.

Again, before we can draw any definite conclusion, we must be entitled to assume that the cause is some one of the factors on the list. But if we make this assumption, we can use what Mill called the *method of difference:* We reason that any factor present in cases in which the effect is absent cannot be the cause. Thus, by process of elimination, we see that eating ice cream must have been the cause of the food poisoning on this occasion.

On still another occasion we again find students being taken ill after eating in the cafeteria. This time we collect the following data:

Student *a* ate one hamburger and got ptomaine with fever of 101°.
Student *b* ate two hamburgers and got ptomaine with fever of 102°.
Student *c* ate three hamburgers and got ptomaine with fever of 103°.

Here we are concerned not with the simple presence or absence of cause and effect but rather with the degree to which cause and effect are present. When we infer from these data that the hamburgers caused the ptomaine, we are employing what Mill called the *method of concomitant variation*. If a factor is present in all and only those cases in which the effect is present, then the more closely its variations in degree are correlated with the variations in degree of the effect, the greater is the probability that this factor is the cause.

Mill regarded these three* methods as useful both as a guide in collecting data and planning new experiments to discover causes and as a guide in reflecting about the strength of arguments that try to prove conclusions about cause and effect. His methods are useful in both these ways: for planning further inquiries and for evaluating results that have been obtained. However, we must not make the mistake of assuming that these simple methods provide an infallible way of detecting causes. Far from it, for in any overall piece of inductive reasoning within which we make use of Mill's methods, we always must evaluate the probability that we have actually included the cause among the factors of which we take account. Unless we are entitled to think it probable that we have done this, use of these methods is not legitimate.

Fallacies involving Mill's methods occur frequently. A crude example is this: Suppose that one day a man eats popcorn while watching television and suffers indigestion; the next day he eats pizza while watching television and suffers indigestion; the next day he eats cheesecake while watching television and suffers indigestion. Using the method of difference, he argues that neither popcorn nor pizza nor cheesecake caused his indigestion, and he concludes that watching television caused it (perhaps because of the electrical radiations). Here the reasoning is absurd, for the list of factors of which he took account omits overeating, which certainly ought to have been considered as a possible cause. Here the cause in general was overeating, but eating too much popcorn was the specific cause on the first

---

* In his *System of Logic,* Mill discusses two additional methods, the joint method of agreement and difference and the method of residues. But these are just slightly more complicated ways of using the method of agreement and the method of difference; they do not introduce any new principle.

night, eating too much pizza was the specific cause on the second night, and so on.

As another example, suppose it is found that in a certain town those young people who regularly attend church relatively seldom get into trouble with the police, while those who do not attend church relatively more often get into trouble with the police. Using the method of difference, the local religious leaders point to these facts as proof that religion causes improvement in the moral fiber of the young. Is this a reasonable conclusion? Not if it is assumed that these data by themselves confer any very high degree of probability upon the conclusion. There are certainly other factors that should be taken into account before we could say that any strong proof had been given. Is it not very possible, for instance, that their wholesome family environment causes some young people both to be religious and to be law-abiding, whereas the unwholesome family environment of others causes them to be neither religious nor law-abiding?

EXERCISE 30

A *Are Mill's methods being employed in the following examples, and, if so, which of them? Discuss the soundness of the reasoning.*

1 Jim drank whisky and soda, and felt great. Bill drank brandy and soda, and felt great. Sue drank vermouth and soda, and felt great. Soda seems to make you feel great.
2 Whenever my electric lights go dim, my television picture shrinks. So I certainly wouldn't want to install dimmer switches for the lights in my house, as that would mean constant interference with the television.
3 Top-flight mathematicians usually are interested in music. So if you want to become a really good mathematician, it would be a good idea for you to cultivate a taste for music.
4 Most of the children born in Arabia grow up to be Moslems. So you'd better not let your children be born there, if you don't want them to become Moslems.
5 You might not believe it, but brushing a dog can cure its ailments. My Irish setter was gravely ill, but I brushed her all night long, and in the morning she was well.

6   A Stanford research team has calculated that the 3 million American males between the ages of twenty-five and thirty-four who have failed to complete high school will earn $237 billion less in personal income over their working lifetimes than will be earned by an equal number of high school graduates. They estimate that it would have cost only $40 billion to put these men through high school. "Each dollar of social investment for this purpose would have generated about $6 per capita of national income, over the lifetime of the group," they stated.

7   According to a study sponsored by the National Institute of Human Development, more teenagers who obtained abortions than teenagers who gave birth were practicing contraception at the time they became pregnant. This indicates that teenagers are not using abortion as a substitute for contraception.

8   In Glasgow a German shepherd lifted his leg in the natural fashion, but his target was a city electricity junction box, and the resulting short circuit blew him into the street. Soon he grew grumpy and distrustful, and bit his master. The owner sued the city for damages, saying that he was off work for eight weeks because of the bite. But the sheriff rejected his claim, declaring that the injury was inflicted by the dog, not by the city.

9   An insurance company's study showed that among 3300 automobile-insurance policyholders the accident frequency for those who said they were nonsmokers was 3.75 per 100 car-years, compared with 6.59 for those who said they were smokers. The company concluded that nonsmokers are significantly better insurance risks.

10 On the average, children born between May and October seem to get slightly higher scores in intelligence tests than children born from November to April. Is it the season of conception or birth that somehow affects the intelligence of children, in so far as these tests can measure it, or is it the intelligence of the parents that influences the season of conception of the child? The second must surely be the explanation: for example, when one compares the average scores of winter and summer children who are brothers and sisters, the difference between them almost completely disappears.   P. B. MEDAWAR, *The Future of Man*

11   It cannot be assumed that economic motives are the only ones which determine the behavior of men in society. The unquestionable fact that different individuals, races and nations behave differently under the same economic conditions in itself proves that the economic factor cannot be the sole determinant.

SIGMUND FREUD, "Thoughts for the Time on War and Death"

12   The unconscious . . . has . . . ways . . . of informing us of things which by all logic we could not possibly know. . . .   I recall one time during World War II when I was returning home from Bollingen. . . .   The moment the train started to move I was overpowered by the image of someone drowning.   This was a memory of an accident that had happened while I was on military service. . . .   I got out at Erlenbach and walked home. . . .   Adrian, then the youngest of the boys, had fallen into the water at the boathouse.   It is quite deep there, and since he could not really swim he had almost drowned. . . .   This had taken place at exactly the time I had been assailed by that memory in the train. The unconscious had given me a hint.

CARL G. JUNG, *Memories, Dreams, Reflections*

B   *Black sprinkled strychnine on the tacos he was serving to Gray; Gray ate them and died within hours.   Discuss the following comments on this incident.*

1   Black's sprinkling of the strychnine cannot have been the cause of Gray's death, since not every strychnine-sprinkled taco causes someone to die.

2   Gray's eating poisoned tacos cannot have been the cause of Gray's death, since not everyone who eats poisoned food dies of it.

3   If Gray had taken an antidote promptly, the poison would not have been fatal.   So the cause—or part of the cause—of Gray's death was that he failed to taken an antidote promptly.

4   Black's sprinkling of the strychnine cannot have caused Gray's death, for there cannot be a lapse of time between cause and effect.   What we ought to say is that Black's sprinkling of the strychnine caused the tacos to be poisonous; Gray's eating them caused an internal bodily condition;

which caused another; which caused another . . . which
caused death.

5 Really, the cause of Gray's death must be the total state of
the universe in the instant just preceding his death.

NUMERICAL PROBABILITIES

We have been using the word "probability" in a sense that has
to do with inductive arguments, identifying the degree of probability with the degree to which it is reasonable to believe the
conclusion on the basis of the evidence. Probability is always a
relative matter, in that it makes sense to call a conjecture probable only relative to some evidence, never just in and of itself.
A conjecture, whether true or false, may have a high degree of
probability relative to one body of evidence and a low degree
of probability relative to some other body of evidence.

Various symbols can be used to represent probability, but
we shall employ a pair of slanting strokes: //. We shall use
strokes between two sentences to form an expression that names
the probability of the first sentence relative to the second. Thus,
if we let "H" be one sentence and "E" another, we write "$H // E$"
as a name for the probability of the former relative to the latter,
that is, the degree to which it would be reasonable to believe
the former if the latter was the evidence one had. According
to this conception, if there were cases in which completely
reasonable men could differ in their judgments about the credibility of a conclusion on the basis of given evidence, in those
cases we could not speak of the probability. For simple normal
cases, however, it seems safe to assume that men could not
disagree without being unreasonable.

In the expression "$H // E$," "H" is the hypothesis (the conclusion) whose probability we are weighing, and "E" is the
evidence (the premise, or conjunction of premises) upon which
the probability is based. If we let "H" represent the sentence
"All swans are white," "H'" represent "The next swan we meet
will be white," and "E" symbolize our evidence regarding swans
that we have observed to be white, then we can write:

$$H' // E > H // E$$

That is, the probability that the next swan will be white is greater than is the probability that all swans are white, relative to our evidence. Here we make a comparison between two degrees of probability, although we have not assigned a definite numerical value to either.

One small reservation is necessary. We shall speak of the probability of a hypothesis sentence relative to the evidence sentence only where the evidence sentence is not a contradiction. Where "E" represents a contradiction, other sentences cannot have any sort of probability, high or low, relative to it, as we are interested in considering the probabilities of hypotheses relative only to evidence that might possibly be true. To put it another way, when an inductive argument is found to have inconsistent premises, we must reject the argument completely; there is no point in thinking that the conclusion possesses any sort of probability, high or low, relative to inconsistent premises.

There is a maximum possible degree of probability. Knowing that a sentence is true occasionally puts one in a position of being equally certain of another sentence. Then the probability of the second sentence relative to the first has the maximum possible value. This happens when (and only when) the first sentence deductively implies the second. For instance, the probability of "Some white things are swans" relative to the evidence "Some swans are white" has this maximum value. It is conventional to correlate the number 1 with this maximum degree of probability. Writing "W" for the first sentence and "S" for the second, we have:

$$W \,/\!/\, S = 1$$

There is also a minimum possible degree of probability. Knowing that "Some swans are white" is true, one is in a position to assign the minimum degree of probability to the sentence "All swans are black" ("B" for short); that is, relative to the known data, the degree to which it is reasonable to believe "B" has hit rock bottom. It is conventional to correlate the number zero with this minimum degree of probability. Thus we say:

$$B \,/\!/\, S = 0$$

This minimum degree of probability arises when (and only when) the hypothesis is contradicted by the evidence.

All other degrees of probability fall between these two extremes. Degrees of probability falling between these extremes sometimes are comparable with one another and sometimes are not. We can say that relative to the historical evidence we now possess, it is more probable that there was such a man as Plato than that there was such a man as Homer, and it is more probable that there was such a man as George Washington than that there was such a man as Plato. But it does not make sense to ask for an exact measure of how much more probable one of these hypotheses is than another. Moreover, suppose someone asks whether, relative to present evidence, the hypothesis that there was such a man as Homer is more or less probable than is the hypothesis that there is no life on Mars. We cannot answer, because there is no answer. The two hypotheses are very different, and there is no basis upon which to compare their degrees of probability.

If there is no reason for calling one probability greater than another, we cannot maintain that they must be equal, for that view would lead to absurdities. For instance, it would lead us to say that the probability that there was such a man as Homer is equal to the probability that there is no life on Mars (since we have no reason for calling one probability greater than the other); it would also lead us to say that the probability that there was such a man as George Washington is equal to the probability that there is no life on Mars (since we again have no reason for calling one probability greater than the other). This would imply that the probability that Homer existed equals the probability that Washington existed; yet these probabilities are not equal. Thus we must conclude that it is sometimes, but not always, possible to compare degrees of probability of this kind.

In certain special but important kinds of cases, however, we not only can compare probabilities, we can compare them so fully that numbers between 0 and 1 can be assigned to represent their degrees. Use of numbers means that every numerical probability is comparable with every other (either greater, smaller, or equal). Also, we can go further and introduce arithmetical operations such as addition and subtraction. In what sort of situation may numbers be used to measure probabilities? The most straightforward kinds of cases in which this is possible are ones like those involved in some gambling games, where the events in which we are interested can be analyzed into certain fundamental possibilities that are equally reasonable to expect.

Consider the rolling of dice. If someone shows us a pair of dice and we have no positive reason for thinking them irregular, the reasonable thing to suppose is that these dice, when rolled, will behave generally as do most other dice. That is, we believe that the various faces of each die will come up just about equally often in the long run, although their sequence will be unpredictable, and that there will be no detectable correlation, in the long run, between the sequence in which faces come up on one die and on the other.

Granting this, what is reasonable to expect regarding the outcome of the next roll of these two dice? It is certain that on the next roll each die must show one and only one of its six faces. (Otherwise a genuine roll would not have been achieved.) We have for each die six mutually exclusive and exhaustive alternatives, which are equally reasonable to expect; therefore, each of these outcomes must be assigned a probability of $1/6$. Then what is the probability of getting, say, a total of 7 with the two dice? Here we must reason as follows: With two dice, each of which can land in just one of six equally probable ways, there are thirty-six equally probable outcomes. We write "1–1" to represent the first die landing with one dot up and the second die landing with one dot up, etc. Of these outcomes there are six (underlined in the list) that yield the result in which we are interested, that is, showing a total of seven dots.

1–1	1–2	1–3	1–4	1–5	1–6
2–1	2–2	2–3	2–4	2–5	2–6
3–1	3–2	3–3	3–4	3–5	3–6
4–1	4–2	4–3	4–4	4–5	4–6
5–1	5–2	5–3	5–4	5–5	5–6
6–1	6–2	6–3	6–4	6–5	6–6

Thus the probability of rolling a 7 equals 6 divided by 36, or $1/6$. Here we are following the general principle that the numerical probability of a result is equal to the number of outcomes favorable to that result divided by the total number of possible outcomes. This principle makes sense only when we use an exhaustive list of mutually exclusive and equally probable outcomes, but it is one way in which we can assign numerical values to some probabilities.

Once we have obtained some numerical probabilities, we can make use of certain elementary laws for deriving further numerical probabilities from ones already known. First there is the law relating the probability of a sentence to the probability of its negation.

Law of negation
$$-p \mathbin{/\!/} q = 1 - p \mathbin{/\!/} q$$

The probability of the negation of a sentence, relative to given evidence, is equal to 1 minus the probability of the sentence itself relative to that same evidence. Notice here that the short dash symbolizes negation—a sentence can have a negation, but a number cannot. The long dash is the subtraction sign—only numbers can be subtracted from one another, not sentences. The strokes are our probability sign, which must not be confused with a division sign, for only sentences are probable relative to one another, and only numbers can be divided by one another.

Let us apply this law of negation to the case of rolling dice. What is the probability of not rolling 7 on the next roll of the dice? This must be 1 minus $\frac{1}{6}$ (the probability of rolling 7), that is, $\frac{5}{6}$. We can see the correctness of this answer if we look at the list and count the number of ways in which the two dice could fall so as to yield a total different from 7. There are 30 out of 36, and so the probability is indeed $\frac{5}{6}$.

Another law is designed for calculating the probability of a conjunction.

Law of conjunction
$$p \mathbin{\&} q \mathbin{/\!/} r = p \mathbin{/\!/} r \times q \mathbin{/\!/} r \mathbin{\&} p$$

This law tells us that the probability relative to given evidence that two things both will come true equals the probability of the first multiplied by the probability of the second when we assume that the first is true. What is the probability that on the next roll of the dice we will obtain a total greater than 4 and less than 7? Using the law of conjunction, we reason as follows:

Table 1

Possible outcomes, throwing two dice once (36)	Outcomes with more than four dots up (30)	Outcomes with less than seven but more than four dots up (9)	1–1, 1–2, 1–3, 2–1, 2–2, 3–1
			1–4, 1–5, 2–3, 2–4, 3–2, 3–3, 4–1, 4–2, 5–1
		1–6, 2–5, 2–6, 3–4, 3–5, 3–6, 4–3, 4–4, 4–5, 4–6, 5–2, 5–3, 5–4, 5–5, 5–6, 6–1, 6–2, 6–3, 6–4, 6–5, 6–6	

The probability of getting a total greater than 4 and less than 7 equals the probability of getting a total greater than 4 (30 divided by 36, since 30 possible outcomes are favorable out of the total of 36) multiplied by the probability of getting a total less than 7, on the assumption that our total is greater than 4 (9 divided by 30, since there are 30 possibilities where the total is greater than 4; of these, 9 are favorable to its being less than 7). Thus we have $^{30}/_{36} \times ^{9}/_{30} = ^{9}/_{36} = ^{1}/_{4}$. If we look at the total list of possible outcomes (Table 1), we see that the law of conjunction has given us the correct result. Table 1 is drawn up to indicate how the law of conjunction has led us to the proper answer in this case.

We can apply the law of conjunction in a simpler way in cases where the happenings that concern us are *independent*; that is, where the probability of q is unaltered by the assumption that p is true. Suppose we want to calculate the probability of getting heads on the first toss of a coin and geting heads also on the second toss. Here we must multiply the probability of getting heads on the first toss (which is ½, when there is no reason to think the coin abnormal) times the probability of getting heads on the second toss (which is again ½). The probability is simply ½ times ½, or ¼, because here the two events are independent in the sense that what happens on the first toss does not alter the probability of getting heads on the second toss. Where the happenings are independent in this way, we can use the law of conjunction in the simple form:

$$p \,\&\, q\,//\,r = p\,//\,r \times q\,//\,r$$

We also have a law designed for calculating the probability of a disjunction; that is, the probability that at least one of two things will come true.

Law of disjunction
$$p \lor q \,/\!/\, r = p \,/\!/\, r + q \,/\!/\, r - p \,\&\, q \,/\!/\, r$$

This law tells us that the probability of a (nonexclusive) disjunction equals the sum of the separate probabilities of its components, minus the probability of their conjunction. For instance, with two dice, what is the probability that either both dice will read alike or that the total will be less than 6? The law tells us that this must equal the probability that both dice will read alike (6 divided by 36), plus the probability that their total will be less than 6 (10 divided by 36), minus the probability that both dice will read alike and have a total less than 6 (2 divided by 36). Thus the probability equals $7/18$. We can confirm the correctness of this result by looking again at the complete list of outcomes (Table 2).

We can calculate the probability of a disjunction in a simpler way if the components cannot both be true. What is the probability that a single die will land with five dots up or with six dots up on a single throw? Here the probability is $1/6$ plus $1/6$ minus zero. We subtract nothing, since the die cannot show two different faces on a single throw. Thus, in cases where the outcomes are mutually exclusive, we merely add the separate probabilities in order to get the probability of the disjunction.

Table 2

	Outcomes when both dice read alike (6)	3–3, 4–4, 5–5, 6–6
Possible outcomes, throwing two dice once (36)		1–1, 2–2
	Outcomes with less than six dots up (10)	1–2, 1–3, 1–4, 2–1, 2–3, 3–1, 3–2, 4–1
		1–5, 1–6, 2–4, 2–5, 2–6, 3–4, 3–5, 3–6, 4–2, 4–3, 4–5, 4–6, 5–1, 5–2, 5–3, 5–4, 5–6, 6–1, 6–2, 6–3, 6–4, 6–5

One of the practical uses of these rules for calculating probabilities is deciding whether a gamble is a reasonable one. Suppose that someone invites you to draw two cards from a well-shuffled bridge deck, the first card to be returned and the deck reshuffled before the second card is drawn. He bets you even money that you will not get a spade on either drawing. Would it be reasonable to accept such a bet?

In order to answer, we must calculate your probability of winning. To win, you must draw a spade either on the first trial or on the second trial. There are thirteen spades in the deck of fifty-two cards, and so your probability of succeeding on the first draw is $^{13}/_{52}$, or $^1/_4$; your probability of succeeding on the second draw is the same. But to obtain the probability of your succeeding the first time or the second time, we cannot simply add these two fractions and call that the answer. (According to that fallacious procedure of reckoning, it would be absolutely certain that you would succeed at least once in four drawings—an absurd result.) By the law of alternation, we must add the two probabilities and then subtract the probability of succeeding both times, which, according to the law of conjunction, is $^{13}/_{52} \times {}^{13}/_{52}$, or $^1/_{16}$. Thus the probability of winning the bet is $^1/_4$ plus $^1/_4$ minus $^1/_{16}$, or $^7/_{16}$. Your opponent's probability of winning, according to the law of negation, is 1 minus $^7/_{16}$, or $^9/_{16}$. He has a greater probability of winning than you have, and if the odds are even money it would normally be foolish to accept such a bet.

If your opponent offers better odds in your favor, it may no longer be unreasonable to accept the bet. If he wagers $9 to your $7, your probability of winning ($^7/_{16}$) multiplied by the amount you stand to win ($9) equals your probability of losing ($^9/_{16}$) multiplied by the amount you stand to lose ($7). The result of multiplying a probability by an amount of gain or loss is called a *mathematical expectation.* We say that a bet is a *fair bet* when the mathematical expectation of gain is equal to the mathematical expectation of loss for each gambler. For it to be reasonable

---

* Gain and loss should perhaps be measured in terms of utility (amount of benefit or harm), not just in terms of money. If winning $9 would merely make one a little less poor, while losing $7 would drive one into bankruptcy, then the expectation of loss on the bet is really greater than the expectation of gain, though not in dollar terms.

to accept a bet, the mathematical expectation of gain should be at least as great as the mathematical expectation of loss.

Now, to say, for instance, that the probability is ⅙ that a pair of dice will land with a total of seven spots up does not mean that we can definitely expect this outcome to occur once in every six rolls of the dice. Far from it; there is only a moderate probability that this will occur exactly once in a given sequence of six throws. And the probability is very low indeed that in a long series of throws every sixth one will yield this particular outcome. What we can say, however, is that it is highly probable that in the long run just about one-sixth of the outcomes will yield a total of seven spots up. The larger the number of throws, the higher is the probability that the fraction of them yielding the outcome 7 will differ from ⅙ by less than any specified percentage. The longer the run, the more probable it is that the relative frequency with which an outcome occurs will closely approximate the probability of that outcome. This principle, which is sometimes referred to as the *law of large numbers,* or the *law of averages,* is fundamental to statistical inference.

> The mathematical notion of limit is needed for a more exact formulation of this principle. Let "x" be the probability of a certain outcome (such as getting a total of 7 in rolling two dice). Let "y" be the number of trials (the number of times the dice are rolled). Let "z" be the fraction of these trials in which that certain outcome occurs. And let "w" be an arbitrarily chosen percentage (such as 1 percent, 0.01 percent, etc.). Then the principle is that, for each choice of w, the probability that the absolute value of the difference between z and x will be less than w increases toward 1 as its limit, as y increases without bound.

Misunderstanding of this principle leads to a common and insidious fallacy, the *Monte Carlo fallacy.* Suppose that a man is playing roulette, and he notices that a certain number has not come up for a long time. He reasons that, because this number has not come up for a long time, there is an increased probability that it will come up on the next spin of the wheel. Or a man is rolling dice, and he notices that 7 has not been thrown as often lately as was to have been expected; he therefore decides to accept at odds of less than 5 to 1 a bet that 7 will be thrown on the next roll of the two dice. In both these cases a fallacy is being committed. Both these men are confused in their thinking and are laying their bets foolishly. The law of large numbers does not tell us anything about the probability of what will happen on the next throw; it tells us only about a long-run probability.

It is a complete mistake to think that in this kind of case the relative infrequency of an outcome in the past makes it more probable that it will occur in the future. This kind of thinking runs directly contrary to the whole basic idea of inductive reasoning: the idea that we should expect for the future the *same* sort of thing that we have observed in the past. Those who commit the Monte Carlo fallacy make the mistake of expecting for the future the opposite of what they have observed in the past, because of their misunderstanding of the meaning of the principle about long-run probabilities.

The Monte Carlo fallacy perhaps is best classified as a fallacy of ambiguity. The arguer assumes that "It is improbable that a certain number will fail to come up in n trials" means "Relative to the evidence that the wheel has spun $n-1$ times, without stopping on that number, it is probable that it will stop there the nth time." Whereas in fact what the sentence means is "Relative to our general evidence about roulette wheels, it is improbable that a wheel will spin n times without ever stopping on that number." Confusion between these two meanings engenders the fallacy.

EXERCISE 31

A *Calculate the following probabilities. Be ready to explain your procedure.*

1 A coin is to be tossed twice. What is the probability of getting heads at least once?
2 A coin is to be tossed twice. What is the probability of getting heads both times?
3 A coin is to be tossed three times. Not to get tails at least once would be the same as to get heads each time. Calculate this probability by two different methods.
4 In a single rolling of two dice, what is the probability of getting: **(a)** 12; **(b)** 2; **(c)** 6; **(d)** 9?
5 In two rollings of a pair of dice, what is the probability of getting 7 at least once? Of getting 7 both times?
6 Two cards are to be drawn from a bridge deck; the first will not be returned to the deck before the second is drawn.

What is the probability that both cards will be spades? That at least one will be a spade?

7   Three cards will be drawn from a bridge deck, and not returned to the deck.   What is the probability that at least one will be a spade?   That all three will be spades?

8   The odds are 2 to 1 against Loppylugs winning the Kentucky Derby.   But the odds are even that he will win the Preakness, if he has won the Kentucky Derby.   What is the probability that he will win both races?   At what odds would it be reasonable to bet on him to win both races?

9   The odds are 3 to 2 in favor of Loppylugs winning the Belmont Stakes, if he has won the Kentucky Derby and the Preakness.   What is the probability that he will win all three races?   At what odds would it be reasonable to bet that he will win the Triple Crown? (Use information given in 8 above.)

10   On earth there are two sexes—male and female—which are equally numerous.   On Mars there are three sexes—alpha, beta, and gamma—which are equally numerous.   Which is more probable: that an earth couple who are going to have two children will have at least one male child, or that a Martian triple who are going to have three children will have at least one alpha child?

B   *Discuss the soundness of the reasoning in the following examples.*

1   The Greens are going to have a child.   The probability is ½ that it will be blond, and ½ that it will be a girl.   So the probability that it will be a blond girl is ½ times ½, or ¼.

2   Gray has an even chance to pass physics, and an even chance to pass mathematics; so the odds are 3 to 1 against his passing both courses.

3   All that we know about the upcoming election is that either a Democrat or a Republican will win.   Therefore, relative to the information we possess, the probability that a Democrat will win equals ½.

4   I have tossed this coin 100 times now, and it has come up heads each time.   By the law of averages, this cannot go on.   So it's more than likely I'll get tails on the next toss.

5   I've been rolling these dice you lent me all day, and have

never got a 7.   If you want to bet with me that I won't get a 7 on the next roll, you'll have to give me better odds than 5 to 1; I want odds of 10 to 1.

6   You've never had an automobile accident?   Well, then, I won't ride with you.   You're probably due for a smashup soon.

7   The odds are 5 to 4 that next winter will be colder than average.   It follows that the odds are 4 to 5 that next winter will be warmer than average.

8   True, you could go to prison for that murder.   But don't worry!   Maybe you won't be indicted; even if you are, maybe you won't be brought to trial; even if you are, maybe the witnesses won't testify against you; even if they do, maybe the jury won't convict you; even if they do, maybe the judge won't send you to prison.   So the probability of your going to prison is really very small indeed.

9   When you play slot machines at the casino, don't play just one machine.   Move around and try many different ones. That way, you'll get diversification, and so you'll have the best prospect of winning.

EXPLANATORY HYPOTHESES

So far, we have considered some special types of inductive arguments and the special considerations that bear upon their strength.   But there is also a more general way of looking at inductive reasoning, a point of view that is often appropriate when we are evaluating the strength of inductive arguments of various types.   We may think of the conclusion of an inductive argument as a hypothesis, a conjecture about the empirical world, and we may think of the premises as data presented in support of that hypothesis.   From this point of view, it is possible for us to ask, Is this hypothesis a plausible *explanation* of the data?   Asking this question can often help when we are trying to form a clear view of the strength of the inductive argument itself.   An inductive argument establishes a high probability for its conclusion, provided that it is possible to regard the conclusion as a hypothesis supplying the best explanation of the data contained in the premises.

To go back to the example used in discussing inductive generalization, let us suppose that we have observed many white swans and have never observed a swan that is not white. How strongly does this evidence support the conclusion that all swans are white? Here it is helpful to adopt this new viewpoint and ask, How well does the hypothesis that all swans are white explain the fact that we have obtained these observations? Our data make the generalization highly probable only if the generalization itself helps to provide the most probable explanation of why these were the data which we obtained. Are there other equally reasonable ways of explaining why it has happened that all the swans we have seen have been white? Is it perhaps that we have looked only at American swans and have missed nonwhite swans in other countries? Is it perhaps that we have looked at swans only in summertime and have missed nonwhite swans in other seasons? In any such case, the inductive argument is weak; if not, it is stronger. Asking ourselves whether the generalization provides the most reasonable explanation of the data is a good way of helping to evaluate the degree of probability that the data confer on the generalization. This general point of view can be helpful in connection with most types of inductive inference.

When we adopt this point of view and ask about the reasonableness of some explanatory hypothesis, we should bear in mind that for any set of data there always are many incompatible ways in which the data might conceivably be explained. Sometimes one line of explanation is definitely very much better than all other conflicting lines of explanation. If the silver spoons are missing from their rack on the dining-room wall; if the maid, who had left hastily, is arrested and found to have the spoons concealed in her car; and if she confesses to having stolen them; then, in the light of these data, by far the most reasonable explanation is that the maid stole the spoons, just as she says. We might well say, "That's the only possible explanation," by which we would mean that this is the best and thus most probable explanation.

Yet even here it is perfectly conceivable that the true explanation could be something different. Conceivably, there may have been an open window through which a crow, attracted by the glitter of the spoons, carried them off one by one and concealed them in the maid's car; she, having been disappointed in love, was in such a low state of mind when apprehended by the police that she readily confessed to the action of which they accused her. This is a conceivable hypothesis, though a very improbable one. The point is that always, if we use imagination, we can think of alternative explanations. We never are absolutely limited to a single hypothesis, since there always are alternative conceivable explanations. We always are faced with choice, and our problem is to choose the most reasonable hypothesis, that is, the one providing the best explanation.

Various factors combine to make one explanatory hypothesis more probable than another. These are not describable in any sharp, precise way, but we can say something about them.

We are likely to think that the extent to which it 'fits the facts' contributes greatly to determining the probability of an explanatory hypothesis. If one hypothesis succeeds in explaining more of the data than another does, this increases the probability of the former. Suppose that only the solid-silver spoons and none of the plated spoons are missing. The hypothesis that the maid stole the spoons explains this, for the maid would know that the plated spoons were of less value, whereas the hypothesis that an unknown crow stole the spoons does not explain this. However, whether a hypothesis 'fits the facts' is not a simple yes-or-no matter. Although the crow hypothesis does not *easily* fit the fact that only the solid-silver spoons are gone, still we could think of some auxiliary hypothesis which, when combined with the crow hypothesis, would provide a conceivable explanation of this troublesome fact. Perhaps there were two crows, both attracted by the shininess of the spoons; the larger crow carried off all the spoons, and then the smaller crow, out of spite, brought back as many spoons as it could but was not strong enough to lift the heavier solid-silver spoons and so returned only the plated ones. This is a far-fetched yet not a totally impossible line of explanation.

There is no limit to the lengths to which we can go in making any hypothesis 'fit the facts,' if we are imaginative enough in thinking of auxiliary hypotheses. In the end, perhaps the best way of looking at the matter is this: We should not think that we have to choose between one single hypothesis and another (e.g., the hypothesis that the maid stole the spoons versus the hypothesis that a crow did). Instead we should think of the choice as lying between whole *sets* of hypotheses (the hypotheses that the maid stole the spoons just as she said and that crows had nothing to do with it, versus the hypotheses that one crow stole the spoons and another brought back some of them, and the maid had a lover who disapointed her, etc.). As we think over the total body of known data, we ask ourselves, Which *set* of hypotheses best explains these data? If one set of hypotheses stands out as giving a much more reasonable line of explanation than does any other set, then all the hypotheses of that set are probably true.

When we compare sets of hypotheses with one another, it is helpful to invoke the notions of *simplicity* and *unifying power*. Other things being equal, the simpler a set of hypotheses and the better it unifies our system of beliefs, the more probable it is as an explanation of the data. Although we cannot define these notions of simplicity and unifying power in any rigorous manner, they can assist us in our reflections. When we supplement the crow hypothesis with auxiliary hypotheses so as to provide a consistent explanation of all the observed data, what makes this line of explanation less reasonable than the line of explanation employing the maid hypothesis? The decisive factor is that the maid hypothesis provides a simpler and more unified line of explanation.

In various ways it is a simpler and more unified explanation. The explanation that makes the maid guilty is simpler because it does not require us to postulate the existence of any entities that have not been observed, whereas the line of explanation making the crow guilty requires us to postulate the existence of two crows and a lover, none of which we have observed. A set of hypotheses is simpler the fewer the entities, and also the fewer the kinds of entities, in which it requires us to believe. Moreover, a set of hypotheses is simpler and more probable if it attributes usual and direct operations to phenomena, rather than elaborate and unusual ones. In this respect too, the crow hypotheses are poor, for they require us to suppose that these crows have carried out a very elaborate operation, which would be very unusual indeed in terms of what we know of crows from our past experience with them and with similar birds.

Occasionally *inconsistency* creeps into an explanation. If there is an inconsistency in the way it treats the facts, an explanation cannot have much probability. To take another example, some people have been puzzled at the paintings of El Greco: the human figures he painted seem strangely distorted, unnaturally tall and thin. Suppose that someone tries to explain this peculiarity of his painting by means of the hypothesis that El Greco suffered from astigmatism, which made him see things in this strangely distorted manner, and as he saw them, so he painted them.

This explanation may sound plausible at first, yet it is wholly unacceptable as it stands, for it deals inconsistently with the facts. If El Greco had bad eyes that made him see everything in a distorted manner, this defect would have been operative not merely when he looked at his models but also when he looked at his canvases. Thus a distorted figure drawn on his canvas cannot have looked the same to him as did his model. This attempted explanation fails to explain; the hypothesis that El Greco had bad eyes could conceivably be true, but it is not supported by the mere fact that he painted in this distorted way. (One could supplement it with the auxiliary hypothesis that he wore corrective glasses when and only when he looked at his canvases; but then we do not have a simple set of explanatory hypotheses.)

A still more extreme inconsistency occurs if the explanatory hypothesis employs a self-contradictory notion. The spoons having disappeared, suppose someone suggests the hypothesis that pixies have carried them off. We point out that no one has seen any pixies, or heard them, or felt or smelled or tasted them. No one has experienced pixies in any way, even though sometimes people have looked for them rather diligently. This person replies, "Well, I think it was invisible pixies that carried away the spoons. These pixies cannot ever be heard or touched or smelled or tasted; not with the unaided senses, nor with scientific instruments either. But I believe they're there, all the same, even though we cannot detect them. Science never will be able to demonstrate their presence, but it cannot prove that they aren't there."

This hypothesis is a queer one. It is advanced as though it were a hypothesis that made sense, that is true rather than false but that never could be verified or refuted. The difficulty here is that we are invited to suppose that there are little manlike creatures which are invisible, intangible, and in every way absolutely undetectable. This hypothesis employs a self-contradictory notion. To say that something is really there is to say that it could conceivably be detected. The notion of a pixie which is there but absolutely undetectable is inconsistent. The hypothesis that there are absolutely undetectable pixies is necessarily false, as much so as is the hypothesis that there are married bachelors.

We have mentioned some of the factors that determine the degree of probability of an explanatory hypothesis. However, when we ask how *good* an explanation is, this comprehends more than just its probability. Probability is one component that helps to make an explanation good, but it is not the only one. Another component is the power of the explanation to illuminate the phenomena for which it aims to account. We commonly seek an explanation for a phenomenon because the phenomenon is strange, out of the ordinary, different from what was to have been expected or, at any rate, isolated, its connections with other phenomena unknown. We ask "Why are the silver spoons missing?" for this is unexpected when in the past they have always been in their rack. We ask "Why does soda fizz?" because this seems strange when most liquids do not, and soda does so only when the bottle is opened. We ask "Why do the planets move in elliptical orbits?" because this fact seems anomalous and isolated, when we do not grasp its relation to other facts.

In answering this sort of question, the explanation tries to remove the strangeness, the anomaly, the puzzle, by showing how the thing being explained harmonizes with other known and conjectured facts. We explain the action of soda water by pointing out that it contains carbon dioxide under pressure, which must escape when the bottle is opened. (This explanation gives the cause.) Newton explained why the orbits of the planets are elliptical by showing how this is a special case of the inertial and gravitational way in which all bodies everywhere in the universe move. (This is not a causal explanation but is none the worse for that.) The point here is that a good explanation not only must be probable, in the light of the data, it also must account for the data in an illuminating way that helps us to grasp their connection with other facts. We can see that there is a difference between probability and explanatory force if we remember the old example (from Molière) of someone asking "Why does opium cause sleep?" and receiving the answer "Because of its soporific power." Here the explanation merely redescribes the data in a totally unilluminating manner. It is certain that opium possesses 'soporific power,' but this is just a way of expressing the fact that needs explaining; it is not a good explanation of it.

> With regard to Newton and gravitation, sometimes we speak of gravitation as *causing* objects to fall, and so on.   Certainly gravitation may be called the cause; but gravitation is not the cause of falling in the sense in which, say, germs are the cause of malaria.   The germs are entities distinct from the pathological results they produce; it would not be senseless to speak of germs without malaria or of malaria without germs.   But gravitation is not some additional entity, over and above moving bodies; to talk about gravitation is to talk about how bodies move.
>
> Thinking of work like Newton's on gravitation, people sometimes say, "Science doesn't tell us why things happen, only how they happen; it doesn't really explain, it only describes."   They say this because they imagine that the only way to explain is to point out the hidden inner entity which is the cause, and they see that science does not do that for gravitation and other fundamental forces.   However, this remark reflects a misunderstanding of the nature of explanation, for not all good explanations point out hidden causes.

EXERCISE 32

In each case, what is the phenomenon being explained, and what explanation is being offered?   Discuss whether it is a good explanation.

1   The windowpanes in our old house rattle frightfully at night.   I think they are being shaken by poltergeists.
2   Astrology undertakes to explain why human beings have different destinies.   And its type of explanation is basically quite plausible.   We can see that the movements of the heavenly bodies probably can influence human beings when we reflect that the moon has a large effect on the tides, so why not on a person—who is about two-thirds water, after all.
3   An ordinary scientific law explains only some kinds of phenomena (the laws of physics explain some physical events, the laws of psychology explain some psychological events, etc.).   But here is a law which is much better and which is of more profound significance, because it explains everything that happens.   The law is: Everything always acts in such a way as to realize its potentialities.   Thus, stones fall because this realizes their potentiality for falling; fish swim because of their potentiality for swimming; and

so on. This law gives the ultimate explanation which explains everything that happens.

4 Since it is obvious that man is far surpassed by many beasts in strength and in other bodily functions, tell me how it is that man excels so that no beast can order him about as he orders many of them. . . . —That whereby we excel the beasts must be something in the soul, since to have a living soul would make us excel dead beasts. They too are living creatures, but there is something lacking in their souls which allows them to be subjected by us, and there is something in our souls that makes us better than they. Now, no one can imagine that that is a trifle, and I know no more correct word for it than reason.

ST. AUGUSTINE, *On Free Will*

5 Soon as the untroubled sleep of death has gotten hold of a man and the nature of the mind and soul has withdrawn, you can perceive then no diminution of the entire body either in appearance or weight. . . . Therefore the whole soul must consist of very small seeds and be inwoven through the veins and flesh and sinews; inasmuch as, after it has all withdrawn from the body, the exterior contour of the limbs preserves itself entire and not a tittle of the weight is lost. Just in the same way when the flavor of wine is gone or when the delicious aroma of a perfume has been dispersed into the air or when the savor has left some body, yet the thing itself does not therefore look smaller to the eye, nor does aught seem to have been taken from the weight, because sure enough many minute seeds make up the savors. . . . LUCRETIUS, *On the Nature of Things*

6 Boy! Lucius! Fast asleep? it is no matter;
Enjoy the heavy honey-dew of slumber:
Thou hast no figures nor no fantasies
Which busy care draws in the brains of men;
Therefore thou sleep'st so sound.

WILLIAM SHAKESPEARE, *Julius Caesar*

7 Among the noteworthy actions of Hannibal is numbered this, that although he had an enormous army, composed of men of all nations and fighting in foreign countries, there never arose any dissension either among them or against

the prince, either in good fortune or in bad. This could not be due to anything but his inhuman cruelty, which together with his infinite other virtues, made him always venerated and terrible in the sight of his soldiers, and without it his other virtues would not have sufficed to produce that effect.   NICCOLÒ MACHIAVELLI, *The Prince*

8   The fact that fish are able to remain motionless under water is a conclusive reason for thinking that the material of their bodies has the same specific gravity as that of water; accordingly, if in their makeup there are certain parts which are heavier than water there must be others which are lighter, for otherwise they would not produce equilibrium.
GALILEO, *Two New Sciences*

9   The love of the man sinks perceptibly from the moment it has obtained satisfaction; almost every other woman charms him more than the one he already possesses; he longs for variety.   The love of the woman, on the other hand, increases just from that moment.   This is a consequence of the aim of nature which is directed to the maintenance, and therefore to the greatest possible increase, of the species. The man can easily beget over a hundred children a year; the woman, on the contrary, with however many men, can yet only bring one child a year into the world (leaving twin births out of account).   Therefore, the man always looks about after other women; the woman, again, sticks firmly to the man; for nature moves her, instinctively and without reflection, to retain the nourisher and protector of the future offspring.
ARTHUR SCHOPENHAUER, *The World as Will and Idea*

10   When we see that the three classes of modern society, the feudal aristocracy, the bourgeoisie and the proletariat, each have their special morality, we can only draw one conclusion, that men consciously or unconsciously, derive their moral ideas in the last resort from the practical relations on which their class position is based—from the economic relations in which they carry on production and exchange.
FRIEDRICH ENGELS, *Anti-Dühring*

11   It happens that the less a man believes in the soul—that is to say, in his conscious immortality, personal and con-

crete—the more he will exaggerate the worth of this poor transitory life. This is the source from which springs all that effeminate, sentimental ebullition against war. True, a man ought not to wish to die, but the death to be renounced is the death of the soul.

MIGUEL DE UNAMUNO, *The Tragic Sense of Life*

12 Many modern political parties will be extremely annoyed by a partial satisfaction of their demands or by the constructive participation of their representatives in public life, for such participation mars the delight of oppositionism. . . . Improvements in the conditions criticized cause no satisfaction—they merely cause discontent, for they destroy the growing pleasure afforded by invective and negation. . . . We all know certain representatives in our parliaments whose criticism is absolute and uninhibited, precisely because they count on never being ministers.

MAX SCHELER, *Ressentiment*

AN EXAMPLE:
SMOKING AND LUNG CANCER

During recent years public health authorities in Western countries have noticed a great increase in the rate of deaths from lung cancer. At the beginning of the present century, only a tiny fraction of all deaths were caused by lung cancer; by the 1970s (in the United States and some other Western countries for which records are available), a much larger percentage of deaths were being attributed to this disease.* How can we explain the change? What cause has been operating?

The cause must be some factor, or factors, more strongly present now than in the past. (Here we think in terms of the method of concomitant variations.) Smoking of cigarettes has increased a great deal during the last few decades, but so have air pollution, nervous tension, the use of automobiles, and many other factors. So far as we can tell by a crude use of the method

---

* For instance, in 1930 in the United States the death rate from lung cancer was 3 per 100,000 persons per year, but by 1955 it was about 25 per 100,000 persons per year. This rise in this death rate has been rapid and steady, year by year.

---

of concomitant variations, any one or any combination of these factors might perhaps be responsible for the increase in deaths from lung cancer. Many hypotheses seem possible: Perhaps the increased use of autos keeps people from walking and so weakens their lungs through lack of exercise; or perhaps air pollution harms the lungs of city dwellers by poisoning their air; and so on. But the hypothesis that smoking is a major factor in the increase in deaths from lung cancer begins to seem more probable than some of the other hypotheses when we remember that cigarettes are known to contain nicotine, which is a poison. If the nicotine in two packs of cigarettes were chemically purified and injected into the bloodstream, the dose would be lethal. Perhaps lung cancer is some subtle form of nicotine poisoning. It seems plausible that a substance that can kill quickly when a large amount of it enters the bloodstream might also kill slowly when small amounts are steadily inhaled into the lungs. This is an argument by analogy, and it is far from conclusive; it merely adds a little to the probability of the hypothesis that the increase in smoking has caused the increase in deaths from lung cancer.

Another argument by analogy which supports this same conclusion is based on the observed fact that when tar extracted from cigarette smoke is smeared on the skins of mice, the mice contract skin cancer. This argument too is far from conclusive, for the skin of a mouse is rather different from the lungs of a man; still, the analogy adds more to the probability of the hypothesis. A further piece of reasoning by analogy is based on the fact that prolonged exposure to some kinds of irritants is known to be capable of producing cancer in men; for instance, it was established in England in the eighteenth century that chimney sweeps, who used to have to crawl through the soot of narrow chimneys, got one kind of cancer much more often than other people did. If exposure to chimney soot can result in human cancer, then by analogy we may suspect that cigarette smoke can produce the same result.

These arguments support the hypothesis that smoking is the main factor in lung cancer, but they are not sufficient to prove this; it is proper to speak of a proof when and only when the inductive probability becomes so strong that there is no longer room for reasonable doubt about the truth of the hypothesis. (There always remains room for conceivable doubt about it, but conceivable doubt is not always reasonable doubt.)

Realizing that much more evidence was needed regarding the possible connection between smoking and lung cancer, medical scientists have carried out dozens of studies. One of the most important of these was a study conducted by Dr. E. Cuyler Hammond, working under the auspices of the American Cancer Society.* Dr. Hammond and his associates began by interviewing American men between fifty and sixty-nine years of age, none of whom then had any serious illness, so far as was known. They found out where these men lived and what the smoking habits of each man were. Over a period of forty-four months they kept track of 187,783 men, of whom 11,870 died during that time. The cause of death was determined as accurately as possible in each case. Of the deaths, 2249 were due to cancer, and in these cases an especial effort was made to determine precisely what type of cancer caused the death. After collecting all these statistics, Dr. Hammond analyzed them and found some striking facts. Some of his finds are shown in the accompanying table. This table does not list men who smoked cigars or pipes, or nonsmokers who formerly had smoked cigarettes regularly, and it lists only those deaths which were very definitely diagnosed as caused by bronchogenic carcinoma, the principal type of lung cancer. The right-hand column in the table is calculated from the earlier columns but includes a correction to allow for the fact that the men of the different groups did not have quite the same average ages (and younger men normally have a lower death rate from lung cancer).

This table shows that, for the group of men studied by Dr. Hammond, there was a very strong correlation, or concomitant variation, between the amount of cigarette smoking and the frequency of death from lung cancer. Do these observations entitle us to make an inductive generalization about the population at large? Or is it likely that these figures are unrepresentative and just reflect some accidental coincidence limited to this observed group of individuals?

For example, is it possible that Dr. Hammond's smokers lived in the cities, where they were subject to air pollution, while his

* E. C. Hammond and D. Horn, "Smoking and Death Rates," *Journal of the American Medical Association,* 166: 1159–1172, Mar. 8, 1958 and 166: 1294–1308, Mar. 15, 1958. This now-classic study has been supplemented but not superseded by more recent research.

Amount of daily smoking	Number of men	Number who died of lung cancer	Age-standardized lung-cancer death rate per 100,000 men per year
(Never smoked)	32,392	4	3.4
Less than one-half pack of cigarettes	7647	13	51.4
One-half to one pack of cigarettes	26,370	50	59.3
One to two packs of cigarettes	14,292	60	143.9
More than two packs of cigarettes	3100	22	217.3

nonsmokers lived in the country, where the air is clean? If this is so, it might be that the real correlation is between air pollution and cancer, rather than between smoking and cancer. But Dr. Hammond looked into this and found that for those of his men who lived in cities the death rate from lung cancer was just about the same as for those of them living in the country. (In another study, it was found that inhabitants of The Channel Islands, where the air is unpolluted, suffered lung cancer just as city dwellers do and that, of those who smoked more, more died of the disease.) Here, because the number of men who were observed was so large and because Dr. Hammond's method of investigation was careful, there is an absolutely overwhelming probability that these figures were not produced by some accident or coincidence.

We definitely are entitled to make the inductive generalization that probably, for the population at large, there is a strong correlation between smoking and lung cancer. If we seek to explain why Dr. Hammond got these results, by far the most probable hypothesis is that these results were representative of the population at large. This conclusion is strengthened still further when we notice that other large-scale studies made by other medical scientists all give results closely similar to Dr. Hammond's. Dr. Hammond also found very ominous correlations between smoking and rates of death from other diseases, especially heart disease; but we shall confine our discussion to lung cancer.

Let us return to the question whether the increase in cigarette smoking *caused* the increase in deaths from lung cancer. We know that cigarette smoking has been greatly on the increase during the last few decades, and we have strong evidence for the generalization that the more people smoke, the more they die from lung cancer. But we must not make the mistake of supposing that the presence of a correlation is sufficient to prove that there is a cause-and-effect connection. So far, there are three possibilities which seem to remain open: (1) Perhaps the increase in smoking was the cause of the increase in lung cancer, either because smoking directly causes lung cancer or because smoking weakens people in some way so that they more easily fall prey to cancer; (2) perhaps the increase in lung cancer in some way caused the increase in smoking, possibly because having cancer creates a craving for tobacco; or (3) perhaps there was some third factor, such as nervous tension, which tended to cause some people both to smoke and to contract lung cancer. We must weigh the plausibility of these three competing hypotheses.

Hypothesis 2 can be dismissed almost at once, for we know that most smokers who died of lung cancer had smoked steadily for many years; their smoking habits became fixed long before they contracted the disease. There is no evidence that people who contracted the disease increased their smoking thereafter. Thus it is very improbable that the disease caused the smoking.

Hypothesis 3 deserves careful consideration. Nervous tension seems to be a very plausible 'third factor.' One piece of evidence against that hypothesis is derived from study of what happened in Norway from 1940 to 1945. During those years the rate of death from lung cancer there showed a sharp reduction; previously it had been rising, and after 1945 it rose again. During those wartime years of 1940 to 1945 Norway was suffering under Nazi occupation; there must have been far more nervous tension than usual for the Norwegians. Cigarettes, however, were scarce. Here, by the method of difference, we argue against hypothesis 3 and in favor of 1. Thus it seems quite improbable that hypothesis 3, with nervous tension as the "third factor,' can be correct.

Might there be some as yet wholly unknown 'third factor' which was responsible? Does some obscure hereditary tendency predispose some people both to smoke and to suffer lung cancer?

Certainly this is logically possible, and at present there is no direct evidence against it. But there is no positive evidence whatsoever in its favor. It would be unreasonable to regard such a hypothesis as probable, if a simpler and more direct explanation is available.

Hypothesis 1 provides the simplest and most direct explanation. Hypothesis 1 is supported by various kinds of further evidence in addition to the arguments by analogy already mentioned. For one thing, it is known that pipe smokers sometimes get cancer of the lip, tongue, or mouth, and it is likely that in these cases the smoking is the cause of the cancer, for the disease affects those very parts which are exposed to the most smoke. (Pipe smokers, like cigar smokers, do not suffer lung cancer nearly as often as cigarette smokers do; this is easily explained by the fact that they do not inhale, whereas most cigarette smokers do so.) If pipe smoke causes cancer of the mouth, it is reasonable to suppose that cigarette smoke can cause cancer of the lungs.

Another kind of evidence is derived from microscopic examinations of tissues from the lungs of persons who died from causes other than cancer. A great many such examinations have been made, and they reveal that in the lungs of heavy smokers there is general widespread scarring and thickening of the tissue, with the formation of spots in which the cells have begun to grow in the distorted manner characteristic of incipient cancer. The tissue of the lungs of persons who have been heavy smokers exhibits these modifications, which are not found in the lung tissue of nonsmokers. The amount of scarring and thickening of tissue seems to be roughly proportional to the amount of smoking that the person has done. These observations strongly suggest that regular exposure to tobacco smoke produces a gradual cumulative deterioration of the lung tissue; in the lungs of some smokers this deterioration goes so far that it becomes lung cancer, but the deterioration is slow enough so that the majority of smokers die of other causes before this can kill them. It seems to be possible for an occasional nonsmoker to suffer lung cancer, perhaps caused by air pollution, but it certainly looks as though smoking is overwhelmingly the most important factor in the incidence of the disease.

It is all too easy for us unconsciously to allow our wishes and personal preferences to influence our thinking about inductive problems.   People who enjoy smoking and who are not accustomed to disciplined thought find it easy to talk themselves out of accepting the unpleasant conclusion that smoking is the main factor causing lung cancer.   They say that we should wait for further evidence before forming an opinion, that we must not be hasty, that it is too early yet to tell, etc.

But imagine that the hypothesis that houseflies produce cancer had gained anywhere near as much evidence in its favor as there now is in favor of the hypothesis that smoking does so. If that were to happen, these same people would be as enthusiastic about accepting the housefly hypothesis as they now are reluctant to accept the smoking hypothesis.   They would demand an immediate government crusade to exterminate the fly.   The difference is that everyone dislikes the housefly anyway and is glad to believe the worst about that insect, whereas people enjoy smoking and want to believe the best about it.   One of the most important kinds of intellectual maturity is to have learned to rise above these emotional prejudices so that one can view evidence impartially, regardless of whether the conclusions toward which it points are pleasing or depressing.

The hypothesis that cigarette smoking is the principal factor in causing lung cancer is now very highly probable in light of the evidence.   It has been highly probable ever since the late 1950s, although it is only much more recently that the public has begun to accept it.   It still is logically possible that some surprising new information might come to light to show that cigarettes are not to blame after all; that is *logically possible,* but present evidence makes any such development *highly improbable.*   We must always be prepared open-mindedly to welcome any new developments that may overturn established hypotheses, for that is the scientific attitude; yet we must not be reluctant to accord due weight to the evidence we now possess, for it is folly to refuse to draw a conclusion when strong evidence already is at hand.   Has it been 'proved' that cigarettes are the main cause of lung cancer?   The evidence is so strong that it constitutes a proof in the sense that there remains no room for reasonable doubt.   But the evidence still falls short of providing us with as complete a proof as we hope to get later, after more research has been done.   There remains much still to be explained, especially about the biochemical process by means of which the cause produces its effect.

EXERCISE 33

Analyze the value of each of the following comments.

1   The weakness of all these studies is that they consider only samples out of the population.   What are a mere 187,000 men, compared with the hundreds of millions of men in the Western world?

2   There is nothing alarming about these statistics concerning increased deaths from lung cancer.   You must expect more people to die of lung cancer nowadays, for the population is considerably larger than it used to be.

3   Dr. Hammond did not include any women in his figures. His sample is not representative of the population at large as regards sex, so why should we expect it to be representative in any way?

4   Some of the other diseases, like cholera and typhoid, are under control now, and so people do not die of them.   Obviously, we have to expect relatively more people to die of lung cancer.   Therefore we need not accuse smoking of doing harm.

5   Air pollution is much worse now than it used to be.   In some cities like Los Angeles and London there have been days anyone breathing the air could taste how bitter it is from chemical pollution.   And the pollutants are dangerous too; we know that smog wilts vegetables and in strong concentrations causes deaths.   Air pollution, rather than smoking, may well be the cause of the increased deaths from lung cancer.

6   No one has proved that there could not be some as yet unknown 'third factor' which causes people to smoke more and also causes them to suffer more lung cancer.   This would mean that smoking and cancer are not cause and effect but are both effects of some unknown cause.   It might be some hidden genetic factor.   Here at the Tobacco Industry Research Institute, we hold the view that something like this must be the explanation.

7   Even if it is something about cigarettes that does cause lung cancer, I don't believe it's the tobacco that is to blame.   The smoke from the cigarette paper may well be the cause.

8   We should set up a committee of impartial scientists who would study all these data and come to a careful, scientific

conclusion about whether cigarettes are harmful. Unfortunately, it is very hard now to find scientists who would be fit to serve on such a committee, because so many of them have already made up their minds one way or the other. We could not appoint anyone from the American Cancer Society or from the Surgeon General's Advisory Committee, because both those groups are no longer impartial; they already have officially declared that they regard cigarettes as the principal cause of lung cancer.

9 "Tobacco has been impeached and indicted, but it has not been convicted in fact," said Congressman Perkins (Democrat, Kentucky). "The case against cigarette smoking is based on statistical associations rather than on scientific evidence."

10 I heard of a man who broke his back just bending over to tie his shoelaces. But do the doctors tell us to give up wearing shoelaces? Smoking may have its risks, but so do all those activities which go to make up living.

CHAPTER 7

APPLICATIONS

We have now discussed a good many aspects of the logic of deductive reasoning of various forms, and we have considered inductive reasoning. There remain some loose ends to be drawn together concerning how knowledge of logical principles should be applied in practice.

CHOOSING THE RIGHT DEDUCTIVE TECHNIQUE

In our study of deductive reasoning we became acquainted with several methods for testing deductive arguments. There were Venn diagrams, the rules of the syllogism, truth tables, the method of quantificational deduction, and so on. If we are to make successful use of these methods in dealing with actual examples, it is important that we take care always to choose a suitable method for the problem at hand. If we are unwise in our choice of method, we may easily arrive at a misleading answer regarding the validity even of an argument correctly symbolized. Unwise choice of method would not lead us to regard an invalid argument as valid, but it might lead us to regard a valid argument as invalid.

Each method is concerned with a *sufficient* condition for deductive validity. Being valid according to a correctly constructed Venn diagram is sufficient to ensure that an argument

279

is valid; being valid according to a correctly constructed truth table is sufficient to ensure that an argument is valid; and so on. But no one test gives a *necessary* condition. That it cannot be shown to be valid by a Venn diagram does not guarantee an argument to be invalid, since it may be valid for some quite different reason. That it cannot be shown valid by a truth table does not guarantee an argument to be invalid, since it may be valid for some quite different reason; and so on. But of course, if an argument has no reason for being valid other than its syllogistic form, then if it cannot be shown to be valid by a Venn diagram, it is invalid. If an argument has no reason for being valid other than its truth-functional form, then if it cannot be shown to be valid by a truth table, it is invalid; and so on.

The method of quantificational deduction studied in Chapter 4, including as it does the laws of truth-functional deduction, is a method powerful enough to show the validity of all valid deductive arguments of all the main types that we have studied (except the identity arguments mentioned in the section on fallacies of ambiguity in Chapter 5). However, it generally is wisest on each occasion to employ the most elementary method that will fit the example. By so doing, we usually reduce the work for ourselves and thereby minimize the chance of error. Moreover, unlike the method of quantificational deduction, the more elementary methods of Venn diagrams, the rules of the syllogism, and truth tables, where they are applicable, can provide negative demonstrations of the invalidity of invalid arguments. Thus, whenever a more elementary method such as that of Venn diagrams is applicable, it is wise to employ it rather than the more complicated method of quantification deduction.

In the same spirit, when symbolizing an argument, it generally is wise to employ the fewest letters that can suffice to exhibit the relevant logical structure of the reasoning. It is not advisable to use more letters than are absolutely needed, for that again increases both the amount of work involved and the risk of error.

Thus, when we are confronted with a deductive argument whose validity we want to investigate, we should use our ingenuity to try to find the simplest legitimate way of interpreting that argument. We want to interpret it as being of the simplest kind, and as having the simplest structure within that kind, which will do justice to the meaning of the sentences involved.

There can be no mechanical procedure for us to follow in finding the best interpretation; we have to use trial and error, and see what will work out. But a growing familiarity with forms of argument will develop one's 'feel' for this.

EXERCISE 34

Show whether each of the following deductive arguments is valid. Try to use the best method in each case.

1 Brown detests anyone as crooked as Gray. No one as crooked as Gray can be invited to the White House. So Brown detests anyone who cannot be invited to the White House.

2 If the engine is running and the oil level is still adequate, oil pressure is maintained. If there is no oil leak, the oil level is still adequate. But oil pressure is not being maintained. So if the engine is running, there is an oil leak.

3 The Athenians exacted tribute from all Aegean islands belonging to the Delian League. But there are some Aegean islands from which they did not exact tribute. So some Aegean islands did not belong to the Delian League.

4 If all bats live on insects, then some that are vampires live on insects. But none that are vampires live on insects. So some bats do not live on insects.

5 No anarchists are tyrants. Some emperors are czars. No czars are nontyrants. So some emperors are not anarchists.

6 Either all states should receive federal money for rivers and harbors, or else none of them should. Not all should. Therefore, none of them should receive it.

7 There is a virus that can destroy any living cell. Phagocytes are living cells. So there is a virus that can destroy any phagocyte.

8 A native of the Low Countries is either from Holland or from Belgium. If he's from Holland, he speaks Dutch; if he's from Belgium, he speaks French or Flemish. So a native of the Low Countries speaks either Dutch, or French or Flemish.

9 Anyone who is being prosecuted by State's Attorney Black will need a superhuman lawyer to gain acquittal. Therefore, unless there are superhuman lawyers, no one being prosecuted by Black will gain acquittal.

10 No Arabian is richer than every Iranian. There are Iranians. Therefore, some Iranian is as rich as any Arabian.

11 Only candidates approved by the chairman will be interviewed and voted on. So if no candidates are approved by the chairman, no one interviewed will be voted on.

12 A negative number has a square root if and only if there is a number such that, when it is multiplied by itself, the product is negative. When a real number is multiplied by itself, the product never is negative. So no negative number has a square root.

THE ENTHYMEME

In ordinary discussion a person often presents an argument without bothering to make explicit what all his premises are. Sometimes he has a premise fairly definitely in mind but does not bother to state it because he regards it as common knowledge, too obvious to need stating. An argument is called an *enthymeme* if at least one of its premises is unstated in this way. Originally the term "enthymeme" was restricted to syllogisms, but nowadays the term is extended to cover all kinds of arguments having unstated premises. And sometimes the term "enthymeme" is extended even further so that it also covers arguments whose conclusions have been left unstated—but such cases are rarer and less important.

Suppose we meet a deductive argument whose conclusion does not validly follow from the stated premises alone. If we want to determine how sound the argument is, we ought to ask ourselves whether there are any unstated premises that the arguer is taking for granted. If there are, we should try to state these premises explicitly so that we can consider whether they are true and so that we can see in full the logical structure of the argument, to tell whether it is valid. Naturally, it is not always easy to be certain what unstated premises a person may have in the back of his mind; but we should simply try to do our best to interpret fairly what it is that the arguer is assuming. In making his argument more explicit, our aim should be to do so in a way that he himself would recognize as expressing what he was thinking. In light of this, there are some obvious guidelines that we should heed when we are considering whether someone's argument has an unstated premise:

1 If the argument candidly expresses the speaker's own actual reasoning, then its premises have to be ones which he believes; this includes any unstated premises. If a sentence expresses an unstated premise of someone's argument, then he must believe quite firmly that what the sentence says is true. If the sentence says something that he would be quite surprised at or would seriously doubt, then it can hardly be a fair interpretation to regard the sentence as expressing a premise of his.

2 If one or more sentences express unstated premises of someone's argument, then the argument with those premises added must be the sort of argument that the person would use. If adding the sentences as premises makes the argument into an argument which the person would not have been likely to use—say, because it is circular in a manner that he would have noticed and avoided—then it cannot be a fair interpretation to regard these sentences as expressing premises of his.

Suppose, for instance, that someone argues, "Robinson must be a lawyer, for he belongs to the bar association." Is his argument a *non sequitur* or is it a valid enthymeme? To classify this argument as a *non sequitur* merely because the premise "Robinson belongs to the bar association" does not by itself logically imply the conclusion "Robinson is a lawyer" would involve an unfair interpretation of the speaker's thinking. Instead, we should realize that in all probability the speaker is employing an unstated premise, "All persons who belong to the bar association are lawyers"; this is a piece of common knowledge and he probably feels that it does not need to be stated outright. When we notice the unstated premise, we see that the reasoning is valid.

However, we do have to avoid the mistake of being too generous about ascribing unstated premises to speakers. Certainly we should not get the idea that all deductive arguments whose conclusions do not follow from their stated premises deserve to be regarded as valid enthymemes. For example, suppose that someone argues "All Marxists are socialists, and so all socialists are Marxists." Should we regard this argument as a valid enthymeme having, say, the unstated premise "If all Marxists are socialists, then all socialists are Marxists"? No, this would be a poor interpretation. To regard the argument in this way would be to think of it as committing a fallacy of begging the question, since this conditional sentence would not be less doubtful than the conclusion of the argument. But the original argument surely did not beg the question; it ought to be regarded as a *non sequitur* instead. The speaker's real mistake most likely lies in thinking that an **A** sentence can be converted. It is a better interpretation to say that the original argument is invalid on account of its form than to say that it is valid but has an unstated premise which makes it beg the question.

An arguer is perfectly justified in leaving unstated some of his premises, provided that these are obvious pieces of common knowledge which his audience will recognize that he intends to assume. He is to blame, however, if the unstated premises upon which his argument depends are dubious and questionable or hard for his audience to fill in for themselves. Still worse, of course, is the mistake of the careless thinker who regards as common knowledge things that not only are not known to be true by the people to whom he is speaking but are not true at all. It is the duty of a really conscientious arguer to make explicit all premises that critical listeners might reasonably challenge and all premises that they cannot readily fill in for themselves. If he fails to do this, he is not presenting his argument as carefully and as candidly as would be desirable.

Some deductive arguments are enthymemes and some are not; those which are can be transformed by making their premises explicit so that they cease to be enthymemes. But when it comes to inductive arguments, they must always be and remain enthymemes, if what was said at the end of the first section of Chapter 6 is correct. With an inductive argument, we never fully succeed in stating all the premises upon which the conclusion depends, so an inductive argument is irremediably an enthymeme. Thus the exercise of making the premises of an argument explicit is a more interesting exercise to undertake with a deductive argument, where the task can be completed, than it is to undertake with an inductive argument, where the task cannot be completed.

EXERCISE 35

*Which of the following arguments should be interpreted as en-
thymemes? What are their suppressed premises?*

1　Our observations of the stars make it evident . . . that the
earth is a sphere of no great size. For . . . the stars seen are
different, as one moves northward or southward. Indeed . . .
some stars seen in Egypt . . . are not seen in the northerly
regions.　　　　　　　　　ARISTOTLE, *On the Heavens*

2　Many argue in this way. If all things follow from . . . the
absolutely perfect nature of God, why are there so many
imperfections in nature, such, for instance, as things corrupt
to the point of putridity, loathsome deformity, confusion,
evil, sin, &c.? But these reasoners are . . . easily confuted,
for . . . things are not more or less perfect, according as they
delight or offend human senses, or according as they are
serviceable or repugnant to mankind.

　　　　　　　　　　　　BARUCH SPINOZA, *Ethics*

3　The present state is short and transitory; but our state in the
other world, is everlasting. . . . Our state in the future
world, therefore, being eternal, is of so much greater importance than our state here, that all our concerns in this world
should be wholly subordinated to it.　JONATHAN EDWARDS

4　Other men die. I am not another. Therefore, I shall not die.
　　　　　　　　　　　　VLADIMIR NABOKOV, *Pale Fire*

5　All that is religious is good, for it is only religious as it expresses a common higher life.
　　　　　　　　FRIEDRICH SCHLEIERMACHER, *On Religion*

6　"For my faith," he continued, "I will not change it. Your
own God, as you say, was put to death by the very men
whom he created. But mine," he concluded, pointing to his
Deity—then alas! sinking in glory behind the mountains—
"my God still lives in the heavens and looks down on his
children."　　WILLIAM H. PRESCOTT, *The Conquest of Peru*

7　The peculiar evil of silencing the expression of an opinion is
that it is robbing the human race; posterity as well as the
existing generation; those who dissent from the opinion,
still more than those who hold it. If the opinion is right,
they are deprived of the opportunity of exchanging error for

truth: if wrong, they lose, what is almost as great a benefit, the clearer perception and livelier impression of truth, produced by its collision with error.

JOHN STUART MILL, *On Liberty*

8 Death is nothing terrible, else it would have appeared so to Socrates.   EPICTETUS

9 Accustom thyself to believe that death is nothing to us, for good and evil imply sentience, and death is the privation of all sentience.   EPICURUS

10 We reject all merely probable knowledge and make it a rule to trust only what is completely known and incapable of being doubted. . . . But if we adhere closely to this rule we shall find left but few objects of legitimate study. For there is scarce any question occurring in the sciences about which talented men have not disagreed.

RENÉ DESCARTES, *Rules for the Direction of the Mind*

11 It seems a proposition, which will not admit of much dispute, that all our ideas are nothing but copies of our impressions, or, in other words, that it is impossible for us to *think* of any thing which we have not antecedently *felt*, either by our external or internal senses. . . . To be fully acquainted, therefore, with the idea of power or necessary connexion, let us examine its impression.

DAVID HUME, *Enquiry Concerning Human Understanding*

12 This is the syllogism. Love (true love, not self-love which only loves the remarkable, the brilliant and consequently really loves itself) stands in inverse ratio to the greatness and excellence of the object. And so if I am of infinitely, infinitely little importance, if in my wretchedness I feel myself to be the most miserable of all: then it is eternally, eternally certain that God loves me.

SÖREN KIERKEGAARD, *Journals*

NONINDUCTIVE REASONING
BY ANALOGY

In Chapter 6 we considered inductive arguments by analogy. One of our examples was the reasoning of a postman who, on the basis of his past experience with boxer dogs that bit, reasons that probably the new boxer looming in his path will bite also if approached. This is an argument by analogy; it is definitely inductive in nature, for the conclusion (that this dog will bite if approached) embodies conjectures regarding what future sense experience can reveal, conjectures that go beyond the present evidence. However, not all reasoning by analogy is inductive in this sense, leading to conclusions embodying empirical conjectures that go beyond the data.

Let us consider an example of an argument by analogy which is not inductive. At a certain university a rigorous honor code specifically lists lying and cheating as punishable offenses. Suppose it is discovered that a student has written a bad check and used it to purchase merchandise. The question now arises whether this student has violated the honor code; is writing a bad check a violation of the rule against lying and cheating? (We shall suppose that whoever first wrote the code never considered this question and that there are no known precedents about it.) Someone might try to dismiss this question by saying, "Well, it's all a matter of definition. If by 'lying' you mean something that includes writing bad checks, then he has violated the rule; and if you don't mean that by the word 'lying,' then he has not violated the rule. It's just a matter of what you choose to mean by a word. Just decide how you want to define your terms, that's all."

This comment suggests that the question about the interpretation of the honor code is just a trivial verbal question. As we remember from our discussion of definitions (Chapter 5), a verbal dispute is one that has no true or false solution and that arises solely because people choose to use words differently, not because they differ in their beliefs about what is so. For example, one person may insist that the fox's posterior appendage is the brush and not the tail; someone else may claim that of course it is the tail, for whoever heard of a brush growing on an animal? Here the issue is purely verbal, for the two parties to the dispute do not disagree about what the fox's appendage is like; they disagree only about what it should be called.

But is the question about the honor code a trivial verbal question, in the way the question about the fox's appendage is? Surely not. The question whether a violation of the honor code has been committed is a serious and substantial question. It cannot be settled by making an arbitrary decision about how to use a word; that would not be fair to the accused student. The decision that is reached will affect our action toward the accused student, and our actions ought not to be arbitrary. We have to engage in some careful thinking if we are to reach a fair decision; we have to weigh the arguments pro and con.

Deductive arguments are likely not to be of much use in this problem. Suppose someone tries to settle the problem deductively by arguing: "All cases of cheating violate the honor code; all cases of writing bad checks are cases of cheating; therefore, all cases of writing bad checks violate the honor code." Although this argument is valid, it does not succeed in proving its conclusion, for if we were dubious about whether the conclusion is true, then we are pretty sure to be at least equally dubious about the minor premise. Here the deduction commits the fallacy of *petitio principii*. No purely deductive line of reasoning is likely to be of much help in settling this problem.

Nor are inductive arguments likely to help much. Whichever conclusion we want to establish here (that writing a bad check is, or is not, a violation of the honor code), in either case the conclusion does not embody any predictive conjecture about future experience going beyond what is already known. No purely inductive line of reasoning would be helpful here, for the conclusion is not of the inductive sort.

What sort of reasoning would be appropriate to this problem? Someone would be making a helpful and relevant contribution to the discussion if he reasoned as follows: "Lying and cheating are indisputably offenses against the honor code; now, writing a bad check is very like lying, because signing your name to a bad check is like falsely stating that you have money in the bank. Also, writing a bad check is very like cheating, for you persuade the merchant to accept the check in exchange for merchandise by deceiving him into thinking the check good. Since writing a bad check is so like lying and cheating in these respects, it therefore resembles them also in being a violation of the honor code." At the heart of this reasoning are the analogies between writing a bad check on the one hand, and lying and cheating on the other hand. The whole argument essentially depends upon these analogies; the argument as a whole is a good argument if and only if these are good analogies.

Here it is worthwhile to notice the distinctive character of this sort of reasoning. This is reasoning by analogy. Hence, unlike deductive reasoning, it does not claim to be demonstrative; at best, the truth of the premises gives us only some good reason for accepting the conclusion. On the other hand, this sort of reasoning by analogy differs also from inductive reasoning. For inductive arguments by analogy lead to conclusions embodying predictive conjectures about what the future course of experience will bring to light, whereas the sort of reasoning by analogy that we now are considering does not lead to that sort of conclusion. (Reaching the conclusion that the student is guilty certainly is not the same as predicting that he will be treated as guilty; nor is it even quite the same as predicting that his conduct will have observable consequences different from those it would have had, had he been innocent.)

Someone may object that this sort of argument ought to be interpreted as an enthymeme having an unstated premise. The idea would be that, if an appropriate additional premise were supplied, the argument would become definitely deductive. But there are two difficulties with this idea. First, in this sort of case it is hard to state another premise which is both known to us and sufficient to render the argument deductively valid. Second, even if we could state such a premise, adding it to the argument would surely make the argument into a *petitio principii*. For instance, the auxiliary premise "Whatever is like lying and cheating ought to count as an honor offense," even if we did not know it to be false, would be more dubious than the conclusion that we are trying to establish. It would seem that someone who insists upon regarding this argument as a deductive enthymeme must say either that the argument is a *non sequitur* or that it depends upon false premises or that it begs the question; in any of these three cases, he will have to say that the argument is of no value for proving its conclusion. But this argument and others like it are not worthless for proving conclusions. They sometimes are very good arguments, whose premises provide real reason for believing their conclusions.

This sort of noninductive reasoning by analogy is a valuable and fundamental type of reasoning, to which we often resort in cases where other types of reasoning are unsuccessful. Although there are no formal rules about when arguments of this sort are good and when they are bad, we can say that the reasoning is good when the analogies are good and that it is bad when the analogies are bad. If one thinks that an argument by analogy employs a bad analogy and reaches a wrong conclusion, one way of attacking it is to point out weaknesses in the analogy.

For example, someone might attack the argument about the honor code, claiming that the analogy upon which it rests is not a good analogy. He might argue that lying and cheating are not that much like writing bad checks; sometimes a person writes bad checks unintentionally, just because he is mistaken about his bank balance, and this is unlike lying, which always is intentional. And even when bad checks are intentionally written, the people who write them often are not intending to defraud their creditors permanently; they just intend to delay the payment for a while. The original argument drew a parallel between bad-check writing on the one hand and lying and cheating on the other; this counterargument claims that the cases are not sufficiently parallel to justify the conclusion that was drawn. We could not decide which viewpoint is more correct until we had reflected very fully about the likenesses and differences between these actions.

A more vivid way of attacking an argument that seems to employ a weak analogy and reach a wrong conclusion is to think of a counteranalogy pointing in an opposite direction. Thus, if someone says, "Maybe this boy did write bad checks, but emotionally he is just a child, and so we should make allowances for him, as we would for a child," someone else might reply, "Well, just because he is childlike, he needs to be dealt with severely, for children who are not sharply corrected persist in their delinquent habits." Here the original analogy is met by a counteranalogy; the weakness of the original argument is brought out by showing that, by reasoning which is no worse, one can reach just the opposite conclusion.

EXERCISE 36

A *In each case, what conclusion is being argued for, and what analogy is employed in the argument? Discuss the soundness of the arguments.*

1 **Black:** That can't be a peace rose. It's purple, and grows on a small bush. Peace roses have to be cream-colored, and grow on large bushes.
   Green: It's a new kind of peace rose. It was developed by selective breeding of traditional peace-rose bushes.
2 **Gray:** I didn't lie to him. I never said a word.
   White: You nodded your head to signal a false answer to his question. You intentionally communicated a falsehood, so it was lying.

3 **Brown:** I wasn't carrying a concealed weapon. All I had was a paperweight bulging out of my pocket.
Green: People can be clubbed to death with paperweights, and its surface wasn't visible. So you were carrying a concealed weapon.

4 **White:** I'm very religious. I go to church every week, and I strictly observe the Ten Commandments.
Gray: You don't actually believe in any supernatural doctrines. You're not really religious.

5 Inflation is a tax; it's a way in which government finances its expenses at the expense of individuals. In a strict economic sense, inflation is the same as counterfeiting. They differ only in that inflation is legal while counterfeiting is not, and inflating is done by the federal government rather than by individuals. Whether the dollar is inflationary or counterfeit, it is a purchase order, and thus is a means by which someone else acquires your capital, giving you nothing in return.

6 The argument in favor of the closed shop in United States industry is that if workers can enjoy the benefits negotiated by the union without joining and paying dues, it will be hard to persuade them to join voluntarily as individuals, even though all workers would be better off if all were members. Imagine depending on voluntary contributions to pay for national defense. It is an analogous situation.

7 A physician is entitled to take refuge under the Fifth Amendment if asked, "Do you assert a right to mix cyanide into your patients' cough medicine?" and an educator is entitled to the same refuge if asked, "Do you assert a right to mix communism into your students' sociology lectures?" But no citizen should be obliged to pay for treatment by such a physician, nor should students pay for instruction from such an educator.

8 Moving parts in contact require lubrication to avoid excessive wear. Honorifics and formal politeness provide lubrication where people rub together. Often, the very young, the untraveled, the naïve, and the unsophisticated deplore these formalities as "empty," "meaningless," or "dishonest," and scorn to use them. No matter how pure their motives, they thereby throw sand into machinery that does not work too well at best.

B *Examine these arguments by analogy.*

1 The man who eats in idleness what he has not himself earned, is a thief, and in my eyes, the man who lives on an income paid him by the state for doing nothing, differs little from a highwayman who lives on those who travel his way.

JEAN-JACQUES ROUSSEAU, Emile

2 It would not seem open to a man to disown his father (though a father may disown his son); being in debt, he should repay, but there is nothing by doing which a son will have done the equivalent of what he has received, so that he is always in debt.   But creditors can remit a debt; and a father can therefore do so too.   ARISTOTLE, *Nicomachean Ethics*

3 "Then you should say what you mean," the March Hare went on.   "I do," Alice hastily replied; "at least—at least I mean what I say—that's the same thing, you know."

"Not the same thing a bit!" said the Hatter.   "Why, you might as well say that 'I see what I eat' is the same thing as 'I eat what I see'!"

"You might just as well say," added the March Hare, "that 'I like what I get' is the same thing as 'I get what I like'!"

LEWIS CARROLL, Alice in Wonderland

4 But me—look at the growth of hair in front.
It hangs before me; down my back it tumbles,
Good, rich, coarse hair all up and down my body.
Don't tell me man-grown hair is out of fashion;
A tree's not beautiful when grey and bare,
A horse without his mane's not fit to look at;
Feathers become a bird as wool does sheep,
So a deep-matted run of hair looks handsome
On any man who has the luck to wear it.

OVID, Metamorphoses

5 That the aggressor, who puts himself into the state of war with another, and unjustly invades another man's right, can, by such an unjust war, never come to have a right over the conquered, will be easily agreed by all men, who will not think that robbers and pirates have a right of empire over whomsoever they have force enough to master, or that men are bound by promises which unlawful force extorts from them.   Should a robber break into my house, and, with a dagger at my throat, make me seal a deed to convey my estate to him, would this give him any title? Just such a title by his sword has an unjust conqueror who forces me into submission.   JOHN LOCKE, *Of Civil Government*

6 A foolish consistency is the hobgoblin of little minds, adored by little statesmen and philosophers and divines. With consistency a great soul has simply nothing to do. He may as well concern himself with his shadow on the wall.
RALPH WALDO EMERSON, "Self-Reliance"

7 A majority taken collectively is only an individual, whose opinions, and frequently whose interests, are opposed to those of another individual, who is styled a minority. If it be admitted that a man possessing absolute power may misuse that power by wronging his adversaries, why should not a majority be liable to the same reproach? Men do not change their characters by uniting with each other; nor does their patience in the presence of obstacles increase with their strength. For my own part, I cannot believe it; the power to do everything, which I should refuse to one of my equals, I will never grant to any number of them.
ALEXIS DE TOCQUEVILLE, *Democracy in America*

8 If the mystical truth that comes to a man proves to be a force that he can live by, what mandate have we of the majority to order him to live in another way? . . . It mocks our utmost efforts, as a matter of fact, and in point of logic it absolutely escapes our jurisdiction. Our own more 'rational' beliefs are based on evidence exactly similar in nature to that which mystics quote for theirs. Our senses, namely, have assured us of certain states of fact; but mystical experiences are as direct perceptions of fact for those who have them as any sensations ever were for us.
WILLIAM JAMES, *The Varieties of Religious Experience*

9 He that pays ready money, might let that money out to use; so that he that possesses anything he has bought, pays interest for the use of it. Consider then when you are tempted to buy unnecessary household stuff, or any superfluous thing, whether you be willing to pay interest, and interest upon interest for it as long as you live; and more if it grows worse by using.   BENJAMIN FRANKLIN, *Poor Richard*

THE RHETORIC OF ASSENT

It is one thing to be acquainted with the general principles of logic; it is another to be able to apply them intelligently when analyzing and criticizing actual arguments. We derive relatively little practical intellectual benefit from an acquaintance with logical principles unless we become able to apply them. To do this effectively takes practice, common sense, general knowledge, and mastery of language.

When we meet a piece of argumentative discourse that we wish to analyze in a systematic manner, a proper first step is to unravel the structure of the reasoning, noting what the conclusions and the premises are. The next step is to classify each bit of reasoning: Is it deductive, inductive, or what? Then we can ask what is its specific type (syllogism? inductive generalization?). Next we can evaluate the validity of each bit of reasoning in terms of the considerations relevant to its type. This should tell us whether the overall reasoning is valid. The final step is to consider whether the reasoning succeeds in proving its conclusion. Is there any fallacy of inconsistency or of begging the question? Are the premises reasonable to believe? Here we must draw upon our general knowledge.

In criticizing reasoning, our task is twofold. We aim to avoid being deceived by unsound reasoning, and we aim to recognize sound reasoning as sound. People with a glib half-knowledge of logic sometimes understand the former aim without comprehending the latter. Having learned the names of a few fallacies, for instance, they conclude that whenever they meet someone else's reasoning the proper procedure is to cry out indiscriminately the name of some fallacy. They think that logical criticism is all negative criticism, always finding fault, always accusing others of having made mistakes. But this attitude is shallow and harmful. A person who develops it is worse off intellectually than he would have been had he never studied any logic or learned the names of any fallacies; what little he has learned he uses so crudely that it does more harm than good.

Even more debased than this are the regrettable intellectual habits of those who, perhaps through experience in debating, learn enough about rhetorical techniques to realize that a vigorous case can be made on either side of almost any issue. They have the idea that the whole point of logic is always to score debating victories over one's opponent. Focusing all their attention on the superficial persuasiveness of arguments, they lose sight of validity and soundness. Sometimes they remain perfectly content with whatever thoughtless opinions they themselves happen to have acquired, and they use all their argumentative talents for the purpose of persuading others that these opinions are right.

Reasoning at its best is not a competitive but a cooperative enterprise. A balanced attitude must involve a willingness on our part to recognize and to accept good reasoning whenever an opponent is able to present it to us, in addition to a willingness to recognize fallacies whenever they occur and not just when they are committed by others. The ideal is that we should be dispassionate and objective as we distinguish between good and bad arguments, and as we evaluate the degrees and respects in which arguments that are neither wholly good nor wholly bad are good and bad.

If by rhetoric we mean an overall view concerning strategy in argumentation, then it may be helpful here to introduce the phrase "rhetoric of assent." In our reasoning, we should be ready and willing to assent to arguments whenever they are sound. Our attitude should not be the merely sophistical attitude of being ready to find excuses for rejecting any argument we meet. A rhetoric which emphasizes negative rejection of arguments may do more harm than would having no overall outlook concerning argumentation at all. The correct attitude is the discriminating one: a willingness to reject and avoid bad arguments, and to accept and employ good ones.

EXERCISE 37

A *The city council is debating finances. One member of the council makes a stirring plea for cancellation of all city tax bills that have remained unpaid for more than five years. He bases his appeal on the statement that poor people have all they can do to make ends meet, and that the city government should wish to appear as protector rather than as oppressor of the unfortunate. You are a member of the council, and are scheduled to speak next in the debate. What will you say? Formulate as good a set of arguments as you can to support your position.*

B In recent years, there has been considerable change in society with respect to marriage and the family. Fewer people are marrying, and more women are choosing to work rather than to raise a family. Over the next twenty or thirty years, will this trend cease, or will it go much further? What do you foresee as the role of marriage and the family in the social life of a generation hence? State your view, and formulate as good a set of arguments as you can in support of it. (Notice that this question is about what is going to happen, not about what ought to happen.)

C In most parts of the United States, and in many other countries, it is now established by law that in spring, and again in the fall, official time shall change its relation to sun time. Clocks are set forward by one hour on a given date in the spring, and are set back by an hour on a given date in the fall. The result is that during the winter twelve o'clock noon is about midway between dawn and sunset, but during the summer 1 P.M. (1300 hours) is about midway between dawn and sunset—thus "saving daylight." Is this a good governmental policy?

1 Emphasizing the idea that it is right for government to regulate time for the convenience of its citizens, write a paragraph, addressed to a general audience, formulating an argument in favor of maintaining this practice.
2 Emphasizing the idea that individuals and organizations are free to change their working hours from season to season and that governmental regulations should not intrude arbitrarily into the personal lives of citizens, write a paragraph, addressed to a general audience, formulating an argument against maintaining this practice.
3 Write a paragraph, addressed to a general audience, presenting your own argument on this matter.

D Mrs. Green is superintendent of schools in Plains City, a community where the law governing hiring of teachers forbids any discrimination on the basis of sexual orientation. In the primary schools, sex education is a required subject, and is taught by teachers to whom the superintendent assigns this special duty. In the past, it has been assigned to teachers who volunteered and who were deemed qualified. For the coming *year, a new situation has arisen: A group of teachers have vol-unteered for this assignment and have passed a test on the factual aspects of the prescribed subject matter; however, they have all publicly identified themselves as homosexuals. Should Mrs. Green assign them to do this teaching?*

1   Emphasizing the idea of tolerance in a liberal society, write a paragraph, addressed to a general audience, formulating an argument in favor of her doing so. Try to make it a logical and convincing argument.
2   Emphasizing the idea that parents have a right to have their children educated along lines which they, the parents, can approve of, write a paragraph, addressed to a general audi-ence, formulating an argument against her doing so. Try to make it a logical and convincing argument.
3   Write a paragraph, addressed to a general audience, giving your own argument(s) as to what she should do.

CHAPTER 8

THE PHILOSOPHY OF LOGIC

We shall conclude with a brief consideration of a few basic philosophical questions concerning the nature and status of logic. The issues selected are ones that emerge rather readily from the discussions of logical reasoning that we have been through in previous chapters.

THE STATUS OF LOGICAL LAWS

We have now spent a good deal of time discussing laws of logic, both deductive and inductive. But what is the nature of these laws? What are they about? What makes them true? Philosophers have long been interested in trying to account for the essential nature of the laws of logic; this philosophical problem deserves our attention. In Chapter 1 some preliminary suggestions were made about the nature of logical laws; now let us try to discuss the matter more fully, considering alternative views. The reader must bear in mind that the issues to be discussed are controversial. Philosophers do not agree about them, and many philosophers would disagree with the things this chapter will say.

When we speak of laws of logic, we are referring to principles such as the following, for example.*

Every sentence of the form "*p* and not *p*" is false.
Every **E** sentence is equivalent to its own converse.
No valid syllogism can have an undistributed middle term.

What kinds of sentences are these laws? How do we know them to be true? How is it that they can be of use to us? Let us consider in turn four different philosophical views as to the nature of these laws. It will suffice if we focus our attention upon quite elementary laws of logic, since the status and character of more intricate laws can be expected to agree with that of the elementary laws.

First let us consider the suggestion that the laws of logic are inductive generalizations, empirical truths about how things in the world behave, like the laws of physical science, though more general. This view has not been very widely held by philosophers, but it deserves our attention. According to this view, we can confirm these laws of logic by making observations of how things happen in the world. This would mean, for example, that past experience is the real basis of our confidence that all sentences of the form "*p* and not *p*" are false. According to this view, just as having observed many ravens that are black and none that is not entitles us to believe that all ravens are black, similarly our having observed many sentences of the form "*p* and not *p*" that are false and none that is true justifies our belief that all such sentences are false. We have met the sentences "Today is Tuesday and it is not," "Snow is white and it is not," and so on; in each case, investigation of the calendar, or of snow, or of whatever is the subject of the sentence has revealed that the sentence is false. Hence we may properly infer by induction that the world probably is so constructed that every sentence of this form is false.

Is this a satisfactory view about the nature of the laws of

---

* Some writers use the phrase "laws of logic" to refer only to sentences that are logically true on account of their form, like "Snow is white or it is not," rather than to sentences that mention other sentences, as our examples do. According to that more pedantic usage, our examples would have to be referred to as "laws of metalogic."

logic?   Like many another view in philosophy, this view offers us a comparison of one thing with another, a comparison partly misleading and partly illuminating.

If we have observed many ravens, all of which were black, we would believe the inductive generalization that all ravens are black, and we would not expect it to be refuted by further observations.   However, we still would understand quite clearly what it would be like for the generalization to be refuted by the discovery of some kind of nonblack raven; if we were to read a report of such a discovery, it would be surprising but not unintelligible.   Our past experience of black ravens is needed to support the generalization precisely because the generalization says something that could conceivably be refuted by experience. A universal sentence saying nothing that experience could conceivably refute (e.g., "All bachelors are unmarried") would not need to be supported inductively by evidence drawn from past experience.   Thus, it is a general characteristic of inductive generalizations that we always can understand fairly clearly the possibility of observations that would refute them.

Are elementary laws of logic like this?   Can we describe what it would be like for observations to refute the logical law that all sentences of the form "p and not p" (when understood in the normal way) are false?   Suppose we meet a creature that claims to be both a man and not a man, or an object which somebody says is both a tree and not a tree.   Suppose, moreover, that the creature insists that it is not merely in some ways like a man and in some ways not like a man; it claims more than that and insists that it both is and is not a man.   The person, similarly, insists that the object is not merely in some ways like a tree and in some ways unlike, but that the object both is a tree and is not a tree.   These claims are unintelligible.   They fail to make sense and are quite unlike the case of the nonblack raven.   No matter what we might observe of the creature or the object, nothing about it could prove to us that it both has and lacks the very same property.   No matter what we might observe, it could not refute our conviction that all sentences of the form "p and not p" are false.

Thus it is misleading to say that the laws of logic are inductive generalizations.   They are unlike inductive generalizations in that they could not be refuted by any describable observations. If they could not be refuted by any describable observations, they cannot need to be supported by evidence drawn from past observation. The view that our knowledge of logical laws rests upon past experience cannot be right. These laws must be known by us in some other way. So much for the misleading aspect of the view that laws of logic are like inductive generalizations.

However, there is also an illuminating aspect to this comparison of the elementary laws of logic with inductive generalizations. Although these laws do not need evidence from experience to show that they hold true, such evidence serves to show their utility. These laws are of use because the world happens to be the kind of world that it is. This is a generalization based upon experience and could be refuted by experience. Suppose, for instance, that the universe was under the governance of a powerful and malicious demon of superhuman intelligence who disliked anybody who reasoned in accordance with logical laws. The demon might see to it that any such person was supplied with misleading evidence—evidence which, when logically interpreted, led to false conclusions. For instance, if there were both white and black swans in the world, the demon would arrange that logical thinkers observed only the white ones; logical thinkers would then infer the false conclusion that all swans are white. The demon might also arrange that illogical thinkers would be supplied with evidence of kinds such that from it, with habitual illogic, those thinkers would infer true conclusions.

If the demon was clever enough and powerful enough, he could cause logical people to reach relatively few true conclusions and illogical people to reach relatively many true conclusions. Under these circumstances, logic would lose its utility, and illogical thinking would be more profitable than logical thinking; this is not to say, however, that the principles of logic would be untrue in such a world. Thus, although our knowledge that these elementary laws of logic are true does not rest upon observation, our knowledge of their utility does, for it is through observations and past experience that we know our world not to be like the far-fetched world just described.

There are some philosophers who have agreed that the elementary laws of logic are necessary rather than empirical sentences, but who still have held that these laws express very general facts about the nature of the universe—facts that cannot be known merely through understanding the meanings of logical words (like "and" and "not") but that must be apprehended in some other way, though not through inductive inference based on sense experience. How can general facts about the universe be known, if not by induction, though?

The answer of these philosophers has been that somehow through the faculty of reason—through the mind's power of rational insight into the nature of things—we can know these laws to be true. According to this view, the logical law that no sentence of the form "p and not p" is true is not primarily a law about sentences, about language, but rather a law about things. Roughly speaking, it would be a law to the effect that no thing in the universe can have a property and at the same time lack that property. We would grasp this general fact about the universe not on the basis of sense experience but rather through the mind's power of rational insight.

This view also embodies a comparison. Knowledge of logical laws is compared to a sort of vision, a nonsensory vision. This comparison, like the preceding one, has both an illuminating and a misleading aspect. Its illuminating aspect is that it emphasizes the difference between logical laws and empirical generalizations, by insisting that knowledge of logical laws is a priori rather than empirical. By speaking of rational insight, this view rightly suggests that we can grasp the truth of elementary logical laws by 'seeing' that they hold, that is, just by thinking about them.

But there is a definitely misleading aspect to this view also. Speaking of insight into the nature of reality suggests that the process by which we come to know logical laws is a kind of seeing with the eye of reason—seeing into the inner essence of things, seeing general facts essentially embedded in the nature of the world. The view suggests that by a kind of penetrating and occult clairvoyance we succeed in gazing into the abstract innards of the universe. This is misleading, for it makes the whole matter seem far more mysterious, far more occult, than need be. It conveys a wrong impression of the reflective thinking that is involved in grasping logical laws. The view seems to suggest that by staring very intently with the mind's eye we come to understand that sentences of the form "p and not p" are false. That is not so, however. We come to understand this through remembering how the words "and" and "not" are used in normal cases, and through fitting together what we remember of this.   Someone who accepted the doctrine of rational insight might be inclined to sit blinking his mind's eye and waiting for his rational vision to clear, when what he should be doing is marshaling what he knows about how he uses certain words when he speaks his own language.   The view we are discussing misleadingly suggests that someone might fully understand the uses of the words "and" and "not" and yet, if his rational insight were clouded, might remain ignorant of the law that sentences of the form "p and not p" are false.   But this could not happen, for if anyone doubts whether sentences of the form "p and not p" (when normally understood) are false, his doubt by itself is sufficient to prove that he does not understand the uses of these words.

Quite a few philosophers have held a third view about the nature of logical laws.   They have believed that these laws describe how the human mind works, that they are generalizations about how people think.   The real meaning of the logical law that all sentences of the form "p and not p" are false would be that the human mind cannot think a contradiction; the human mind lacks the power to believe a sentence of the form "p and not p," for it is under a compulsion to reject all inconsistency. According to this view, in studying logic we are studying the capacity of the human mind to maintain certain types of beliefs and the compulsions to which the mind is subject that prevent it from maintaining certain other beliefs.   Most of those who hold this view would not seek any explanation of why the human mind is subject to such compulsions, except perhaps that God benevolently made it so or that there is evolutionary survival value in having these compulsions.

This view embodies a comparison between logical laws and laws of psychology.   Again, there is an illuminating aspect to the comparison, although there is a misleading aspect also.   The value of the comparison lies in the fact that logical laws are related to what the mind can believe.   For example, it is rather as though the human mind were subject to a compulsion not to believe contradictions, for truly the more fully a person comprehends that a belief is a contradiction the harder it is for him to believe it.   People often hold contradictory beliefs, but only when they do not fully recognize what they are doing.

However, this view that logical laws describe how the mind works is misleading insofar as it tends to suggest that logic is a branch of empirical psychology, which is not the case. The principle that people cannot full knowingly believe contradictions really is not an inductive generalization belonging to psychology. Instead, it is a necessary truth reflecting something about what it means to understand a contradiction; part of what it means to say that someone fully understands a contradiction is that he does not believe it. Logic, indeed, has very little to do with empirical facts about human minds. (Empirical facts about human psychology enter into logic, if at all, only in connection with the discussion of logical fallacies.) When logic tells us that no sentence of the form "p and not p" is true, this is best regarded as a remark about sentences, not as a remark about minds. Mental phenomena are not the subject matter of logic; its subject matter consists of sentences and arguments, which may be about anything whatever. Logic is not a branch of psychology, for psychology is an empirical, inductive study of how people and animals think and behave, whereas logic is a nonempirical, noninductive study of such matters as the validity of arguments.

Some recent philosophers have advocated still another view about the status of the laws of logic, the view that these are verbal conventions. The logical law that all sentences of the form "p and not p" are false is compared to a stipulative definition. According to this view, the meaning of the law is that we have arbitrarily decided always to apply the word "false" to that sort of sentence containing "and" and "not." We maintain this stipulation because it proves to be a convenient way of speaking but not for any other reason.

According to this view, the logical law cannot be regarded as a necessary truth; it really is neither true nor necessary, for all it does is express an arbitrary verbal convention, which we could alter if we decided that it would be convenient to do so. Perhaps it would never prove convenient to alter this particular verbal convention, but some thinkers have actually urged that we alter the corresponding law stating that all sentences of the form "p or not p" are true. They have suggested that it would be more convenient to do without the principle of the excluded middle. According to this view, such a proposal is perfectly legitimate, and a logic that regards some sentences as neither true nor false might be more convenient for some purposes than is our standard logic.

This view compares logical laws to stipulative definitions, and, like the earlier views, has both illuminating and misleading aspects. The view rightly calls to our attention that the elementary laws of logic are embedded in our language and that it is the character of language, more than the character of the world, that is revealed by logical laws. To have learned to use the words "not" and "and" in their standard sense is to have learned that sentences of the form "p and not p" are false. Somebody who thinks that a sentence of this form might be true thereby shows that he does not understand the standard meaning of the words "and" and "not." Furthermore, how words are used is a matter of arbitrary convention. It is a matter of historical accident that we use the word "and" to express conjunction and the word "not" to express negation. These conventions certainly could be changed legitimately, if we decided to do so.

There is a misleading element in this view, however. For it holds that logical laws are arbitrary in nature and that the laws themselves might perfectly well have been otherwise if we had chosen to have them otherwise. But what would it be like for our present logical laws to be untrue? What would it be like for the world to contain, say, things that both were and were not trees—in the standard senses of "and" and "not"? This does not make sense. The law that all sentences of the form "p and not p" are false, when understood in the normal way, is a law that cannot be false. Since it cannot be false, we certainly could not *make* it false.

Confusion arises here because of an ambiguity. The proponent of this view neglects the difference between a logical law considered merely as dealing with sentences of the form "p and not p" and a logical law considered as dealing with these sentences *understood in the standard manner*. If a logical law dealt merely with marks and sounds, the law could arbitrarily be changed merely by changing the meanings we attach to the marks and to the sounds. For instance, we could decide to let "and" express disjunction; that would certainly change the law. But when the logical law is understood as dealing with sentences understood in a particular way, the law cannot be changed by any human power, or by any power at all, for it is necessarily true.

Looking back over these four views, we see that each contributes something to our understanding of the matter, yet none is adequate. It is not good enough to describe the laws of logic as inductive generalizations about how things in the world behave; it is not good enough to call them rational insights into the nature of the universe; it is not good enough to call them generalizations about how human minds work; nor is it good enough to call them arbitrary verbal conventions. This may encourage us to return to the account suggested in the final section of Chapter 1. Putting it in a more positive way, we may say that the laws of logic are necessary truths about sentences and arguments, which hold true in virtue of the ways words are used and which we grasp through mastering our language.

EXERCISE 38

Discuss the assertions made in the following dialogue. Which points are well taken; which are confused?

1 **Gray:** Logic is about thinking, and thinking is a mental process. So the old view that logic deals with the laws of thought is basically right.
2 Logic deals with the way we must think; and it is the structure of our brains that determines how we must think. So, at least indirectly, logic is a study of brain structure.
3 It would obviously be pointless to draw up a system of logic whose rules were ones in accordance with which we could not think.
4 **Black:** Rubbish. Logic has nothing to do with the brain, or with human psychology. Laboratory research would simply have no relevance to logic.
5 Our laws of logic, both deductive and inductive, are true by definition. They do not describe thinking, or the world, or anything else. All they do is express the prescribed rules of our language. They are linguistic conventions.
6 If we grant this, it obviously leaves open the possibility that we could have employed other, different linguistic conventions instead.
7 For example, our familiar logic allows just two truth values; in it, every sentence must be either true or false. But there could be a different logic in which three values were allowed, so that every sentence had to be, say, true, false, or indeterminate. In a logic of this latter kind, some forms of argument that count as valid in our familiar two-valued

logic would not be valid. For instance, *reductio ad absurdum* is not valid within the three-valued logic; showing that a sentence is not true would not suffice in three-valued logic to show that the sentence was false—it might be indeterminate.

8   This illustrates how validity is always *relative* to a specific kind of logic. Since different kinds of logic are possible, there is no such thing as absolute validity. All we are entitled to say is that relative to the usual two-valued system of logic, *reductio ad absurdum* reasoning is valid; but relative to a three-valued system it would not be valid; and so on. Therefore, we cannot just study an argument and determine whether it is valid or invalid; before we do that, we must choose the logical system relative to which validity is to be assessed.

9   How then do we choose among different but equally legitimate systems of logic? The choice must be made on the basis of considerations lying outside the systems of logic among which we are choosing. One of the criteria for the choice of systems seems to be primarily psychological: The logic we usually employ is the one that is generally accepted by common sense, the one that is familiar and natural to us.

10   Another criterion for the selection of systems is utility. For ordinary practical purposes, the common two-valued logic probably is the most useful. But in special situations some other system might be more convenient.

11   Just because there is no ultimate necessity determining the choice of logical systems, it does not mean that logic is irrational, or based on whims. One must, of course, have a set of logical principles that is consistent; no logic could be useful that was inconsistent. And beyond that, our logic should be as psychologically satisfying and as useful as possible.

12   **Gray:** Well, I'm glad that you came around to my viewpoint, after all. You agree with me, then, that the nature of human psychological processes dictates what logical principles are to be accepted.

13   **White:** I cannot agree with Black about utility. How can we explain why one kind of logic is more useful than another? Would a logic that was not true be likely to be use-

ful? The simplest explanation of why the normal two-valued logic is the most useful kind of logic for us to use is that its principles are the correct ones.

14 Why do we need to go searching around for some subject matter for logic to be about, such as the psychology of thinking, or the rules of language? Why not just say that logical laws are about negation and conjunction and categorical statements, and so on? And that when logical principles are correct, they express the truth about these matters?

15 Also, Black speaks about the consistency of different systems of logic, and speaks of it as if it were something not relative. Thus he is employing the notion of an absolute consistency. (Systems that were consistent only relative to some other systems would not be preferable to those that weren't, surely.) So if it is all right to speak of absolute consistency, why should it not be all right to speak of absolute logical validity? Thus Black's whole relativistic outlook collapses.

PROBLEMS ABOUT DEDUCTION AND INDUCTION

If we start thinking specifically about deductive reasoning in contrast with inductive reasoning, a problem arises about each. These two problems have perplexed philosophers of the past.

Does All Deductive Reasoning Beg the Question?

The distinctive feature of deductive arguments is that they are, or claim to be, demonstrative; that is, a deductive argument makes the claim that since the premises all are true, the conclusion must necessarily be true also. Put another way, the deductive argument claims that there would be an outright contradiction involved if any person were to assert the premises but deny the conclusion. If the conclusion said anything wholly new and independent of the premises, there could not then be any contradiction involved in asserting the premises but denying the conclusion; the argument could not then have the conclusive character of a valid deductive argument. Thus we see that if an argument is to be both deductive and valid, its conclusion cannot say something new or independent of its premises. In this sense, the conclusion of a valid deductive argument cannot go beyond the content of its premises; it can only bring out what is already contained in the premises. But this fact gives rise to a philosophical puzzle.

This puzzle has troubled philosophers since the time of Plato, but the classic statement of the puzzle was offered by John Stuart Mill.* Mill was particularly concerned with the categorical syllogism, because in traditional logic the syllogism was regarded as the fundamental kind of deductive argument. Mill considered the syllogism, noted that its conclusion must always be contained in the premises if the argument is to be valid, and concluded that this makes the syllogism a worthless style of reasoning.

Consider the syllogism "All teetotalers are avaricious; Mr. White is a teetotaler; therefore Mr. White must be avaricious." Mill charged that an argument like this is worthless because it must beg the question. How could you really know that all teetotalers are avaricious, unless you had already observed each and every teetotaler and found him to be avaricious? But in doing this, you would have had to observe Mr. White himself and note that he is avaricious. Thus you would have had to learn that the conclusion is true *before* you could have learned that the major premise is true. This makes the syllogism worthless as a means of proving the conclusion. The syllogism is a *petitio principii*, for anyone who was in doubt about the conclusion should be at least equally in doubt about the premises.

Not all syllogisms are quite like this example. We might have a syllogism that involved no circularity of reasoning with respect to its major premise, for instance, "All bachelors are unmarried; Aristotle was a bachelor, and so he must have been unmarried." This syllogism has a necessary major premise, and we do not have to observe all bachelors including Aristotle before we can know that all of them are unmarried; we know this in virtue of the meanings of the words involved. Even in this example, however, there still remains a circularity in the reasoning. For how could we know that Aristotle was a bachelor unless we first had found out that he was unmarried? If we did

* J. S. Mill, *A System of Logic,* book II, chap. III.

not know that he was unmarried, we could not possibly know that he was a bachelor. Thus again we have to know the conclusion *before* we can know a premise. Here the circularity arises with respect to the minor premise rather than the major, but the reasoning again is a begging of the question.

Mill considered that all deductive reasoning suffered from this sort of circularity. No deductive argument could ever be used really to prove anything, for always one would have to know the truth of the conclusion before one could know the truth of all the premises; always the premises would be at least as dubious as the conclusion itself. Because all deductive reasoning seemed to him to be useless, Mill came to the conclusion that all genuine reasoning that proves anything is what we would call inductive in nature.

Suppose I am trying to prove that Mr. White is avaricious. The evidence from which I really reason is that Mr. Brown, whom I've met, is an avaricious teetotaler; that Mr. Gray, whom I've met, is an avaricious teetotaler; and so on. The actual evidence that I have is about other particular individuals. This is the evidence upon which I must rely if I am to make a useful inference about whether Mr. White is avaricious. An argument of this type, in which one reasons from evidence about some individual cases to a conclusion about another individual case, is what we have called an inductive argument by analogy. Mill contended that this was the fundamental type of argument that we use in our thinking whenever we are employing reasoning that can really prove anything.

Is Mill right about this? Can it be true that deductive reasoning, which we have spent so much time studying, always is basically worthless and never can prove anything? The idea that deductive reasoning always commits the fallacy of begging the question sounds very paradoxical and puzzling; yet can we maintain that deduction is of any use when we admit that the conclusion of a valid deductive argument has to be contained in its premises?

Mill surely was right in insisting that inductive reasoning is extremely important in our thinking and that our empirical beliefs about the phenomena of nature, about past history, and about future predictions ultimately involve inductive reasoning and not deduction alone. How do we know that the sun will rise tomorrow? Our knowledge of this is based upon our observations of the regular behavior of the sun and other heavenly bodies in the past. How do we know that the Washington Monument is still there on the mall and has not vanished into thin air overnight? It is because of our past observations of the durability of buildings. As we go speeding down the highway, what right do we have to assume that the pavement continues out of sight around the bend rather than plunging into a fiery pit? It is because of our past experience with the reliability of United States highways.

No doubt we can justify some of the facts that we know about the world by deducing them from other more general facts that we know about the world. But, in the end, those more general facts must themselves be established inductively if we are to know them. Mill is surely right that induction (as we call it; he used the word somewhat differently) is very important and that merely deductive proofs of empirical conclusions would never be complete. He rightly emphasizes the importance of induction and the limitations of deduction in our reasoning about empirical matters.

However, Mill surely puts his point too strongly. It is a serious exaggeration to say that whenever we have an argument whose conclusion is deductively contained in its premises, there we always have a fallacy of begging the question. It is true that whenever we have the fallacy of begging the question, there we have an argument whose conclusion is contained in its premises, but the converse does not hold true. Sometimes we can have arguments which are deductively valid, whose conclusions are indeed contained in their premises, yet which are of real value as proofs.

Suppose that a man lives in the suburbs but works in the city; he commutes every day. He knows perfectly well that it takes him ten minutes to get from his house to the station, thirty-five minutes by train into the city, ten minutes by subway, and then five minutes to walk to his office, and the same on the way back. And he knows perfectly well that 10 plus 35 plus 10 plus 5 equals 60, and that there are sixty minutes in an hour. He knows these separate facts very well indeed. But it may come as a surprise to him, and perhaps a shock, if someone now points out that he is spending two full hours every working day of his life just traveling back and forth. This conclusion follows deductively from the premises; the man knew perfectly well that the premises of the argument are true, but he had never before noticed the conclusion contained in the premises.

An argument begs the question if its conclusion is contained in its premises in such a way that a person would not know the premises to be true without having noticed that the conclusion is true too. The example just given is a simple deduction that does not beg the question. Its conclusion is indeed contained in its premises, but it takes some thinking to detect that the conclusion is there, and so the argument can succeed in showing a person something important that he had not noticed before. This is the kind of case in which deduction has its value. The point of deductive reasoning is that it helps us to grasp consequences that we had not noticed but that are contained in what we already believe. And naturally in more complicated cases the conclusion might be far more deeply hidden. This happens often in mathematical reasoning, where very elaborate deductive arguments sometimes are employed in order to bring out the consequences of sets of premises.

Is All Inductive Reasoning Invalid?

Mill believed that he had discovered a fatal weakness in deductive reasoning, and so he put his faith in inductive reasoning instead. But is inductive reasoning really legitimate? Here too a philosophical puzzle arises.

The Scottish philosopher David Hume in the eighteenth century had already raised a serious question about induction.* He asked: What right do we have to trust inductive reasoning? In any inductive argument the conclusion goes beyond what the premises say and makes some kind of prediction or conjecture which further observations may or may not support. There never is any logical contradiction involved in asserting the premises of an inductive argument but denying the conclusion. This means that there never is any logical certainty that the conclusion must be true, just because the premises are. If this is so, how can an inductive argument have any logical force at all? If the truth of the premises does not guarantee the truth

* David Hume, *Enquiry Concerning Human Understanding,* sec. IV.

of the conclusion, why should we trust or rely upon inductive reasoning?

Consider examples. In our past experience we have always found that bread is nourishing to eat and arsenic is poisonous. We have observed many occasions when people have eaten bread and stayed healthy, and we have observed some occasions when people ate arsenic and died. But have we any logical right to believe that this must continue to be so in the future? It is logically possible that from tomorrow onward people who eat arsenic will be nourished by it whereas those who eat bread will be poisoned by it. If this is so, how can we claim that what we have observed in the past gives us any real reason for making inferences about what must happen in the future? How can we claim really to know anything about what will poison us and what will not?

Hume came to the conclusion that we do not have any reason for trusting inductive arguments. Inductive reasoning is invalid and never really enables us to know anything, he felt. Thus Hume was led to a sceptical point of view, doubting that we ever can know anything about as yet unobserved phenomena. Hume recognized that people constantly indulge in inductive thinking, and he developed a theory to explain why people do this. He theorized that human minds are constructed in such a way that they have a certain built-in tendency to expect for the future the same sort of thing they have experienced in the past. Whenever a person has observed something happening often in the past, he expects to find that same thing happening in the future; the more frequent the past experience has been, the stronger is the expectation for the future. But this is an irrational tendency in human nature, Hume thought; our minds work this way, but there is no logical justification for it.

Some philosophers, seeking to escape Hume's sceptical conclusion, have thought that we may justify inductive reasoning by noticing how successful it has been in the past. Looking at our past experience, we see that inductive thinking has frequently led us to true conclusions. Is this not a good reason for trusting induction for the future too? This sort of argument is unsatisfactory as a reply to Hume's scepticism; it offers an inductive argument in favor of the reliability of induction, and that begs the question so far as the sceptic is concerned. Since he is dubious of the legitimacy of induction, he will be at least equally dubious regarding this particular piece of inductive reasoning. Here is a subtler kind of *petitio principii,* in which it is the form of reasoning itself that is begging the question.

Other philosophers have thought that we may justify inductive reasoning by introducing the assumption that nature is uniform and regular and that the kinds of things that have happened in the past will continue to happen in the future. If we take it as an additional premise in our reasoning that things in nature happen uniformly, this supposedly gives us reason for believing, say, that arsenic which has always poisoned in the past will continue to do so in the future. The idea is that if we assume the 'uniformity of nature,' we can infer that what has happened in the past will continue to happen in the future. However, there are two difficulties about this theory.

First, it is very hard to see how we could formulate a sentence that would adequately perform the role required of this proposed additional premise. (What kind of uniformity would it be, and how much?) Second, even if we were able to word such a sentence satisfactorily, we would have no way of knowing it to be true, except by induction. There is nothing else we know from which we could deduce such a sentence. Our thinking would be circular if we used inductive reasoning to justify the sentence that itself is introduced for the purpose of justifying inductive reasoning. Thus it seems that we have no way of justifying induction.

The conclusion that we have no real reason for believing that bread is not going to poison us or that arsenic is going to do so is paradoxical and puzzling. We use inductive thinking all the time; can it really be an illogical process without any justification?

Hume's criticism of induction was a valuable contribution to philosophy, for Hume made it because he had recognized that inductive arguments are not demonstrative in that one always can consistently deny the conclusion without contradicting the premises. Earlier philosophers had not clearly understood this and had not fully grasped the difference between induction and deduction.

Hume was surely not correct, however, in believing that this fact means that inductive thinking is not good reasoning at all, that it has no logical force whatever. The difficulty is that Hume thought deductive reasoning to be the only legitimate type of reasoning; when he found that inductive arguments are not deductive in nature, he rejected them as illegitimate. But deduction and induction are two different yet equally important types of reasoning, neither of which can be reduced to the other. It is a misunderstanding to criticize induction just because it is not deductive. We have no more right to do that than we would have to criticize deduction for not being inductive.

The misleading aspect of Hume's sceptical viewpoint becomes clear if we notice what it implies. Hume says that we have no real reason for accepting inductive conclusions; this would imply that someone who chooses to eat arsenic in preference to bread is just as reasonable as someone who elects the opposite menu. Hume thinks we have no rational basis for predicting the future; this implies that one kind of thinking is no more logical than any other kind of thinking for making predictions about the future. It implies that the careful scientist who makes predictions is thinking in no more rational a way than the careless person who relies on 'intuitions' or superstitions. They are all in the same category, all completely irrational in their reasoning, if induction really is illogical.

This viewpoint, however, embodies a misuse of the words "rational" and "logical" (and the whole family of words associated with them). For if we use these words in their normal sense, we have to say that the scientist is more rational and logical in his thinking than is a superstitious person. That is part of what it means to be rational and logical: that one uses carefully scientific inductive methods of thinking rather than carelessly superstitious ones. There is no confusion or mistake involved in this normal use of the terms. The mistake arises only in the minds of people who misunderstand their normal use.

The great merit of Hume's ideas about induction is that Hume succeeded in distinguishing, much more clearly than had earlier philosophers, between induction and deduction. He discovered how our thinking involves two quite different types of reasoning. But he himself, like many a discoverer, was misled by what he found. Because he thought that deduction was the only genuine reasoning, he was led to the conclusion that since induction differs from deduction, it cannot be good reasoning. What we should try to recognize is that though they differ, they are both genuine types of what is meant by reasoning.

This at any rate is a line of thought in terms of which one can try to work out an account of how Hume's problem should be resolved. There remains room for much further philosophical study of inductive reasoning, both with regard to how its principles are to be formulated, and with regard to the reasonableness of its principles. Hume's view of induction, if indeed it is mistaken, cannot be regarded as involving just a simple or trivial mistake. It raises deep and difficult philosophical problems, which are by no means settled in present-day philosophy.

EXERCISE 39

A *Discuss the following questions.*

1 Do all deductively valid syllogisms tend to beg the question? Do they all have an equal tendency to do so?
2 Do all deductively valid truth-functional arguments beg the question? Do they all have an equal tendency to do so?
3 Do all deductively valid quantificational arguments beg the question? Do they all tend to do so equally?
4 Do some invalid deductive arguments beg the question?
5 Can an inductive argument beg the question?
6 Can a single argument beg the question to a differing extent, depending on the context of discussion within which it is used?

B *Discuss the following quotation, and consider its bearing on the problem of induction.*

In all inference, form alone is essential: the particular subject-matter is irrelevant except as securing the truth of the premises. This is one reason for the great importance of logical form. When I say, "Socrates was a man, all men are mortal, therefore Socrates was mortal," the connection of premises and conclusion does not in any way depend upon its being Socrates and man and mortality that I am mentioning. The general form of the inference may be expressed in some such words as, "If a thing has a certain property, and whatever has this property has a certain other property, then the thing in question also has that other property." Here no particular things or properties are mentioned: the proposition is absolutely general. All inferences, when stated fully, are instances of propositions having this kind of generality. If they seem to depend on the subject-matter otherwise than as regards the truth of the premisses, that is because the premisses have not been all explicitly stated.
    BERTRAND RUSSELL, *Our Knowledge of the External World*

abusive ad hominem argument Any *ad hominem* argument that tries to refute a view by attacking the character, qualifications, or motives of the person who advocates the view, rather than by offering direct reasons why the view is false.

ad baculum argument (appeal to force) Strictly speaking, an *ad baculum* argument is any argument that fallaciously employs a threat as though it were a logical reason for believing a conclusion. In a looser sense, when someone stops offering arguments and resorts to force, he may be said to be resorting to the *ad baculum* 'argument.'

addition A form of deductive argument in which from a premise a conclusion is derived that is a disjunction having one component that is just the same as the premise. This is schematically represented as "$p, \therefore p \lor q$."

ad hominem argument Any argument whose premises, rather than containing evidence having a direct bearing on the conclusion, talk instead about the opponent who refuses to agree to the conclusion. Such arguments are often, though not always, fallacious.

adjunction A form of deductive argument where from two premises a conclusion that is their conjunction is derived. This is schematically represented as "$p, q, \therefore p \& q$."

ad misericordiam argument (appeal to pity) Any argument whose premises, rather than containing evidence having a direct bearing on the conclusion, instead give reasons why acceptance of the conclusion would prevent someone's misery.

ad verecundiam argument (appeal to authority) Any argument whose premises, rather than containing evidence having a direct bearing on the conclusion, instead give evidence that some supposed authority advocates the conclusion. Such arguments are often, but not always, fallacious.

affirmative sentence Any categorical sentence is affirmative if it is in **A** or **I** form.

affirming the consequent A form of reasoning in which one premise is a conditional and the other premise is the same as the consequent of that conditional. This is schematically represented as "$p \supset q, q, \therefore p$." This form of reasoning is not deductively valid.

alternation Disjunction.

ambiguity To say that an expression is ambiguous is to say that it is unclear which of two or more quite different meanings the expression has.

ambiguity, fallacy of Any *non sequitur* in which some ambiguity in the argument leads people to misunderstand the logical form of the argument, thus making them regard the argument as valid when it is not.

analogy A similarity between different things. Sometimes analogies are used for purposes of description, sometimes for purposes of reasoning.

analytical definition Any definition that aims to describe the accepted meaning of a word or symbol.

antecedent In a conditional sentence, the component governed by the word "if."

a posteriori sentence Empirical sentence.

appeal to authority *Ad verecundiam* argument.

appeal to force *Ad baculum* argument.

appeal to pity *Ad misericordiam* argument.

a priori knowledge Knowledge that we can possess without possessing supporting evidence drawn from sense experience.

a priori sentence Any sentence that can be known to be true or known to be false a priori.

argument A formulation in words of one or more premises and of a conclusion that the speaker infers from them or wants his hearers to infer from them.

association Principles to the effect that in a conjunction of more than two components, or in a disjunction of more than two components, grouping does not matter. Schematically represented, "$(p \& q) \& r$" is equivalent to "$p \& (q \& r)$," and "$(p \lor q) \lor r$" is equivalent to "$p \lor (q \lor r)$."

atomic sentence Any sentence not containing any other shorter sentence as a component of itself.

begging the question *Petitio principii*.

biconditional sentence Any sentence of the form "p if and only if q."

black-and-white thinking Thinking in extremes; because a sentence is false, it is inferred that some very contrary sentence must be true.

bound variable To say that a variable in a quantificational formula is bound is to say that the variable there is governed by a quantifier.

broad To say that an analytical definition is too broad is to say that the definiens applies to some things to which the definiendum does not apply.

categorical sentence Any sentence in **A, E, I,** or **O** form.

chain argument (hypothetical syllogism) An argument consisting of three or more conditionals. This is represented schematically by "$p \supset q, q \supset r, \therefore p \supset r$."

circumstantial ad hominem argument Any *ad hominem* argument that offers reasons why the opponent would want to accept the conclusion, rather than reasons why the conclusion is true.

collectively To speak of the members of a group collectively is to speak about the whole group considered as one unit. What is said may not be true of the members of the group considered individually.

commutation Principles to the effect that in a conjunction and in a disjunction the order of the components does not matter. Represented schematically, "$p \& q$" is equivalent to "$q \& p$," and "$p \lor q$" is equivalent to "$q \lor p$."

complex question Any question worded so as to contain a concealed questionable assumption.

complex question, fallacy of Any fallacy caused by the presence of an unjustified assumption concealed in a question.

component The simpler sentences that together make up a compound sentence are called its components.

composition, fallacy of The fallacy of inferring a conclusion that speaks of a group collectively from a premise that speaks of the group distributively, when such a conclusion does not follow.

compound sentence Any sentence containing one or more shorter sentences as part of itself.

conclusion In an inference, that which is inferred from the premises.

conditional sentence Any "if-then" sentence.

conjunction Any "and" sentence.

conjunction, law of Law for calculating the probability of a conjunction. The probability of one event *and* another equals the probability of the first, times the probability that the second would have, assuming that the first is true.

conjunctive argument Any of various forms of argument that depend upon conjunction; as represented schematically, especially "$-(p \& q), p, \therefore -q$."

consequent In a conditional sentence, the component not governed by "if."

consistency A group of sentences is consistent if and only if it is not necessarily impossible that all of the sentences may be true.

contingent sentence A sentence whose meaning is such as to leave open both the possibility that the sentence may be true and the possibility that it may be false. Empirical sentences are contingent.

contradiction Any sentence that is necessarily false. Also, to say that one sentence contradicts another is to say that they necessarily cannot both be true.

contradictory sentences Two sentences are contradictories (or negations) of each other if and only if they are necessarily opposite as regards truth and falsity.

contradictory terms Two terms are contradictories (or negations) of each other if and only if it is impossible that there could be anything to which both terms apply, yet one or the other must apply to each thing.

contraposition The contrapositive of a categorical sentence is got by making subject and predicate trade places and negating each. The contrapositive of a conditional is obtained by making the antecedent and consequent trade places and negating each.

contrary sentences Two sentences are contraries of each other if and only if they cannot both be true but might both be false.

contrary terms Two terms are contraries of each other if and only if it is impossible that there could be anything to which both apply but possible that there may be things to which neither applies.

conversion, by limitation The converse by limitation of a universal categorical sentence is got by making subject and predicate trade places and changing the quantity to particular.

conversion, simple The simple converse of a categorical sentence is got by making subject and predicate trade places. The converse of a conditional is got by making antecedent and consequent trade places.

copula In categorical sentences, the words "are" and "are not," serving to link subject with predicate.

counteranalogy An argument by analogy constructed for the purpose of countering or opposing some other argument by analogy.

deduction Inference in which the conclusion follows necessarily from the premises, or at any rate in which the speaker claims that it does so. Also, an argument is called a deduction in a narrower and more special sense if it is formally arranged in a series of lines so that each line either is a premise or is inferred from earlier lines by means of some standard principle of inference.

definiendum In a definition, the word or symbol being defined.

definiens That part of a definition which gives the meaning of the word or symbol being defined.

definition A verbal formation of the meaning of a word or symbol; a rule or recipe for translating sentences in which a word or symbol occurs into equivalent sentences that do not contain it. But, in a different and looser sense, any description of the essential nature of a thing is called a definition.

definition in context A definition that shows how to translate sentences containing the definiendum into sentences that do not contain it. This definition does not provide any one fixed combination of words or symbols that can always be substituted for the definiendum.

demonstrative argument Any argument whose conclusion strictly follows from its premises so that if the premises are true the conclusion must necessarily be true also.

De Morgan's laws Laws that the negation of a conjunction is equivalent to a disjunction of negations and that the negation of a disjunction is equivalent to a conjunction of negations. Schematically represented, "$-(p \mathbin{\&} q)$" is equivalent to "$-p \vee -q$," and "$-(p \vee q)$" is equivalent to "$-p \mathbin{\&} -q$."

denying the antecedent Form of argument in which one premise is a conditional and the other is the same as the negation of its antecedent. This is represented schematically by "$p \supset q, -p, \therefore -q$." This is not deductively valid.

dilemma Form of argument having three premises, two of which are conditionals and the other a disjunction. A simple dilemma contains three distinct basic components; a complex dilemma contains four. In a constructive dilemma the components of the disjunctive premise are the same as the antecedents of the conditional premises; in a destructive dilemma the components of the disjunctive premise are negations of the consequents of the conditionals.

disjunction (alternation) Any "or" sentence.

disjunction, law of Law for calculating the probability of a disjunction. The probability of one event or another equals the probability of the first plus the probability of the second minus the probability that both will occur.

disjunctive argument Any of various arguments that depend on disjunction; represented schematically, especially "$p \vee q, -p, \therefore q$."

distribution, law of Principle that a conjunction one of whose components is a disjunction is equivalent to a disjunction both of whose components are conjunctions, and that a disjunction one of whose components is a conjunction is equivalent to a conjunction both of whose components are disjunctions. Thus, represented schematically, "$p \mathbin{\&} (q \vee r)$" is equivalent to "$(p \mathbin{\&} q) \vee (p \mathbin{\&} r)$," and "$p \vee (q \mathbin{\&} r)$" is equivalent to "$(p \vee q) \mathbin{\&} (p \vee r)$."

distribution of terms The subject, S, of a categorical sentence is distributed in that sentence if and only if the sentence says something about every kind of S; the predicate, P, of a categorical sentence is distributed in that sentence if and only if the sentence says something about every kind of P.

distributively To speak of the members of a group distributively is to say something that applies to each member of the group considered singly. What it said need not be true of the group considered as one unit.

division, fallacy of Fallacy of inferring a conclusion that speaks of a group distributively from a premise that speaks of the group collectively, when such a conclusion does not follow.

double negation Principle that the negation of the negation of a sentence is equivalent to the sentence itself; represented schematically, "$-(-p)$" is equivalent to "p." Also, the principle that the negation of the negation of a term means the same as the term itself; e.g., "non-nonS" means "S."

empirical knowledge Knowledge that a person having only ordinary faculties can possess only if he has evidence drawn from sense experience to support it.

empirical sentence Any sentence that people who possess only ordinary faculties can know to be true or know to be false only on the basis of evidence drawn from sense experience.

enthymeme Any argument one or more of whose premises is unstated.

equivalence Two sentences are equivalent if and only if they must necessarily be alike as regards truth or falsity. When two sentences are equivalent because of their truth-functional form, they are said to be truth-functionally equivalent; when two sentences are equivalent because of their quantificational form, they are said to be quantificationally equivalent.

equivocation, fallacy of Any fallacy of ambiguity in which the ambiguity of some particular word or phrase causes the fallacy.

exclusive disjunction Any "or" sentence whose meaning is such that the sentence is false if both components are true.

existential instantiation (E.I.) Rule of inference according to which we may infer from an existential quantification any instance of it, with the restriction that the name in the instance must be new to the deduction.

existential quantification Any symbolized sentence that starts with an existential quantifier whose scope is all the rest of the sentence.

existential quantifier The expression "$(\exists\ )$," where any variable may be put in the gap. "$(\exists x)$" means "At least one thing x is such that."

existential viewpoint In discussing the interrelations of categorical sentences, any viewpoint from which one takes for granted the existence of things of some or all of the kinds under discussion.

explanation Any way of fitting some strange or puzzling phenomenon into the fabric of one's knowledge, by pointing out its cause or by showing that it is a special case of some more general phenomenon. Explanation differs from proof at least in this respect, that one asks for an explanation of a phenomenon only when one is ready to grant that it does occur; one asks for a proof of a phenomenon only when one is not ready to take for granted that it occurs.

explicit definition Any definition giving as the definiens a single word or phrase that can be substituted for the definiendum.

exportation A principle of equivalence involving conditionals. Represented schematically, "$p \supset (q \supset r)$" is equivalent to "$(p \, \& \, q) \supset r$."

expression Any word or symbol, or combination of words or symbols.

extension of a general term All those things to which the term applies.

fair bet A bet is fair when every party to the bet has the same mathematical expectation of gain and the same mathematical expectation of loss.

fallacy Any logically defective argument that is capable of misleading people into thinking that it is logically correct.

figure In a categorical syllogism, the pattern of arrangement of the terms.

forgetful induction Invalid deductive reasoning in which the mistake is that some of the relevant available data have not been taken into account.

formal fallacy Any fallacy in deductive reasoning in which the mistake arises because of pure misunderstanding of logical principles.

formula Any sentence written with logical symbols; also any expression containing logical symbols which, though not itself a sentence, displays some logical structure that a sentence could have.

free variable In a symbolized quantificational formula, a variable not governed by any quantifier.

general term Any word or phrase that would make sense if used as subject or predicate in categorical sentences.

hasty induction In inductive reasoning, the fallacy of overconfidently inferring a sweeping conclusion from weak evidence.

hypothetical sentence Any conditional sentence.

hypothetical syllogism Chain argument.

hypothetical viewpoint In discussing the interrelations of categorical sentences, the viewpoint from which one leaves it an open question whether there exist things of the kinds under discussion.

identity To say that x and y are identical is to say that they are one and the same thing. The verb "is," in one of its senses, expresses identity.

ignoratio elenchi Fallacy of irrelevance.

illicit obversion Fallacious obversion, in which the mistake arises because the term that ought to be replaced by its contradictory is replaced instead by a contrary term.

illicit process In categorical syllogisms, the fallacy of allowing a term to be distributed in the conclusion when it is not distributed in a premise.

immediate inference Deductive inference in which a categorical conclusion is inferred from a single categorical premise.

implication To say that one sentence, or group of sentences, implies another sentence is to say that if the former is true then the latter must necessarily be true too. Where the implication results from the truth-functional forms of the sentences, it is called truth-functional implication; where it results from their quantification forms, it is called quantification implication.

inconsistency, fallacy of The fallacy of reasoning from premises that are inconsistent with one another.

inconsistent sentences A group of sentences are inconsistent with one another if and only if it is necessarily impossible for them all to be true. An inconsistent group of sentences either contains sentences of the form "p" and "$-p$" or it implies them.

induction Nondeductive inference in which the conclusion expresses an empirical conjecture that goes beyond what the premises say; that is, the conclusion implies something, not implied by the premises, that can be confirmed or refuted only on the basis of evidence drawn from sense experience.

inductive analogy Inductive reasoning that reaches a conclusion about a single case on the basis of a similarity between that case and other previously observed cases.

inductive generalization Inductive reasoning that passes from evidence about some observed members of a class to a conclusion about the whole class.

inference The deriving of a conclusion from premises.

instance In the logic of quantification, an instance of a quantification is a sentence exactly like the quantification except that the quantifier has been removed and a name has been substituted for the variable of quantification. In inductive reasoning, individual cases to which a generalization applies or which bear out an analogy are called instances of that generalization or instances of that analogy.

intension of a general term All those characteristics that a thing must necessarily possess in order that the term correctly apply to it.

invalidity To say that an argument is invalid is to say that the conclusion does not follow from the premises, or, at any rate, that it does not follow with the degree of probability that the speaker claims for it.

irrelevance, fallacy of Any *non sequitur* that is neither a pure fallacy nor a fallacy of ambiguity. A fallacy of this sort is misleading when something about the premises distracts attention from the fact that they have no logical bearing upon the conclusion.

large numbers, law of   Statistical principle to the effect that if, for example, a coin is to be tossed (in this case the probability of heads in a single toss is ½) then the greater the number of tosses, the higher is the probability that the fraction of them yielding heads will closely approximate the probability of the single case (i.e., ½).

logical analogy   Reasoning by analogy which aims to show that an argument is invalid (or that it is valid) by pointing out that other similar arguments are invalid (or valid).

logical form   In a sentence or an argument, the logical structure obtained if all nonlogical words are removed, leaving only such logical words as "all," "some," "not," "and," "or," etc.

logical laws   Principles about what kinds of sentences are true because of their logical form; principles about what sentences may be inferred from others; and so on.   Also, in another sense, a sentence that is necessarily true because of its logical form may be called a law of logic.

major premise   In a categorical syllogism, the premise containing the major term.

major term   In a categorical syllogism, the term that is the predicate of the conclusion.

mathematical expectation   In a gambling situation, the amount the gambler stands to gain (or lose) multiplied by the probability that he will gain (or by the probability that he will lose).

method of agreement   A method of reasoning about causes, using the principle that the cause of a phenomenon must be a factor that is present in every case in which the phenomenon occurs.

method of concomitant variations   A method of reasoning about causes, using the principle that the cause of a phenomenon must be present to the same degree as is the phenomenon.

method of difference   A method of reasoning about causes, using the principle that any factor present when the phenomenon does not occur cannot be the cause of it.

middle term   In a categorical syllogism, the term that occurs in both premises but not in the conclusion.

Mill's methods   Ways of finding the causes of phenomena, based on the general principle that the cause of a phenomenon must be present when and only when the phenomenon occurs.

minor premise   In a categorical syllogism, the premise containing the minor term.

minor term   In a categorical syllogism, the term that occurs as subject of the conclusion.

modus ponens   A form of conditional argument.   It is represented schematically by "$p \supset q, p, \therefore q$."

modus tollens   A form of conditional argument.   It is represented schematically by "$p \supset q, -q, \therefore -p$."

Monte Carlo fallacy   In inductive reasoning, the fallacy of inferring that, because an event has occurred less often in the recent past than was to have been expected, there is therefore an increased probability of its occurring in the near future.

mood   In a categorical syllogism, the forms of the sentences in the syllogism; thus, a syllogism is in the mood **EAE,** for instance, if its major premise is an **E** sentence, its minor an **A,** and its conclusion an **E.**

narrow   An analytical definition is too narrow if the definiendum applies to some things to which the definiens does not apply.

necessary condition   If all cases of *A* are cases of *B*, then *B* is said to be a necessary condition of *A*.   For example, having a middle term that is distributed is a necessary condition of being a valid syllogism.   The fact that *A* is a necessary condition of *B* may itself be a necessary truth, or it may be an empirical truth.

necessary sentence   Any sentence which, if true, is necessarily true and could not have been false, or which, if false, is necessarily false and could not have been true.   The truth or falsity of a necessary sentence can be known a priori.

negation   Any "not" sentence.

negation, law of   Law for calculating the probability of a negation; the probability that something is *not* so equals 1 minus the probability that it is so.

negation of a sentence   The result of writing the sentence with "It's not the case that" prefixed to it as a whole.   This result is contradictory to the original sentence.

negation of a term   The result of writing the term with "non" prefixed to it as a whole.   This resulting term is contradictory to the original term.

negative analogy   In inductive reasoning by generalization or analogy, the extent of the observed differences among the previously observed cases.

negative sentences   Categorical sentences are said to be negative if and only if they are in **E** or **O** form.

nonexclusive disjunction   Any "or" sentence that counts as true if both components are true.

noninductive reasoning by analogy   Reasoning by analogy in which the conclusion does not express any empirical conjecture going beyond the statements of the premises.

non sequitur   Any invalid argument, where the conclusion does not follow from the premises.

obversion   A categorical sentence is obverted by changing its quality and negating its predicate.

particular sentence   Any categorical sentence that is in **I** or **O** form.

petitio principii (begging the question)   Fallacy of using a premise (or a form of inference) whose acceptability is bound to be at least as doubtful as is that of the conclusion supposedly being proved.

positive analogy In inductive reasoning by generalization or analogy, the extent of the observed similarities among the already observed instances.

post hoc, ergo propter hoc In inductive reasoning about causes, the fallacy of inferring that just because one thing happened after another, the later was caused by the earlier.

predicate In a categorical sentence, the term after the copula.

premise In an inference, an assumption upon which the conclusion depends.

probability In inductive reasoning, the degree of confidence that it is reasonable to accord to the conclusion, relative to the available evidence.

proof Any argument that succeeds in establishing its conclusion.

pure fallacy Any *non sequitur* that arises purely from misunderstanding of logical principles and not from ambiguities of language or irrelevant distractions.

quality To specify the quality of a categorical sentence is to state whether the sentence is affirmative or negative.

quantifier A word or symbol that indicates how many things a sentence is talking about; the words "all," "no," and "some" and the symbols "(x)" and "($\exists$x)" are quantifiers.

quantity To specify the quantity of a categorical sentence is to state whether the sentence is universal or particular.

real definition Many traditional philosophers believed that there is one and only one correct way of describing the nature of each natural being; such description they called a real definition.

reasoning Thinking that includes the making of inferences.

reductio ad absurdum Deductive reasoning in which a conclusion is established by showing that its negation leads to something necessarily false. Schematically, one form is "$p \supset (q \,\&\, -q), \therefore -p$."

relevance In inductive reasoning by generalization or analogy, the extent to which one's background knowledge makes it reasonable to expect that one thing will be associated with another.

revelatory definition Any description that, by means of a metaphor or in some other way, attempts to point out something fundamental about the nature of the thing being described.

scope of a quantifier In a symbolized sentence containing a quantifier, that portion of the sentence governed by the quantifier.

self-contained argument Any argument whose premises can be stated completely so that, in determining whether the conclusion validly follows from them, one need take no account of the truth or falsity of any other sentences (except for sentences expressing logical laws).

sentence   Any combination of words that can serve as a complete utterance, according to the rules of language.   In logic the concern is with sentences used to make true or false statements.

simplification   Conjunctive argument whose single premise is a conjunction and whose conclusion is the same as one component of that conjunction.   This is represented schematically by "$p \,\&\, q, \therefore p.$"

singular sentence   A sentence containing at least one singular term.   An example is "Socrates is mortal"; this example can be symbolized "All S are M" (if "S" is taken to mean "persons identical with Socrates") or it can be symbolized as "Ma" (if "a" stands for Socrates).

singular term   A word or phrase whose meaning makes it purport to apply to exactly one thing.   Proper names are one kind of singular term.

slothful induction   In inductive reasoning, the mistake of underrating the degree of probability with which a conclusion follows from evidence.

sorites   An argument whose conclusion is derivable from premises through use of a series of two or more categorical syllogisms.

square of opposition   A traditional diagram for illustrating the logical interrelations of the different forms of categorical sentence, when all have the same subject and all have the same predicate.

statement   An assertion.   To make a statement is to utter (or write) a sentence in such a way as to say something true or false.   Strictly speaking, the same sentence might be used on different occasions to make different statements.   (By uttering the sentence "You're stupid" while addressing Smith one may make a true statement, yet by uttering that same sentence while addressing Jones one perhaps makes a false statement.)   In logic a sentence is called true when the statement that the sentence would normally be used to make is a true statement.

stipulative definition   A definition that arbitrarily assigns a new meaning to the word or symbol being defined.

subcontraries   To call two sentences subcontraries is to say that they cannot both be false but may both be true.

subject   In a categorical sentence, the term between the quantifier and the copula.

sufficient condition   To say that A is a sufficient condition of B is to say that all cases of A are cases of B.   Having an undistributed middle term is a sufficient condition for being an invalid categorical syllogism.

syllogism   A categorical syllogism is any deductive argument consisting of three categorical sentences that contain three different terms, each term occurring twice, in two different sentences.

symmetry of a relation   To say that a relation is symmetrical is to say that, whenever it holds between a first thing and a second, then it holds also between the second and the first. This is represented schematically by "(x) (y) $(Rxy \supset Ryx)$."

tautology Any sentence that is necessarily true in virtue of its truth-functional form.

term In categorical sentences, the words or phrases occurring as subjects and predicates are called terms. More generally, any word or phrase that it could make sense to apply to a thing is called a term. (But not all words are terms; the word "not" is not a term, for it makes no sense to say "This thing is a not.")

transitivity of a relation To say that a relation is transitive is to say that, whenever it holds between a first thing and a second and between the second and a third, then it holds also between the first and the third. This is represented schematically by "(x) (y) (z) $[(Rxy$ & $Ryz) \supset Rxz]$."

truth function To say that a compound sentence is a truth function of its component sentences is to say that the truth or falsity of the compound is settled once the truth or falsity of each component has been settled.

truth table Table that shows whether a compound sentence is true or whether it is false, for each possible combination of truth and falsity of its components.

undistributed middle, fallacy of For a categorical syllogism to commit this fallacy is for its middle term to be distributed neither in the major nor in the minor premise.

universal instantiation In deductive reasoning, the principle that allows one to infer from a universal quantification any instance of it.

universal quantification A symbolized sentence that starts with a universal quantifier whose scope is all the rest of the sentence.

universal quantifier The expression "$(\ )$," where any variable may be put in the gap. "(x)" means "Each thing x is such that."

universal sentence To call a categorical sentence universal is to say that it is in **A** or **E** form.

vagueness To say that a word is vague is to say that there is no way of telling where the correct application of it is supposed to stop, as things vary in degree.

validity To say that an argument is valid is to say that its conclusion logically follows from its premise, as the argument claims. A deductive argument is valid if and only if the relation between premises and conclusion is such that the truth of the premises would strictly guarantee the truth of the conclusion. A deductive argument valid on account of its truth-functional form is called truth-functionally valid; if valid on account of its quantificational form, it is called quantificationally valid. An inductive argument is valid if and only if the degree of support which it claims that its premises provide for the conclusion is indeed the degree of support that the premises do provide for the conclusion.

variable Any of the letters "x," "y," "z," etc., as used in quantificational symbolism.

variable of quantification In a universal quantification or an existential quantification, the variable whose occurrences are governed by the quantifier that comes at the beginning.

verbal dispute A disagreement caused not by any difference of opinion concerning anything true or false but merely by a difference in verbal usage; one speaker prefers to use a word in one way, while his opponent prefers to use the word in another way.

GLOSSARY OF SYMBOLS

Letters

A, E, I, O: These four boldface capital letters refer to the four forms of categorical sentence.

A, B, C, etc.: Italic capital letters are used in several ways. In Chapter 2 they are used as abbreviations for terms; thus "All *S* are *P*" can symbolize "All Slavs are prudes." In Chapter 3 they are used as abbreviations for whole sentences; thus "*S ⊃ P*" can symbolize "If Socrates was wise, then Plato was wise." In Chapter 4 they are used in quantified sentences to express properties and relations; thus "*Sx*" can symbolize "x is a Slav" and "*Pxy*" can symbolize "x precedes *y*."

a, b, c, etc.: Small italic letters from the beginning of the alphabet are used in Chapter 4 as names of particular objects; they function as proper names do.

p, q, r, etc.: Small italic letters starting with "*p*" are used in Chapter 3 to display the logical skeletons of compound sentences; they function as ellipses do: "*p* v *q*" is like ". . . or ///."

x, y, z, etc.: Small italic letters from the end of the alphabet are used in Chapter 4 as variables; they function as pronouns do.

Truth-Functional Symbols

−: The dash expresses negation. "−*p*" is read "not *p*," or "it is not the case that *p*."

&: The ampersand expresses conjunction. "*p* & *q*" is read "*p* and *q*."

v : The wedge expresses disjunction, in the nonexclusive sense. "*p* v *q*" is read "*p* or *q*."

⊃ : The horseshoe expresses the conditional, in its truth-functional sense. "$p \supset q$" is read "if p then q," or "p only if q."

≡ : The three lines express the biconditional. "$p \equiv q$" is read "p if and only if q."

Quantificational Symbols

(x): Any variable enclosed within parentheses is a universal quantifier. "(x)" may be read "each thing x is such that."

(∃x): Any variable preceded by a backwards "E" and enclosed within parentheses is an existential quantifier. "(∃x)" may be read "at least one thing x is such that."

Probability Symbol

//: The double stroke is used to express probability. These two strokes appear between one sentence and another to form an overall expression that refers to the probability of the first sentence relative to the second. "$p // q$" may be read "the probability of p, given q."

INDEX